QUMRAN
IN CONTEXT

QUMRAN IN CONTEXT

Reassessing the Archaeological Evidence

YIZHAR HIRSCHFELD

HENDRICKSON PUBLISHERS

© 2004 by Yizhar Hirschfeld

Hendrickson Publishers, LLC
P. O. Box 3473
Peabody, Massachusetts 01961-3473

ISBN 1-56563-612-0

Printed in the United States of America

First Printing — October 2004

Cover art: Combs and a necklace found at Qumran. Photo Credit: Mariana Salzberger; Courtesy Israel Antiquities Authority. Used with permission. Photo of Qumran site appears courtesy of Yizhar Hirschfeld. Used with permission.

Library of Congress Cataloging-in-Publication Data

Hirschfeld, Yizhar.
    Qumran in context : reassessing the archaeological evidence / Yizhar Hirschfeld.
      p. cm.
    Includes bibliographical references and indexes.
    ISBN 1-56563-612-0
    1. Qumran community. 2. Qumran Site (West Bank)—Antiquities. 3. Excavations (Archaeology)—West Bank. 4. Dead Sea Region (Israel and Jordan)—Antiquities. I. Title.

    BM175.Q6H57 2004
    933—dc22

                      2004018367

To my colleagues at Dumbarton Oaks
where the surroundings were an inspiration for this book

Table of Contents

Foreword

This book really does not need an introduction; no doubt both the topic and the author speak for themselves. Qumran is one of the most famous and, perhaps for that reason, most controversial sites in the ancient Levant. After more than 50 years of intensive research, the site and the scrolls found in caves nearby still evoke a fascination not only to a lively and exceedingly diverse academic community, but also to the educated public—though in the US certainly more than in my native Germany.

Yizhar Hirschfeld is one of the most prolific excavators in Israel. His fields of research extend from the Byzantine monasteries in the Judean desert to the Roman baths at Hammat Gader on the Yarmouk River. In 2000 Yizhar published a fascinating report on the Herodian farm at Ramat Hanadiv. That volume and a series of articles on rural settlement in ancient Palestine prove him to be one of the leading experts on rural life and architecture. Through his surveys in the Dead Sea region and his large scale excavations in En Gedi (just concluded in 2002 and, of course, also soon to be published), Yizhar is one of the few scholars of our days who has intensively worked at several sites in the region around Qumran and is equally familiar with its unique physical features and its rich cultural history. Yizhar probably knows the region better than his own backyard!

From very early on since the discovery of the Dead Sea Scrolls and research into them, archaeology has played a major role in attempts to reconstruct the character of the Qumran settlement and the identity of its inhabitants. To this day, the most influential model with respect to the settlement and its inhabitants was formulated by Roland de Vaux, the excavator of Qumran. De Vaux integrated archaeological data into a comprehensive interpretive model that connected the inhabitants of the Qumran site with the authors of the scrolls found in eleven caves nearby and associated them with the Essenes, an ideally pious Jewish group mentioned in the works of ancient authors such as Philo, Pliny the Elder, and Flavius Josephus. De Vaux's systematic account *Archaeology and the Dead Sea Scrolls* (Oxford: Oxford University Press, 1973) has become a true classic and describes better than any other book a position that is usually called "consensual theory"—mainly by those colleagues who adopted it. A short time ago, de Vaux's position was in part modified, but in general defended, in Jodi Magness' book *The Archaeology of Qumran and the Dead Sea Scrolls* (Grand Rapids: Eerdmans, 2002). The basis for the "consensus model" is the assumption that the main elements of the apocalyptic, separatistic, and ascetic ideology of the Essenes, as reconstructed from a conflated reading of ancient sources and selected passages from the scrolls, are accurately reflected in the isolation of the site, its unique layout, and its austere inventory (e.g., its pottery). Isolation and uniqueness are seen as the prime characteristics of Qumran. The strength of this argument, however, mainly is a result of the formative power of a particular reading of the texts. In the "Qumran-Essene-Theory" the role of archaeology is largely affirmative and illustrative. Archaeological features figure as important only insofar as they support the "consensus." When those features do not support that consensus, they are often ignored or played down. Good examples for this approach are the little significance given to glass finds and to trade and regional connectivity. The so-called "consensus" never really took the archaeology of the site seriously as an independent source of information and knowledge, but, rather, concurred with a widespread tendency of scholars who mainly deal with texts to deny archaeology its very own power to formulate concepts and ideas about the past (see John Moreland, *Archaeology and Text,* London: Duckworth, 2001).

In the late 1980s and early 1990s, however, the first serious doubts were raised challenging the "Qumran triangle" of (1) allusions in the scrolls, (2) one particular interpretation of the archaeology of the site, and (3) the group named "Essenes." Norman Golb's claim that the scrolls might not be of Qumran origin, but may have come from Jerusalem, motivated scholars to reconsider the connection between the scrolls and the Essenes. Now it is generally accepted that only a small fraction of scrolls actually shows sectarian affinities. Surveys in the region, additional excavations at sites neighboring Qumran, and especially new information on the pottery, glass, and other small finds from the huge, still unpublished, fundus of Qumran finds stored in the École Biblique, have expanded our picture widely enough to encourage scholars to propose alternative theories about the archaeology of Qumran. Most prominent among these scholars were Robert Donceel and Pauline Donceel-Voûte in the early 1990s who, by pointing to an agricultural context for Qumran, triggered a very controversial discussion that opened up a completely new perspective. In the following years, one unique "Essene" feature of Qumran after another collapsed. The more data became available the more Qumran moved away from the isolated fringes of Judah back into the network of a culturally and economically diverse late Hellenistic/early Roman Dead Sea region.

In archaeology, innovation comes from new data or new approaches to old data. A second volume of the official Qumran final reports, edited by Jean-Baptiste Humbert and Jan Gunneweg, has just been published. It is filled with studies on pottery, the cemetery, graffiti, and natural-scientific reports on various other aspects of the vast array of finds. And much more data can be expected from the ongoing publication process. In this respect, any synthetic study of the archaeology of Qumran still is preliminary. Despite the fact that much data from Qumran are not yet available, one still can look closely at the vast material that *has* been generated in the *region* during the last decades and which has not been properly assessed in Qumran studies. Not always is the simplest or the most accepted theory the best, but the theory that allows one to correlate and, if possible, integrate a highly diverse and complex set of data on the basis of their context. *Context* is the key word!

Now Yizhar Hirschfeld's book marks a new step in Qumran archaeology because, for the first time, he systematically takes the *region* as prime context of the settlement. Not isolation, but analogy and comparison, are the appropriate ways to look at Qumran. By following a strictly archaeological agenda, by bringing new material data into the discussion, and by adopting a consequential regional approach, Hirschfeld lays his hands on the methodological and material foundations of the current debate, urging us to review and rethink commonly-held positions about the alleged "isolation" and "uniqueness" of Khirbet Qumran. Hirschfeld does not "ignore" the relevant texts. On the contrary, only a meaningful assessment of the archaeology as an independent, but not unrelated, source can help the reading of the texts for their own value and thus avoid the traditional harmonistic circle of reading one assessment into the other.

Much in this book will certainly be hotly debated, and this is exactly what we need—a discussion about hidden concepts and agendas, about reconstructive imagination, about how to correlate texts and material culture, about new readings of relevant texts—in all, about how to read the archaeology of Qumran as *archaeology* for the first time. Maintaining a "consensus" never was a value in itself; it is all about facts and arguments. The debate is opened again. One may disagree with Hirschfeld about details, but one cannot dismiss nor ignore his overall argument.

It is a particular honor and joy for me to introduce *Qumran in Context: Reassessing the Archaeological Evidence.* During the last couple of years Yizhar and I have discussed many issues in Qumran research, not always agreeing on everything. We soon learned from each other that forging a consensus is not the first thing scholars should seek. Given the fragmentary nature of our sources, it is much more appropriate to listen to the details, be surprised by new insights they reveal, and risk swimming against the tide when composing a new picture. The truth is out there; we just have to open our eyes! As ever, Yizhar's book is most stimulating, and I recommend it to everybody who takes arguments as what they are: means to trigger our reason and imagination to venture into unknown territory and in new directions.

Jürgen Zangenberg
Wuppertal, Germany

Preface

Khirbet Qumran, in the northwestern Dead Sea Valley, is a controversial site. Was it, as prevalent theory sees it, a community center of the Essene sect, a kind of monastery in which the members of the sect gathered for communal meals and prayers? Did these same Essenes copy the scrolls—now known the world over as the Dead Sea Scrolls—that were found in the nearby caves? Or as more and more scholars have become convinced, did these scrolls originate in Jerusalem, brought from the capital at some time during the First Revolt (66–70 C.E.) and concealed in the caves near the site? Adherents to the latter view tend to give Qumran a secular interpretation as a complex built for some practical purpose: economic, military, or governmental. In this spirit, Qumran has been variously defined as a fortress, a road station, or the center of an agricultural estate that also included the nearby oasis of 'Ein Feshkha. I will be discussing all of these interpretations, which are not necessarily mutually exclusive.

Few Palestinian sites have attracted as much scholarly attention as has Qumran, primarily because of the abundance and importance of the scrolls discovered in the caves near the site. My intention here is to examine the archaeological remains at Qumran in their own right, without the religious connotations ascribed to them by their first excavator, Father Roland de Vaux, and in isolation from the content of the scrolls that were indeed found near the site but not within its remains.

I arrived at the study of Qumran and associated issues by an indirect route. During the 1980s and 1990s I conducted extensive excavations at two sites of the early Roman period (first century B.C.E.–first century C.E.) at Ramat Hanadiv northeast of Caesarea. At each site the excavations uncovered not only a fortified complex with a tower but also agricultural installations, such as wine and oil presses and *columbarium* towers for the raising of pigeons. When I began to analyze the excavation finds from the two sites at Ramat Hanadiv, their similarity to the remains of Qumran was striking.

---

[1] In the following text, the names of sites and places are given in the form in which they most commonly appear in the literature; thus En-Gedi and 'En Boqeq (Hebrew), 'Ein Feshkha and 'Ain ez-Zara (Arabic). *'En, 'ein,* and their variations mean "spring."

In 1996 I began a large-scale excavation in the oasis of En-Gedi, which continued for seven consecutive seasons until 2002. During these excavations I became increasingly aware of the unique character of the resources, natural landscapes, and sites of the Dead Sea region. During those years I carried out several surveys and limited excavations at 'Ein Feshkha and Khirbet Mazin (Qasr el-Yahud) to the south of Qumran, at Rujum el-Baḥr (Ma'aganit ha-Melah) to its northeast, and at Qumran itself. I also revisited the large sites of the Dead Sea area, the palaces of Herod at Jericho and Masada. Thanks to the peace agreement with Jordan, I was also able to visit the important sites on the eastern shore of the Dead Sea. Among these, the most important are the large cemetery of Khirbet Qazone on the peninsula of the Dead Sea, Callirrhoe ('Ain ez-Zara) on the northeastern shore, and Zoar (as-Safi) at the sea's southern extremity. Thus, in the course of my research I have accumulated information not only on Qumran but also on sites around the Dead Sea and sites of the Herodian period in different parts of the Judean kingdom. In this way I am able to bring a unique regional perspective to the study of Qumran, which makes it possible to examine the Dead Sea Scrolls and the site of Qumran in a new way—in a wider historical-geographical context.

The first chapter of this book presents the historical-geographical background of the Dead Sea region in the Second Temple period, together with the history of research devoted to Qumran. The second chapter, on the discovery of the Dead Sea Scrolls and the finds made in the caves near Qumran, addresses the question of the scrolls' origin: Qumran or Jerusalem? The third chapter analyzes the archaeological finds at Khirbet Qumran, discussing the remains in chronological order according to the occupation strata found at the site. The fourth chapter presents the remains discovered in the oasis of 'Ein Feshkha south of Qumran. The fence wall that connects these two sites implies that they functioned as one complex, that is, that the abundantly watered oasis was the agricultural estate of which Qumran was the center. The fifth chapter, which examines the integral part played by Qumran and 'Ein Feshkha in the general settlement picture of the Dead Sea in the Second Temple period, discusses a fascinating issue, the presence of the Essenes, John the Baptist, and other hermits in the western Dead Sea region in this period. The concluding chapter addresses the three central questions asked by Qumran scholars today: What is the origin of the scrolls? Who owned the property at Qumran? And who lived there?

I also take the opportunity to correct the misimpressions left by the unusual and sometimes eccentric vocabulary that the first excavator, because of his monastic background and the usage in his native French, inserted into the study of Qumran. Such vocabulary has led to a loss of proportion regarding many aspects of Qumran. I hope to restore this proportion by describing the remains of Qumran in the objective terminology used by archaeologists.

The tendency to ignore finds that did not fit into preconceived theories has also contributed to this loss of proportion. This book contains the most up-to-date references to these "neglected" finds, which shed intriguing new light on the site.

Another fascinating question is the Christian context of Qumran. The study of the site and its surroundings reveals a pattern of settlement in the first century C.E., the period of Jesus. One of the components of such settlement was the hermitic lifestyle of the ascetics among the Essenes. Everything recorded about John the Baptist in the New Testament leads to the conclusion that he was a member of the Essene sect, or at least close to their faith and way of life. Therefore the study of Qumran in its context gives us background for the beginnings of Christianity.

During the writing of this book, I benefited from much useful advice. My colleagues Katharina Galor and Jürgen Zangenberg read the manuscript and made many useful suggestions. I am particularly grateful to Jürgen Zangenberg for introducing me to Hendrickson Publishers, who spared no efforts in the production of this handsome volume. My thanks to Sue Gorodetsky, who translated parts of the text from Hebrew and edited the final manuscript; to Robert Amoils and Jill Rogoff for translating and editing previous versions; and to Miriam Feinberg Vamosh, whose advice contributed to the editing of the final manuscript. Most of the plans and drawings in the book are the work of Dov Porotsky. Dov Porotsky also drew some of the reconstructions, together with Balizs Balogh, Shlomo Rotem, Anna Yamim, and Tanya Gornstein. The photographs were taken by the author, as well as by Zeev Radovan and Gabi Laron; my thanks to all those who helped me produce this book.

The final manuscript was completed in 2002–2003 during my stay at the Dumbarton Oaks Research Library in Washington, D.C. I am most grateful to Edward Keenan, the director of Dumbarton Oaks; to Alice-Mary Talbot, the director of Byzantine studies; and to Michel Conan, the director of studies in landscape architecture, for the hospitality that I enjoyed during my stay and the ideal conditions for research and writing.

Washington, D.C.

List of Illustrations

Scrolls

Stone work

Miscellany

Site Photographs

Aerial views

Architectural features at Qumran

Regional sites and views

Water supply system at Qumran

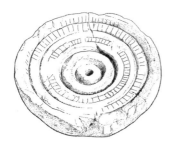

Abbreviations

General

B.C.E.	before the Common Era
ca.	*circa*, about
C.E.	Common Era
ch(s).	chapter(s)
cm	centimeter(s)
e.g.	*exempli gratia*, for example
fig(s).	figure(s)
frag.	fragment
ft	feet
i.e.	*id est*, that is
kg	kilogram(s)
km	kilometer(s)
m	meter(s)
mm	millimeter(s)
p(p).	page(s)
pl.	plural; plate
sq	square

Bible

Lev	Leviticus
Num	Numbers
Josh	Joshua
2 Sam	2 Samuel
1–2 Kgs	1–2 Kings
1–2 Chr	1–2 Chronicles

Isa	Isaiah
Matt	Matthew
2 Tim	2 Timothy

Josephus

Ant.	*Jewish Antiquities*
J.W.	*Jewish War*
Life	*The Life*

Mishnah, Talmud, and Related Literature

b.	Babylonian Talmud
m.	Mishnah
t.	Tosefta
y.	Jerusalem Talmud
B. Bat.	*Baba Batra*
ᶜErub.	*ᶜErubin*
Šabb.	*Šabbat*
Soṭah	*Soṭah*

Other Ancient Works

Diodorus Siculus
  Bibl. hist.   *Bibliotheca historica*
Eusebius
  Hist. eccl.   *Ecclesiastical History*
Pliny the Elder
  Nat. hist.   *Natural History*
Strabo
  Geogr.   *Geographica*
Theophrastus
  Hist. plant.   *Historia plantarum*

CHAPTER 1

The Study of Qumran

1.1. The Enigma of Qumran

Khirbet Qumran, or Qumran in abbreviated form, is one of the most fascinating and enigmatic sites in the Levant. The site's Arabic name, which means "the gray ruin," apparently derives from its location on light-colored marl.[1] It is located on a natural plateau at an elevation of 325 m below sea level. From this elevation, about 90 m above the Dead Sea, it commands a magnificent view of Jericho and the mouth of the River Jordan to the north, the massive ridge of the mountains of Moab to the east, and the end of the Dead Sea to the south. Behind Qumran on the west rises a steep cliff, 200 m high, which is part of the long Syrian-African rift system. The site is bounded on the south by the steep cliff of the north bank of Wadi Qumran and on the west and north by ravines (fig. 1). On the east, extending over the sloping ground, is the cemetery of Qumran.

The British explorer Gurney Masterman, who visited Qumran in 1900–1901, described its location in these words:

> The whole of these ruins stand on a commanding position, surrounded on all sides, and especially to the south, by steep declivities; at one point at the south-west corner, however, a narrow path connects it with the plateau to the west. From this site every point of the 'Ain Feshkhah oasis and all its approaches can be overlooked; it is, also, a fresher and healthier situation than any spot in the plain below. I found a fresh breeze there when on all the lower ground it was hot and still. The site is just such a one as would have been chosen in, say, Roman times to protect the springs and the road passing through the district to the south, a road which very possibly in such times may have been continued along the shore round Ras el-Feshkhah.[2]

The modern access road reaches the site from the east. It branches off Route 90, which runs south from Jericho via Qumran to En-Gedi. In the Second Temple period, three ancient roads converged at Qumran (fig. 2). The main road ran from Jericho in the north,

---

[1] Palmer 1881, 345. According to Cross (1958, 38, n. 3), the name actually derives from the Arabic word *qmr*, meaning "lit by the moonlight." On the metamorphosis of the Arabic name of Qumran, see Cansdale 2000; Taylor 2000a. According to Masterman (1902, 161), there was a second name: Khirbet el-Yahud.

[2] Masterman 1902, 152.

Figure 1. Aerial view of Qumran, looking south.

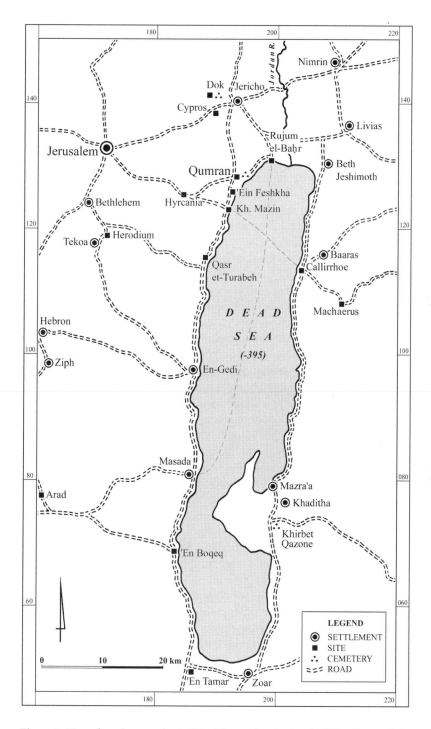

Figure 2. Map of road system in the Dead Sea region during the Herodian period.

running along the marl plateau at the foot of the cliff and ending at Wadi Qumran. The second road arrived from En-Gedi and Masada in the south. It took a straight course along the Dead Sea shore to 'Ein Feshkha and then mounted the plateau on which Qumran is situated. This was the main artery connecting the Dead Sea sites of the period with Jericho, and from there with Jerusalem; the existence of this road is demonstrated by the occurrence of several Second Temple period sites along its line. The third route reached Qumran directly from Jerusalem to the west. It set out from Jerusalem's southern gates, one of which was called "the gate of the Essenes."[3] It runs along the ridge leading eastward from Jerusalem to Abu Dis and Mount Muntar. From the southeastern slope of the mountain the route leads to the fortress of Hyrcania, crosses the Valley of Hyrcania (el-Buqei'a in Arabic) and reaches the top of the path known as Ma'aleh Qumran (the Hebrew word *ma'aleh* means "ascent"). At the edges of this relatively easy route are remains of ancient retaining walls, attesting that the path was paved in antiquity.[4] The path arrived directly in Qumran at the foot of the slope. This was an important road, since it was the shortest route between Jerusalem and the northwestern coast of the Dead Sea and its 25-km length could be walked in one day.

Qumran was thus situated at a major crossroads and on a site that controls its immediate surroundings, and its location on the eastern frontier of the kingdom of Judea in the early Hasmonean period was also one of great strategic importance.

Qumran is outstanding in the abundance of archaeological finds at the site itself and in its surroundings. Of course, the discovery that made the site world-famous was the cache of scrolls found in eleven caves near the site. These are the Dead Sea Scrolls—hundreds of texts (principally in Hebrew), including most of the books of the Old Testament, the rules of a sect of some kind, and postbiblical apocryphal works of the Second Temple period. After the discovery of the scrolls, excavations on a large scale were held at the site, directed by Father Roland de Vaux, an archaeologist from the École Biblique in Jerusalem. The site was almost totally excavated in five consecutive seasons from 1951 to 1956.[5]

Hundreds of coins of the Second Temple period were discovered in the well-preserved structures, along with a varied and rich assemblage of pottery and glass vessels, cosmetic items, stone weights, metal utensils, artifacts made of organic materials (mats and baskets), and ostraca (inscribed potsherds) bearing typically Hebrew names attesting to the fact that the inhabitants of the site in that period were Jews.

But unlike at other sites, the abundance of written materials and finds do not make identification of the site easier. On the contrary, the more the finds, the more the mystery and controversy.

The two main interpretations of the finds are diametrically opposed, and sometimes proponents vociferously attack the other position. The debate rages because the biblical nature of the scrolls has the potential to make the subject cross the line from the scholarly to the spiritual. The debate focuses on two issues: the origin of the scrolls and the identity of the inhabitants of Qumran.

---

[3] Josephus, *J.W.* 5.145.

[4] Masterman (1903, 265) was able to lead his horse down this ancient path to Qumran.

[5] Lankester L. Harding conducted the first excavation season jointly with de Vaux; see Harding 1952. For preliminary reports of de Vaux's excavations, see de Vaux 1953a; 1953b; 1954; 1956.

The traditional interpretation, beginning with de Vaux, has influenced two genera-tions of scholars. It regards Qumran as a communal center of one of the Essene groups, a monastery of sorts, in which the members of the sect assembled for collective meals, im-mersion in ritual baths, and the copying of the scrolls that have been found in the nearby caves. This interpretation describes Qumran as a cultic site, the center of a sect whose members had retreated to the desert in their quest for a remote and isolated place in which to seek spiritual fulfillment. Few other sites have been given such numerous and diverse appellations of religious significance. For example, Magen Broshi and Hanan Eshel have dubbed it "the first monastic community in the Western world."[6] Hartmut Stegemann de-scribes Qumran as a kind of production center for sacred writings, and André Lemaire re-gards it as a house of study *(bet midrash)* of sorts.[7] Even the term "a communal building" ("un édifice communautaire"), first used by de Vaux to describe the remains there, refers in French to a site of religious character.[8] The "Essene-Qumran" hypothesis, as it is termed in the research literature, maintains that most, if not all, of the scrolls originated in Qumran and that they belonged to a local library of the Essene sect.[9] This interpretation, first propounded by de Vaux, is presently accepted by most scholars and serves as the cornerstone of numerous studies dealing with the scrolls and their contents.

On the other hand, there is growing support for the theory maintaining that the scrolls originated in Jerusalem, that is, they were brought from the capital on the eve of the destruction and were hidden in caves adjacent to the site. The German scholar Karl H. Rengstorf initially put forward this theory in the 1960s,[10] and the American researcher Norman Golb gave it definitive form in the 1990s.[11] In his book *Who Wrote the Dead Sea Scrolls?*, Golb suggests that the scrolls came not from a single library in Jerusalem but from several different ones. In an important study of Qumran and the Essenes, the Australian scholar Lena Cansdale proposes that some of the scrolls came from Jerusalem and others from Jericho.[12] These and other scholars have called for a complete severance of any con-nection between Qumran and the Essenes.[13]

By suggesting that Jerusalem is the source of the scrolls, we liberate Qumran from the burden of religious significance that has clung to it. It allows us to give the site a secular in-terpretation, not as a monastery but as a complex of utilitarian buildings constructed for some commercial, military, or administrative purpose. In this spirit, the remains at

---

[6] Broshi and Eshel 1999a, 267.

[7] Stegemann 1998, 51–53; Lemaire 2000, 40.

[8] de Vaux 1954, 210. The historical conclusions relating to the scrolls and Qumran were already presented by de Vaux in the preliminary report on the first season of excavations at the site. Subse-quently, even in his summary books in French (de Vaux 1961) and in English (de Vaux 1973), he did not change his mind.

[9] On the metamorphoses of the Essene-Qumran hypothesis in the scholarly literature, see Campbell 1999, 813–14; Hutchesson 2000, 17–28.

[10] Rengstorf (1960) suggested that the scrolls originated in the temple library in Jerusalem.

[11] Golb (1995, 143–49; 1999) has summarized the Jerusalem hypothesis of the scrolls' source.

[12] Cansdale 1997, 96–97.

[13] Golb 1999, 828–29; Cansdale 1997, 192. Roth (1959) rejected the connection between the owners of the scrolls at Qumran and the Essenes. Davies (1990, 507–8) and Goodman (1995, 161) have also expressed similar reservations.

Qumran have been variously interpreted as a fort,[14] a road-station,[15] or the industrial center of an agricultural estate that included within its area the nearby oasis of 'Ein Feshkha. A number of scholars now accept the interpretation of Qumran as the center of an agricultural estate.[16]

The Dead Sea Scrolls were found in the vicinity of the site, but not among the remains themselves. By reexamining the vestiges of Qumran on their own terms, in isolation from the content of the scrolls, we can release Qumran from the interpretive impasse in which it has become trapped, whereby the scrolls explain the finds and the finds explain the scrolls. As Edna Ullmann-Margalit points out, a vicious circle characterized de Vaux's interpretation.[17] On the one hand, he conferred cultic significance on the excavation finds in accordance with the spirit of the scrolls and the description of the Essenes in the writings of Josephus Flavius and Philo. This allowed him to conclude, "The community [of Qumran] was religious in character, with special religious observances of its own."[18] On the other hand, the same finds are presented as archaeological evidence for the identification of the writers of the scrolls and the inhabitants of Qumran with the Essenes; according to de Vaux, "the Essenes . . . are the community of Qumran."[19]

Recently published archaeological data indicate that Qumran was not isolated but functioned within the specialized economy of the Dead Sea region. The proximity of Jerusalem, the political and religious center of the Jews in the Second Temple period, must be taken into consideration as well.[20]

1.2. The Physical Setting

The Dead Sea Valley is long and narrow, running from north to south and delimited by high mountains on the west and east. To the west of Qumran, the Judean mountains attain a height of about 1,000 m above sea level. To Qumran's east, the peaks of the mountains of Moab are about 1,500 m above sea level.

The Dead Sea region is one of the driest and hottest on earth. The average annual rainfall is low, ranging between 100 mm in the north and below 50 mm in the south.[21]

---

[14] It was Golb (1994, 37–41) who proposed that the archaeological remains at Qumran should be interpreted as a fort. On the different interpretations of the site, see Murphy 2002, 350–55.

[15] On Qumran as a fortified road-station on the main road between En-Gedi and Jerusalem, see Cansdale 1997, 123–24.

[16] See Donceel-Voûte 1994, 34; Donceel and Donceel-Voûte 1994, 26–27; Kapera 1996; Hirschfeld 1998, 182; Zangenberg 2000a. On the other hand, the proposal made by Sapiro (1997) that Qumran should be regarded as a production center for papyrus lacks supporters.

[17] Ullmann-Margalit 1998.

[18] Vaux 1973, 87.

[19] Ibid., 136.

[20] In this approach I have adopted the view of scholars such as Jürgen Zangenberg and Gabriele Fassbeck, who examine the site in its regional context. See Zangenberg 2000a; forthcoming; Fassbeck 2000.

[21] This description of the physical setting of the Dead Sea region is based on Raz 1993; Potcher 2000; Hadas 2002, 7–16.

The temperatures are high throughout the year; during the summer the average maximum daily temperature is 33–38°C, and the winter is mild, with an average maximum daily temperature of 20–22°C. The lowest temperature ever recorded is 3°C, indicating that the region never suffers from frost. The relative-humidity values are low even during the winter.

In his description of the region, Josephus says that the climate in winter "is so mild that the inhabitants wear linen when snow is falling throughout the rest of Judaea."[22] On the other hand, he says that in summer "the surrounding region is so parched up, that one can scarcely venture out of doors."[23] The skeletal remains recovered from the Second Temple period tombs to the west of Jericho demonstrate the advantages of the region. According to anthropologists Baruch Arensburg and Patricia Smith, the age and sex distributions of the 192 individuals identified "point to lower infant mortality and a higher percentage of adults surviving beyond the age of 50 in Jericho than in Jerusalem. These differences may be climate-related; winters in Jericho are warm and mild, while in Jerusalem they can be very cold and damp."[24] This is probably why kings and aristocrats from Jerusalem built palaces and villas at Jericho, Masada, Callirrhoe (on the eastern shore of the Dead Sea), Machaerus, and other places around the Dead Sea.

The Dead Sea is defined as a terminal lake, that is, one that water enters but does not exit. Because of the low elevation, high temperatures, and high evaporation rate, this is one of the saltiest bodies of water in the world: about 30 percent of its water consists of dissolved salts and minerals of various kinds. It is composed of two basins, the northern basin, 56 km long, and the southern basin, 13 km long. A peninsula known as "the Tongue" (ha-Lashon in Hebrew, Lisan in Arabic) separates the two basins. The earlier shape of the Dead Sea is known from maps of the 1940s and 1950s, when its water level was –392 m (i.e., 392 m below sea level). Today the southern basin is dry, just as it appears in the late-sixth-century/seventh-century C.E. Madaba mosaic map, discovered in Jordan. The reason for this is that the water level has changed.[25] The elevation of the threshold between the two basins is –402 m. In dry periods like the present-day one, the level drops below –402 m and the southern basin dries up. When the Madaba mosaic map was made, the Dead Sea's level was probably below –402 m.

The Dead Sea is fed by a small number of permanent water sources, such as the Jordan River, Wadi Mujib (Nahal Arnon), and Wadi Hasa (Nahal Zered), and the springs that flow in the oases on its shores. Its most important water source, however, is the powerful winter floods that gush in from all directions (fig. 90, color). The Dead Sea is an exceptionally large drainage basin that extends over about 40,000 sq km and includes parts of six states: Israel, the Palestinian Authority, Jordan, Syria, Lebanon, and Egypt (fig. 3). Since floods constitute its principal water source, the water level of the Dead Sea varies from time to time in accordance with global climatic changes. In periods of low precipitation, the level drops by dozens of meters, whereas in periods of high humidity and increased rainfall the

---

[22] Josephus, *J.W.* 4.473 (Thackeray).
[23] Josephus, *J.W.* 471 (Thackeray).
[24] Arensburg and Smith 1983, 136.
[25] On the Dead Sea levels, see Amiran 1997.

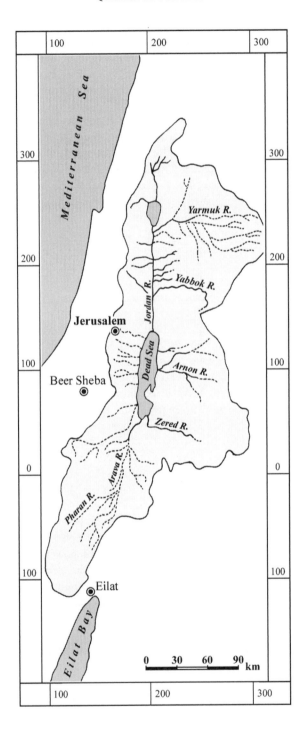

Figure 3. Map of the Dead Sea watershed.

level rises.[26] These fluctuations of the water level had a decisive impact on the road system in the Dead Sea region and on the potential for agriculture in the oases along its shores.

Scholars who support the Essene-Qumran hypothesis generally emphasize the barrenness of the Dead Sea area and the salinity of its springs. Thus, for example, Jodi Magness claims that the springs of 'Ein Feshkha, 'Ein el-Ghuweir, and 'Ein et-Turabeh are saline (fig. 4).[27] In support of her statement, Magness quotes the testimonies of several nineteenth-century travelers and explorers of the Dead Sea Valley, saying that the waters of 'Ein Feshkha are brackish and have a salty taste.[28] Her conclusion is that in the immediate vicinity of Qumran there are no permanent sources of fresh water.

Magness, however, overlooks the fact that periodic, climate-induced fluctuations of the Dead Sea have a significant effect on the salinity of the springs along its shores. Hydrological research has shown that climatic change influences both the flow of the springs and the level of the Dead Sea. Increased rainfall in Jerusalem raises the level and increases the flow of fresh water in the springs. In contrast to the dry climate of the nineteenth century, the first half of the twentieth century was much wetter, and the level rose to –393 m.[29] Indeed, the accounts of travelers and explorers of the early twentieth century inform us that the water of the springs of 'Ein Feshkha, 'Ein el-Ghuweir, and 'Ein et-Turabeh was sweet.[30] Today the situation is almost catastrophic; their water level at the time of the writing this book is –418 m, and it is falling rapidly at a rate of 0.8 m per year. As a result, the springs along the Dead Sea shore are extremely saline.

The important issue here, however, is the fluctuation of the level of the Dead Sea during the Hellenistic and early Roman periods. Geological and archaeological data seem to indicate that the level was relatively high, around –395 m.[31] Three ancient harbors, at Khirbet Mazin, Rujum el-Baḥr, and Callirrhoe confirm that this was the Dead Sea's level in this period.[32] This high level shows that the climate in the Second Temple period was wet, like that of the early twentieth century. It may be assumed that oases along the Dead Sea such as 'Ein Feshkha, 'En Boqeq, and others had an abundant supply of sweet water.

---

[26] Underhill 1967; Frumkin 1997; Frumkin and Elitzur 2001. In the past these changes were due to natural processes and occurred relatively slowly. Today, however, they are mainly the result of human intervention and take place much more rapidly.

[27] Magness 2002, 19–21.

[28] Ibid. Magness quotes from the descriptions of Robinson and Smith, who visited the Dead Sea region in 1838, and de Saulcy, who visited it in the mid-nineteenth century.

[29] Underhill 1967, 48, table 1; Schattner 1962, 105–7; Mazor and Molcho 1972; Mazor 1997.

[30] It is of interest to trace the changing descriptions of visitors to 'Ein Feshkha over time. Thus, e.g., in 1873 Conder and Kitchener (1883, 171) described the water as "slightly brackish." Masterman (1902, 164–65), who visited the oasis in 1900–1901, mentions the fresh water of 'Ein Feshkha and describes another small spring to its north, named 'Ein Mabneyeh, as a "fresh limpid stream of water." In 1934 a group of fourteen travelers headed by Raphi Tahoon found among the rocks a "fresh, sweet spring" (Tahoon 1990, 255). These three accounts accord with the data on the rise of the Dead Sea's level in the early twentieth century.

[31] Frumkin 1997, 243–44; Hirschfeld 2004c.

[32] For the most recent information on Khirbet Mazin, see Hirschfeld 2002; for Rujum el-Baḥr, see Bar-Adon 1989, 1–14; for the harbor at Callirrhoe, see 'Amr et al. 1996, 441. These sites will be discussed below in ch. 5.

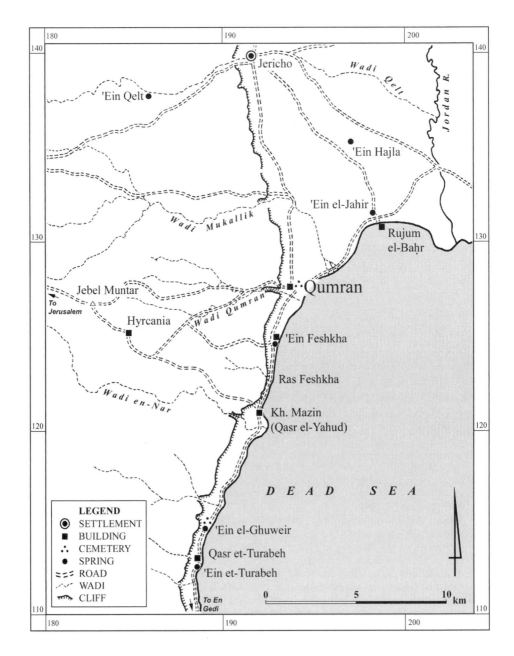

Figure 4. Map showing the springs south of Qumran: 'Ein Feshkha,
'Ein el-Ghuweir, and 'Ein et-Turabeh.

Indeed, it is when the level of the Dead Sea is around −395 m that the inhabitants of the region enjoy the best of both worlds. When the level is above −390 m, as it was, for example, in the early Byzantine period,[33] the Dead Sea covers the coastal plain, and oases such as that of ʿEin Feshkha contract. The water reaches the cliff of Ras Feshkha (Rosh Tsuqim) (see below), and road transportation along the shore is impossible. On the other hand, when the level is below −400 m, many of the springs dry up and some become brackish. Consequently, the inhabitants of Qumran and other sites in the Dead Sea Valley in the first century B.C.E. and first century C.E. enjoyed the most favorable conditions that the region can offer.

The archaeological evidence supports this assessment. Surveys and excavations conducted since the 1950s have shown that the entire region witnessed a building boom in the Second Temple period, when most of the territory around the Dead Sea came under the control of the Hasmoneans and later of Herod. These include Jericho, Qumran, En-Gedi, Masada, and ʿEn Boqeq along the western shore and Callirrhoe, and Machaerus along the eastern and southern shores.[34]

In the late Hellenistic and early Roman periods, the Dead Sea region supported vigorous economic activity. The cultivation of date palms was and still is the backbone of the regional economy. These trees are indigenous to the region and cope very well with the extreme climate and the salinity of the aquifer. Since date palms filter much of the salt from the water and provide shade, they create ideal conditions for the cultivation of other crops, such as barley and vegetables, between the rows. Dates were the source of date honey (*silan*), an important element of the ancient diet.[35] In addition, palm trees provided the raw material for construction, furniture, and countless useful utensils. Balsam was intensively cultivated in the region and assured even greater earnings.[36] A description of the gardens of Jericho toward the end of the nineteenth century may give us an impression of the region's fertility in the later Hellenistic and Roman eras as well: "In these gardens every kind of vegetable is grown. . . . The grapes, trained on trellises four feet high, grow to good size. Wheat and barley is also of good quality."[37]

In addition to date palms, balsam shrubs were cultivated, from which costly perfumes and ointments were produced. Other plants also yielded ointments and perfumes (such as myrrh, frankincense, and nard), and fruits were also grown. The sea itself was a source of minerals, such as bitumen and edible salt.[38] Because of the constant demand, natural bitumen, sulfur, and salt gave a high return on a minimal investment of effort and connected the Dead Sea Valley with international trade networks leading to Egypt and even Rome.[39]

The excavations conducted in the desert oases of En-Gedi, ʿEn Boqeq, and Callirrhoe have revealed villas, farmhouses, workshops, and installations of these periods.[40] These are

---

[33] On the level during the Byzantine period, see Hadas 2002, 13–15; Hirschfeld 2004c.

[34] Fischer, Gichon, and Tal 2000, 143–44, gives a similar list of sites.

[35] Ayalon 1987, 78–79; Hadas 2002, 34–36.

[36] Patrich and Arubas 1989; Donceel-Voûte 1998; Gichon 2000.

[37] Conder and Kitchener 1883, 189.

[38] Beit Arieh 1996; Gichon 2000, 93–102; Hadas 2002, 28–55; Zangenberg forthcoming.

[39] See Hammond 1959 on the value of bitumen to the inhabitants of the Dead Sea shores; and Amar 1998a on the production of salt and sulphur in the region.

[40] For En-Gedi, see Mazar 1993; for ʿEn Boqeq, see Fischer, Gichon, and Tal 2000; for Callirrhoe, see Clamer 1997.

in addition to the palaces and fortresses built by the Hasmonean dynasty and by Herod at Jericho, Masada, and Machaerus. Consequently, in the relevant period Qumran was far from being a backwater but, rather, was located in a busy area, close to routes that connected the sites of the Dead Sea with the regional capital of Jericho and the capital city of Jerusalem in the hills. Broshi and his colleagues admit that Jerusalem is only "one day's donkey journey away" from Qumran, and Jericho is only "a two-hour walk."[41] He also draws our attention to the harbors, which were a crucial element in the local traffic network. To those at Khirbet Mazin and Rujum el-Baḥr we can add the harbor of En-Gedi and that of Callirrhoe on the eastern shore, which served as the main approach to Machaerus.[42] Thus, a complex network of routes connected all the settlements around the Dead Sea and also linked the entire region with the Judean Hills to the west and Peraea and the mountains of Moab to the east. In addition, the series of sites along the western shore of the Dead Sea also indicate that Qumran was located on a central crossroads.[43]

The question of Qumran's function is related to its location within the road system of Judea in the late Hellenistic and early Roman periods and its proximity to the eastern frontier of the kingdom of Judea, bordering on the Nabatean kingdom. Scholars who endorse the Essene-Qumran hypothesis generally point to what, in their view, was the isolated location of Qumran. Thus, for example, Broshi points to the promontory of Ras Feshkha, which protruded into the Dead Sea and prevented traffic along it: "No major roads passed by Qumran. . . . Only narrow trails connected Qumran to the rest of the world, no more than that. No north-south roads passed by it." [44]

The southern end of the oasis of 'Ein Feshkha is indeed bounded by a steep cliff known in Arabic as Ras Feshkha.[45] The cliff, about 60 m high, descends almost vertically to the shore, leaving only a narrow passage (fig. 91, color). In 1900 one of the boulders at the foot of Ras Feshkha was marked with the initials P.E.F. (which can still be seen above the sign and under a carved horizontal line about three-fourths of the way up the large rock) on behalf of the Palestine Exploration Fund (fig. 5). At that time the mark was 14 ft (4.2 m) above the sea level of ca. −393 m. Between the water line and the P.E.F. Rock was a narrow path.[46] Broshi writes that the elevation at the foot of the P.E.F. Rock is −399 m and that therefore "the level of the Dead Sea must be below −400 m. to enable traffic along the foot of Ras Feshkha."[47]

At my request, a team of qualified surveyors measured the elevation at the foot of Ras Feshkha. They found that the elevation is −393 m, 6 m higher than that given by Broshi.[48] Consequently, in the late Hellenistic and early Roman periods, when the Dead Sea's level

---

41 Yellin, Broshi, and Eshel 2001, 65.

42 Strobel 1977; Strobel and Clamer 1986. On the harbor at En-Gedi, see Hadas 1993.

43 Bar-Adon 1981, 348; Walker 1993; Cansdale 1997, 104–6; Hirschfeld 1998, 171–74; Zangenberg forthcoming.

44 Broshi 1999, 273.

45 Markus 1970.

46 Underhill 1967, 45–48, table 1; Masterman 1902, 156.

47 Broshi 1999, 273.

48 My thanks to Avi Blumenkrantz and Shomroni, who carried out the measurement on June 23, 2003. The absolute height of the ground at the foot of the P.E.F. Rock is −391.75 m.

Figure 5. The P.E.F. Rock at Ras Feshkha, looking west (enhanced).

was around −395 m, the route leading south from Qumran via Ras Feshkha to En-Gedi and Masada was open (fig. 6).

The major route from Jerusalem and other settlements in the Judean Hills in the west to Jericho and the northern part of the Dead Sea follows the riverbed of Wadi Qelt (Nahal Prat). Additional secondary routes follow other riverbeds to reach the sites along the western shore of the Dead Sea. Ma'aleh Qumran has been mentioned above. A path named Ma'aleh Feshkha climbs to the west from 'Ein Feshkha. This is a relatively comfortable ascent that permits traffic of pedestrians and pack animals from the oasis on the shore of the Dead Sea to the Valley of Hyrcania to the west, and from there to Jerusalem.[49] Other paths ascend the cliffs to the west of the major sites, such as Khirbet Mazin, En-Gedi, Masada, and 'En Boqeq.[50]

Because of the extreme climate and barrenness of the Dead Sea region today, Qumran appears to be the perfect habitat for a self-contained, isolated, and ascetic community. Thus, for example, in her book on the archaeology of Qumran—a site with an exceptional number of workshops and installations—Magness overlooks the unique economy of the area. Consequently, the word "balsam," which is mentioned by ancient authors such as Josephus, Strabo, and Pliny as the source of a highly prized perfume, does not appear at all in Magness's book.[51]

All evidence points to the fact that far from being an out-of-the-way hermitage, Qumran, in fact, had an important place within the highly developed agriculture-based economy of the Dead Sea region in the late Hellenistic and early Roman periods.[52]

1.3. The History of Research: Fieldwork

In 1873, long before the discovery of the Dead Sea Scrolls, the British surveyors Claude Conder and Herbert Kitchener visited Qumran. Among the ruined buildings, they described a pool lined with unhewn stones and a flight of steps leading down into it. They noted "the immense numbers of graves occupying the plateau and the eastern slope," which they estimated as numbering "some 700 or more."[53] They observed that the north-south orientation of the graves rules out the possibility that these are burials of Muslims. They excavated one of the graves and found the remains of a skeleton with its head to the south.

A year later, in 1874, the French archaeologist Charles Clermont-Ganneau visited the site and, like Conder and Kitchener, excavated one of the graves.[54] As noted above, the British scholar Masterman visited the sites of Qumran and 'Ein Feshkha several times in

---

[49] Markus 1986, 134; Magness 2002, 203.
[50] On the roads in the Dead Sea region, see Dorsey 1991, 147–50; Cansdale 1997, 104–7.
[51] Magness 2002, general index (pp. 236–38).
[52] On the economy of the Dead Sea region, see Porath 1986; Fischer, Gichon, and Tal 2000, 139–46; Hadas 2002; Zangenberg 2000a; forthcoming.
[53] Conder and Kitchener 1883, 210. On the research of Khirbet Qumran in the nineteenth century, see Taylor 2002a.
[54] Clermont-Ganneau 1899, 14–16.

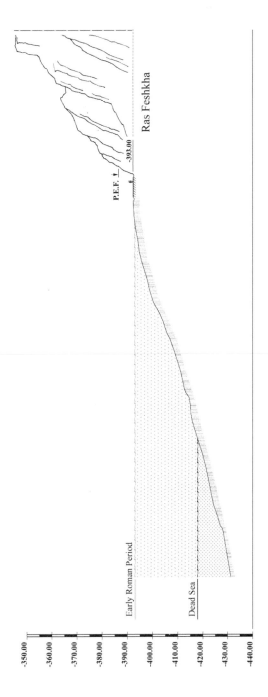

Figure 6. Cross-section showing the levels of the Dead Sea. Scale is meters below sea level.

1900–1901. Masterman described the ancient roads leading to the site, which in his opinion "may very well have been once a small fortress,"[55] and was the first scholar to describe Qumran's rock-cut aqueduct. Subsequent research has confirmed Masterman's assumption that "this little aqueduct was made to fill with the winter rains the cistern or cisterns connected with the building now known as the ruin Kumrân."[56]

Next to explore Qumran, in 1914, was the German scholar Gustav Dalman.[57] Like his predecessors, Dalman described the ruins of buildings (including a column base) and the water conduit running from Wadi Qumran. Like Masterman, he concluded that the site might have been a fortress.

The first scrolls were famously discovered by Bedouin in 1946–1947 in Cave 1 about 2 km north of Qumran (fig. 7). Some of the scrolls came into the hands of Eliezer Lippa Sukenik of the Hebrew University of Jerusalem, who was the first to suggest a connection with the Essenes.[58] In 1949 de Vaux and Lankester Harding, the chief inspector of antiquities in Jordan, located and excavated Cave 1 (fig. 8).[59] In addition to pottery, pieces of linen cloth, and other artifacts, they found fragments of additional manuscripts. They also surveyed the site of Qumran and excavated two graves in the cemetery.

Excitement about the scrolls was growing. Sukenik had already identified the biblical book of Isaiah among them, and this fired the imagination of people throughout the world. Harding and de Vaux therefore returned to Qumran in 1951 to carry out the first season of excavations. De Vaux alone conducted later seasons. The Bedouin continued their search of the caves for manuscripts. In 1951 they found scrolls in Cave 2, prompting archaeologists to carry out a systematic survey of the caves in the cliffs behind Qumran.[60] During this expedition (in 1952), the archaeologists discovered Cave 3, which yielded the enigmatic *Copper Scroll*. But it was next to the site itself that Bedouin workmen accidentally discovered the richest cave of all, Cave 4, containing about six hundred scrolls. Cave 5 was found near Cave 4 (fig. 9), and during the excavation of Cave 4, Cave 6 was discovered in the limestone cliffs behind Qumran. Caves 7, 8, and 9 were found at the southern end of the marl plateau on which Qumran is situated.[61] Cave 10, near Cave 4, lacked scrolls but yielded archaeological finds. Bedouin discovered Cave 11, the last one containing scrolls, south of Cave 3 in 1954.[62] Since the mouth of the cave was blocked, the twenty-five scrolls that it contained had been preserved in relatively good condition. Thus, eventually eleven caves containing about 850 scrolls and thousands of fragments were discovered in the vicinity of Qumran.

The first season of excavations at Qumran was carried out five years after the discovery of the first scrolls, and so it was inevitable that to a great extent the excavations would be conducted under the powerful impact of the scrolls. De Vaux was an active participant

---

[55] Masterman 1902, 161.
[56] Masterman 1903, 267.
[57] Dalman 1914, 9–11.
[58] Sukenik 1948, 16.
[59] Harding 1949, 112–15; 1955, 5–7.
[60] de Vaux 1962, 4–31; Reed 1954, 9–13.
[61] On the excavation of Cave 4, see de Vaux 1977, 9–21.
[62] On the discovery of Cave 11, see Harding 1958, 17.

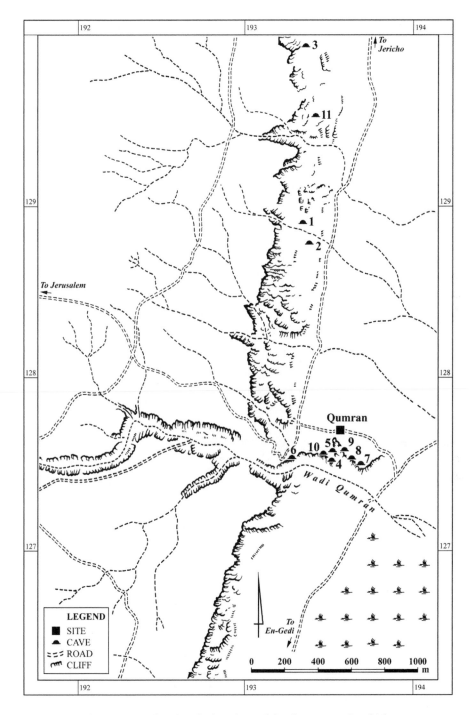

Figure 7. Map showing the locations of the eleven caves in which
the Dead Sea Scrolls were found.

Figure 8. The opening of Cave 1, looking west.
(Courtesy of Israel Antiquities Authority.)

Figure 9. Caves 4 and 5 (foreground) southwest of Qumran, looking southwest.

in the discovery and deciphering of the scrolls. A member of the Dominican order in Jerusalem, he saw the scrolls as making a huge contribution to the understanding of the birth of Christianity in the Dead Sea region. It was only natural for him to identify the inhabitants of the site with the people who concealed the scrolls found in the nearby caves.

This approach accorded with the general tendency of biblical archaeology in the twentieth century to attribute to cultic activity anything that could not otherwise be explained.[63] In de Vaux's time, the site of Qumran was indeed anomalous in many respects. In the early 1950s, the large-scale excavations of Masada, En-Gedi, and Jericho had not yet taken place, nor had the smaller excavations at 'En Boqeq and Callirrhoe. Qumran was the forerunner of all these excavations, and consequently many of its finds were unique at the time. For example, the large number of mikvehs (Hebrew *miqva'ot;* stepped pools used by Jews for ritual immersion), which we know today is a common feature of Second Temple period sites, was a startling discovery for de Vaux.

The finds of the first season prompted de Vaux to undertake large-scale excavations at Qumran during four seasons, from 1953 to 1956. During Qumran's last season and again in 1958, de Vaux also excavated at 'Ein Feshkha.[64]

Few other sites of the Second Temple period (among them is Masada) have been uncovered to such a great extent. Other sites that bear similarities to Qumran have been only partially excavated. Therefore items that we know from Qumran may actually also be present at these other sites without our knowledge. For example, in Qumran even the garden area outside the building was intensively excavated. The other sites may also have kitchen gardens yet to be revealed. In my opinion, the extensive exposure of Qumran is its outstanding feature. Another noteworthy element is the fact that the dry climate preserved organic materials—such the scrolls, made of parchment, and textiles—to a greater extent than would be possible in wet areas. And Qumran's isolation in later periods meant that its remains lay undisturbed. In the Byzantine period, for example, when other areas of the country were extremely populated, even in the desert, Qumran was not settled.[65]

The excavation seasons at Qumran and 'Ein Feshkha were long and employed many local Bedouin laborers. In the first two seasons, the main building was exposed. The third season was devoted mainly to the industrial quarter to the southeast of the main building, and the fourth season to the industrial quarter to its west. As part of the project, de Vaux excavated forty-three graves in the cemetery to the east of the site.[66]

In the excavations of Qumran and 'Ein Feshkha, each architectural space (room, hall, courtyard, or installation) was numbered as a separate locus, though in a few cases the same

---

[63] Yeivin (1973, 163) pointed to what he saw as a deplorable tendency in biblical archaeology, the tendency of scholars "to regard every more or less unusual find as something connected with ritual and holy places, whether it is the remains of a building or vessels or their sherds." It seems to me that these words are also applicable to the archaeology of Qumran.

[64] For the preliminary report of the excavations at 'Ein Feshkha, see de Vaux 1959b.

[65] In my recent excavation at En-Gedi, we realized that at the beginning of the fourth century the Dead Sea totally covered the Roman bath built at the beginning of the second century. It may be assumed that most of the oasis of 'Ein Feshkha was submerged during this period also. See Hirschfeld, 2004a.

[66] For a summary of the excavation of the cemeteries at Qumran and 'Ein Feshkha, see Donceel 2002.

installation was given two numbers (e.g., the stepped pool in the eastern wing of the main building was designated Locus 48/49). The excavated graves were numbered from 1 to 43.

The numerous caves near Qumran were also numbered. As noted, scrolls were found in eleven caves. Five of these, 1Q, 2Q, 3Q, 6Q, and 11Q, are natural karstic caves in the limestone cliffs behind the site. The other six, 4Qa–b, 5Q, 7Q, 8Q, 9Q and 10Q, are man-made caves cut into the marl plateau on which the site is located. In 1952 an expedition headed by de Vaux surveyed the area around the site. Of the caves discovered in this short time, 230 were barren of artifacts and only 40 contained pottery and other items.[67]

Qumran was much richer in finds than the nearby site of 'Ein Feshkha. De Vaux discovered hundreds of coins, vessels, and other artifacts under the debris of Qumran's destruction by the Roman army during the First Revolt. The small finds from Qumran and 'Ein Feshkha were divided between two institutions in Jerusalem: the Rockefeller Museum, at that time under the auspices of the Department of Antiquities of Jordan, and the École Biblique, with which de Vaux was associated.

Several excavations have taken place at Qumran since those of de Vaux. Two small excavations were conducted in the 1960s. One, under the direction of R. W. Dajjani, was part of restoration work at the site shortly before the 1967 War, when the site was still under Jordanian control.[68] In 1965–1967 Solomon H. Steckoll excavated twelve tombs in the cemetery.[69]

In the 1980s and 1990s, Israeli archaeologists investigated the caves. In 1984–1985 Joseph Patrich of the Hebrew University conducted a systematic survey and excavations of caves in the Qumran region.[70] During the survey seventeen caves were found to contain archaeological remains, such as pottery and small finds. In 1986–1991 Patrich excavated five caves. In one of them, known as the "Balsam Oil Cave," a Herodian juglet wrapped in palm fibers and containing remains of a viscous oil was found (fig. 10).[71] According to Patrich, the survey and excavations provided evidence that temporary residents such as shepherds, laborers, or refugees inhabited the caves near Qumran.

In the winter of 1995–1996, a team headed by Broshi and Eshel conducted excavations in several caves north of Qumran.[72] Like previous researchers, they uncovered only portable objects such as pottery, and they found no permanent installations. Nevertheless, they claimed that the owners of the site used the caves in the vicinity of Qumran as living quarters.

From 1996 to 2002 Itzhak Magen and Yuval Peleg of the Israel Antiquities Authority carried out the most significant excavation at the site of Qumran since de Vaux's work. In a conference at Brown University in 2002 on the archaeology of Qumran, Magen and Peleg presented the remarkable discoveries of that dig.[73] They unearthed hundreds of artifacts,

---

[67] On the survey of the caves and the small finds discovered in them, see above, n. 61

[68] Donceel and Donceel-Voûte 1994, 11 n. 37.

[69] Steckoll 1968; Kapera 1994, 9; Norton 2003, 123.

[70] Patrich 1994a.

[71] Patrich and Arubas 1989.

[72] Broshi and Eshel 1999b.

[73] Magen and Peleg 2002. Magness (2002, 121) mentions these excavations only briefly and does not take the opportunity to discuss their data. The papers of this conference will be published in 2005 (Galor, Humbert, and Zangenberg, forthcoming).

Figure 10. Herodian juglet containing balsam oil (?). Scale is in cm.
(Courtesy of J. Patrich.)

including pottery, glass and stone vessels, coins, jewelry, bronze objects, and organic materials, and discovered new installations and workshops.

During restoration work undertaken at the site by the Nature and Parks Authority in 1997–1999, I was able to examine the water system and take measurements of the reservoirs and mikvehs at the site. A team of surveyors headed by Israel Vatkin carefully surveyed the cemetery and counted the graves.[74]

In April 2001 I conducted a short season of excavations at 'Ein Feshkha.[75] The excavations focused on two areas, the *villa rustica* of the early Roman period excavated in 1956 and 1958 by de Vaux (Area A) and the remains of a small tower of the late Iron Age that were discovered during our work (Area B). I also carried out a survey of the oasis between Wadi Qumran and 'Ein Feshkha.

Two additional investigations complete this list of archaeological activities in and around Qumran. In 1996 James E. Strange of the University of South Florida conducted a geophysical survey on the plateau south and east of the site. In one of the probes under the surface of the soil to the south, a potsherd inscribed in Hebrew was found.[76] The Israel Museum in Jerusalem now exhibits this sherd, which has become known as the Yahad Ostracon.

In the summer of 2001, Broshi and Eshel led an expedition to map the cemetery of Qumran.[77] A year later, in the summer of 2002, the expedition excavated the remains of a small building (designated Building B by de Vaux) on a low hill at the easternmost end of the cemetery. The skeleton of a male between thirty-five and forty-five years old with his head toward the Dead Sea was found in what is now known as Tomb 1000. On the basis of this scant evidence, Broshi and Eshel suggested that this individual was one of the leaders of the Yahad community at Qumran (*Mevaqer Tzedek* in Hebrew), mentioned in the sectarian scrolls as the leader of the community.

1.4. The History of Research: Scholarly Work

Despite the importance of Qumran and the fact that the Dead Sea Scrolls were discovered not on the site but in the nearby caves, the vast majority of scholarly works have been devoted to the scrolls, with only a few synthetic scholarly works focusing on its archaeology. The conference held at Brown University in 2002 was the first dedicated to the archaeology of Qumran. Even scholars who purported to take a comprehensive look at Qumran, such as Magness (who is the first since de Vaux to attempt the task), do not devote nearly enough space to the archaeology. The lack of expertise in archaeology among some outside the field may also have impeded their efforts. In the case of Magness, however, even though I do not agree with her conclusions, her description of the finds from an archaeological perspective is excellent.

---

[74] The survey was carried out in coordination with two staff members of the Nature and Parks Authority, Assi Shalom and Amnon Bar-Or.

[75] Hirschfeld 2004a.

[76] Cross and Eshel 1997.

[77] Broshi and Eshel 2003, 71.

During the excavations at Qumran and 'Ein Feshkha, de Vaux published preliminary reports in the *Revue biblique,* the periodical of his institution in Jerusalem.[78] Later, in 1961, de Vaux published an overview of the archaeology of Qumran in French, and an expanded English version was published in 1973, two years after his death.[79]

Our understanding of Qumran still very much depends on de Vaux's publications. His writing, however, suffers from two major drawbacks: overinterpretation and the omission of evidence. The tendency to overinterpret relatively simple and well-known objects and architectural features can be traced throughout his publications. For instance, he describes a hall that was probably used for dining as the main assembly hall, also used for ritual meals; animal bones found in a cultivated area outside the buildings as ritual deposits; an oven as a communal bakery oven; and so on.[80]

Overinterpretation is not an uncommon weakness among us archaeologists. It is natural to be tempted to exaggerate the special features of a site. Much more serious is de Vaux's habit of omitting evidence that might undermine the Qumran-Essene hypothesis. In his publications, he disregards various finds attesting to the wealth of the inhabitants of Qumran. For example, his publications give scant attention to decorated architectural elements, including molded stucco. He does not mention at all other finds that are crucial for our ability to identify the people of Qumran, such as stone and glass vessels, fine potteryware, cosmetic utensils, and spindle whorls.

The English version of de Vaux's overview, entitled *Archaeology and the Dead Sea Scrolls,* played a crucial role in shaping the unique vocabulary of the archaeology of Qumran. Perhaps because of his French background, as mentioned, or his eagerness to present Qumran as a sectarian site, de Vaux established some eccentric terms to describe the remains. For example, he dubs the plateau on which Qumran lies "the esplanade," and the settling tanks that were installed at the openings of most of the cisterns and stepped pools (a standard device for cleaning the rainwater and collecting silt sediments to enrich the gardens) are strangely termed "decantation basins."[81] These terms, and many others, became part of the vocabulary of many archaeological works dealing with Qumran.

The unique vocabulary, however, was not limited to technical terms. Thus, rather than using the standard term "stratum," de Vaux uses the term "period" to describe the chronological layers of the site. A site such as Qumran, which dates basically from one major period and has a coherent plan, is usually described as a complex or compound. A complex may be a fortress if it is fortified, a farmhouse if there are signs of agricultural activity, or a villa or palace if there are signs of grandeur. The site of Qumran, however, is described by de Vaux as "the establishment of a community."[82] By using such terminology, de Vaux gave Qumran a vague definition that enhances a sense of its uniqueness and so accords with the sectarian interpretation. Other advocates of the Qumran-Essene hypothesis use

---

[78] de Vaux 1953a; 1954; 1956; 1959b.

[79] de Vaux 1961; 1973.

[80] de Vaux 1973, 11–12 (for the dining hall), 12–13 (for the animal bones), 26 (for the oven). On the overinterpretation that characterizes de Vaux's publications, see Davies 1988.

[81] de Vaux 1973, 3 ("esplanade"), 4 ("decantation basin").

[82] Ibid., 10.

similar terminology. For instance, Magness defines Qumran as "a sectarian settlement" although in archaeology the term "settlement" usually refers to a village or town.[83]

The hypothesis that the Essenes were the people who lived at Qumran and who wrote the Dead Sea Scrolls appeared at the very beginning of Qumran studies, and until the 1980s, the interpretation proposed by de Vaux was widely accepted. Such notable scholars as André Dupont-Sommer,[84] John M. Allegro,[85] Geza Vermes,[86] Frank Moore Cross,[87] J. T. Milik,[88] and E. F. Sutcliffe,[89] most of whom had a background in history, epigraphy, or theology, supported and developed the consensus.

A surprise in this regard was the Israeli archaeologist Yigael Yadin. In *The Message of the Scrolls*,[90] he adopted de Vaux's conclusions in their entirety although at that time he was unable to visit the site of Qumran and examine the excavation finds for himself. In addition, Yadin was known to have been a sharp critic of his fellow archaeologists, yet he accepted de Vaux's interpretation without reservations. It is difficult to explain Yadin's sweeping support for de Vaux's interpretation.[91]

Yadin's influence on the study of Qumran and the scrolls has been great and long-lasting: he was involved in the translation and deciphering of some of the scrolls, and it was on his initiative that the Shrine of the Book, in which parts of the scrolls and some of the excavation finds are exhibited to the general public, was built in Jerusalem. For many years Magen Broshi, an ardent advocate of the Essene-Qumran hypothesis, headed the Shrine of the Book.[92] Since Yadin and Broshi accepted de Vaux's conclusions, most of the scholars dealing with Qumran, whether historians, epigraphists, or archaeologists, reached a consensus in favor of this hypothesis. It was only in the 1980s and 1990s that other voices seeking the total rejection of the Essene-Qumran hypothesis were first heard.

Ernest-Marie Laperrousaz, who took part in the excavation, made an important contribution to the study of Qumran and 'Ein Feshkha in 1976.[93] His book presents a useful summary of the data from both sites and complements the preliminary reports of de Vaux.

---

[83] As early as page 5 of her book, Magness (2002) writes, "At Qumran we can distinguish at least three successive occupation levels . . . during the relatively brief existence of the sectarian settlement," although the sectarian nature of the site remains to be demonstrated.

[84] Dupont-Sommer 1954.

[85] Allegro 1956.

[86] Vermes 1956.

[87] Cross 1958.

[88] Milik 1959.

[89] Sutcliffe 1960.

[90] Yadin 1957a (Hebrew); 1957b (English).

[91] On Yadin's contribution to creating consensus among Qumran scholars, see Silberman 2000, 921. In his celebrated biography of Yadin, Silberman (1993) rightly emphasizes Yadin's uniqueness as "a maker of historical myths." Shanks (1998, 14–15) gives a vivid description of Yadin's emotional involvement in purchasing the scrolls.

[92] Adolfo Roitman, Broshi's successor as director of the Shrine of the Book, in the exhibition catalogue, which he edited in the spirit of Yadin's legacy, wrote, "The basic assumption underlying the exhibition is that Khirbet Qumran and its surroundings were home to a Jewish sect of Essenes" (Roitman 1997, 7).

[93] Laperrousaz 1976.

In 1986, on the initiative of the École Biblique in Jerusalem, a team was set up to publish the final report of the excavations of Qumran and 'Ein Feshkha. It included two Belgian archaeologists, Robert Donceel and Pauline Donceel-Voûte of the Catholic University of Louvain. They had been invited by Jean-Baptiste Humbert, who is now the staff archaeologist at the École Biblique. The team worked for three years on the small finds: coins, lamps, glassware, pottery, stone vessels, metalware, and other artifacts. The preliminary reports published by the Donceels are a landmark in the archaeological research of Qumran. In a lavishly illustrated article published in 1994, Donceel-Voûte presented the wealth and variety of the small finds from Qumran.[94] For the first time, photographs of the stone vessels, glassware, and the rich assemblages of pottery discovered by de Vaux became accessible. In a joint article published in the same year, the Donceels gave a detailed survey of the small objects discovered by de Vaux.[95] This evidence is proof of the affluence of the owners of Qumran and their many contacts with Jerusalem and other centers in Judea and beyond.

Two beautiful catalogues illustrate the richness of the finds from Qumran, including those from the caves. The first catalogue, *Scrolls from the Dead Sea,* published in 1993 by Ayala Sussmann and Rutha Peled, accompanied an exhibition of scrolls and archaeological finds from the collections of the Israel Antiquities Authority.[96] The catalogue contains excellent photographs of items such as coins, stone vessels, pottery, leather objects such as sandals, and artifacts made of organic materials, such as linen cloth and straw basketry. The second catalogue, published in 1997 by Adolfo Roitman, is even richer.[97] It presents many archaeological items that have never been previously published, such as agricultural tools.

Although we still await a final excavation report, in 1994 Humbert together with Alain Chambon published a large volume described as the first in a series.[98] It contains the raw data of the excavation: plans, photographs from the time of the excavation, and de Vaux's original summary of each of the 144 loci excavated at Qumran and 36 loci at 'Ein Feshkha.[99] This publication for the first time enables analysis of de Vaux's working methods and points up the deficiencies that led to incorrect conclusions.

Three books dealing with the archaeology of Qumran were published in 2002. The first is that by Magness. Her claim that it "represents the most recent survey of the archaeology of Qumran"[100] is misleading because she ignores most of the recent publications de-

---

[94] Donceel-Voûte 1994.

[95] Donceel and Donceel-Voûte 1994. For the glassware of Qumran, see Donceel 1999/2000.

[96] Sussmann and Peled 1993.

[97] Roitman 1997; see also above, n. 93.

[98] Humbert and Chambon 1994. The volume contains an impressive quantity of data: 48 line drawings (maps and plans of the area) and 538 black-and-white photographs of the remains at Qumran at the time of their exposure. The original French edition has been translated into German, and has recently appeared in English (Pfann 2003).

[99] The editors added the last eight loci (nos. 145–152) in 1992 (ibid., 338–39). According to Donceel and Donceel-Voûte (1994, 15–18), de Vaux left eight notebooks containing handwritten descriptions of the excavation finds and an additional typed notebook summarizing the loci in numerical order. The last-mentioned notebook, which contains no measurements, elevations, or section drawings, is the one that was published in the preliminary report on the Qumran excavations.

[100] Magness 2002, 4.

scribing the small finds from Qumran, such as the works of the Donceels and the two catalogues. Magness admits that she had access only to the finds at the Rockefeller Museum,[101] and this means that she has seen only one-third of the material from Qumran. She did not pay a visit to the excavations of Magen and Peleg although they started in 1996, long before the publication of her book. Thus, her book is based mainly on the selective material published long ago by de Vaux. It is therefore not surprising that Magness comes to the conclusion that "all the available evidence supports de Vaux's interpretation of Qumran as a sectarian settlement."[102]

The second book, by the American scholar Catherine Murphy, deals with wealth in the Dead Sea Scrolls and at the site of Qumran.[103] Chapter 6 of her book presents a detailed survey of the small finds of Qumran and their significance. The third book, by Minna and Kenneth Lönnqvist of Finland, is a speculative work in which the authors attempt to show the wider connections of Qumran with Alexandria and the entire universe.[104] In 2002 the first conference dedicated exclusively to the archaeology of Qumran was held at Brown University in Providence, Rhode Island. This provided opportunity for the researchers involved in the archaeology of Qumran to exchange previously unpublished data and to communicate directly. The discussions clearly showed that the old consensus concerning Qumran, the Dead Sea Scrolls, and the Essenes is no longer valid.[105] The latest publication concerning the archaeology of Qumran appeared in 2003 as the second volume of the Final Report Series. The volume edited by Jean-Baptiste Humbert and Jan Gunneweg discusses several topics such as the cemetery, the miqvehs, the textiles, and an analysis of the pottery provenance. It does not, however, include a complete presentation of the small finds such as the pottery, glassware, stone vessels, metal objects, etc.[106]

Thus, there is still a need for a reassessment, based on all the currently available data, of the issues raised by Qumran. Chronologically, the discovery of the scrolls preceded the excavation of the site. The next chapter will therefore discuss the scrolls and the question of their provenance: Qumran or Jerusalem?

---

[101] Ibid., 3.

[102] Ibid., 15.

[103] Murphy 2002.

[104] Lönnqvist and Lönnqvist 2002. E.g., one of their chapters is entitled "Archaeoastronomy and the Settlement at Qumran."

[105] See Zangenberg and Galor 2003.

[106] Humbert and Gunneweg 2003.

CHAPTER 2

The Origin of the Scrolls: Qumran or Jerusalem?

2.1. The Discovery of the Scrolls

Yigael Yadin describes the 850 parts of scrolls discovered between 1947 and 1956 in the vicinity of Qumran as "the most important discovery made in Palestine in the fields of Bible, history and the annals of Judaism and Christianity."[1] From the archaeological point of view as well, this is truly one of the most important discoveries of all time.

Most of the scrolls are in Hebrew; some are in Aramaic or Greek or even in code. About twenty scrolls are complete whereas the others are preserved to varying extents. In addition to the complete and fragmentary scrolls, numerous scraps of scrolls were found. (Some estimates of their number run as high as fifteen thousand!)[2]

Scrolls have been discovered at other sites in the Judean Desert, such as Masada, Nahal Hever, Nahal Zeelim, and Wadi Murabba'at south of Qumran, and Ketef Jericho and Wadi Daliyeh to its north (fig. 11). They are known collectively as the Judean Desert scrolls.[3] Still, the interest of both scholars and the general public has focused on the scrolls from the caves near Qumran. The reason is simple. Most of the Judean Desert scrolls are prosaic in nature, comprising receipts, marriage and property contracts, and lists of various kinds, and belonged to people whose identity can be established, such as refugees who took shelter in the caves during the Bar Kokhba revolt. In contrast, the Dead Sea Scrolls, from the caves near Qumran, are overwhelmingly literary or religious in character. About a third of them are biblical, another third are sectarian, and the rest are general Jewish compositions that lack sectarian features, including, among others, tractates of Jewish religious law

---

[1] Yadin 1957a, 9.

[2] For up-to-date reviews of the scroll finds, see Woude 1998; Dimant 2000. More than ten thousand items appear in the bibliography of Martínez and Parry 1996; the number has probably doubled since then.

[3] For a general survey of caves in the Judean Desert in which scrolls have been found, see Eshel 2000. For the discoveries at Ketef Jericho, see Eshel and Zissu 2000. The finds from Nahal Hever have been published by Cotton and Yardeni 1997. For Wadi Murabba'at, see Benoit, Milik, and de Vaux 1961.

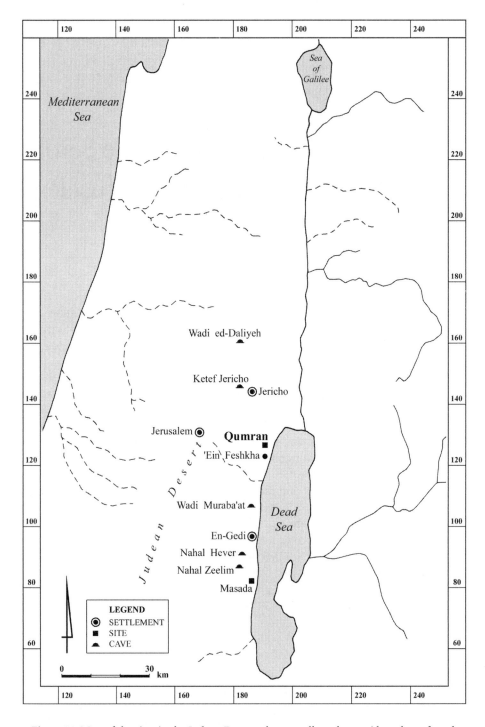

Figure 11. Map of the sites in the Judean Desert where scrolls and papyri have been found.

(halakah), wisdom literature, hymns, biblical commentaries, prayers, and apocalyptic and magic texts.

The great literary variety of the Dead Sea Scrolls is typical of the Jewish literature of the Second Temple period. The combination of biblical scrolls, sectarian texts, and general Jewish literature marks the scrolls as a collection of compositions written in various periods and by different authors. Since the sectarian scrolls were the first to be published, they gave the mistaken impression that the entire collection reflects a separatist group of the Second Temple period. Today there is more and more support for the thesis that the Dead Sea Scrolls are in fact Jewish scrolls that originated in Jerusalem, not in a separatist group.[4] The generally accepted explanation for the placing of the scrolls in the caves refers to the First Revolt. The assumption is that the members of the sect, faced with the inevitability of Qumran's destruction, deposited their precious scrolls in the caves to ensure their safety. The huge number of scrolls, however, testifies that this was the collection of a public library. Additional evidence for this is the fact that there are multiple copies of some books: thirty-six copies of Psalms, twenty-seven copies of Deuteronomy, and twenty-one copies of Isaiah. On the other hand, only two copies of Proverbs and Joshua and single copies of Chronicles, Ezra, and Nehemiah were found.

As mentioned, the first scrolls were found in 1947 by Bedouin—three shepherds of the Ta'amireh tribe, whose territory is in the Dead Sea region.[5] While seeking a goat that had gone astray about two km north of Qumran, they came upon a cave that contained ten jars. In one of the jars in this cave, later designated Cave 1, they found three scrolls wrapped in linen cloth: a complete copy of Isaiah (Isaiah[a]), a short commentary (pesher) on the book of Habakkuk *(Pesher Habbakuk)*, and a work that was later to become known as the *Rule of the Community* (or Manual of Discipline) *(Serek Hayaḥad)*.

The Bedouin returned to the cave and found four more scrolls: another copy of Isaiah (Isaiah[b]), the *War Scroll* (or War of the Sons of Light and Darkness) *(Milḥama)*, *Thanksgiving Hymns[a]* (or Thanksgiving Scroll) *(Hodayot[a])*, and the *Genesis Apocryphon.* Sukenik obtained the first three scrolls during 1947, and Yadin later acquired the remaining four scrolls. All seven scrolls from Cave 1 thus found their way to the Shrine of the Book in the Israel Museum in Jerusalem.[6]

These seven scrolls are typical of the composition of the Dead Sea Scrolls. Two of them are copies of the biblical book of Isaiah. The *Rule of the Community* lays out the regulations of some kind of sect, whose identity is disputed. It describes the initiation procedures of the community and details the punishments for those who transgress its laws. The great similarity between the laws of the community and the descriptions of the lifestyle of the Essenes by Josephus, Philo, and Pliny led Sukenik, and after him many other scholars, to identify the authors of the scrolls with the Essenes.[7] The *Rule of the Community,* which

---

[4] Tov 1998, 10; Golb 1999, 840–41; Dimant 2000, 171–72.

[5] Harding 1955, 5–6, contains one of the earliest accounts of the discovery of the first scrolls. Almost every book on Qumran since then has repeated it; see, e.g., de Vaux 1973, 95–97; VanderKam 1994, 3–59; Magness 2002, 25–29.

[6] On the acquisition of the scrolls, see Yadin 1957b, 15–52.

[7] For Sukenik's suggestion that the writers of the scrolls were the Essenes, see Sukenik 1948, 16. For a discussion of the scrolls of Cave 1, see Golb 1995, 15–94.

has dominated all discussion of the origin of the scrolls, was believed to provide the proof that Qumran was the motherhouse of the Essenes.

Several of the scrolls speak of "the desert," which, in the view of many scholars, refers to the Judean Desert. In the *Rule of the Community,* however, it seems clear that the passages refer to a symbolic desert and are taken from Isa 40:3: "A voice cries out: 'In the wilderness prepare the way for the LORD, make straight in the desert a highway for our God.'" These citations are metaphors for the "secrets" of the Torah and cannot be considered references to a specific location in the desert.

Pesher Habakkuk from Cave 1 is one of several commentaries among the Dead Sea Scrolls. This scroll comments on the book of Habakkuk in light of the realities of the Second Temple period. It mentions the leader of the sect, the "Teacher of Righteousness," and his opponent, the "Wicked Priest."

The *War Scroll* belongs to the apocalyptic literature. It describes the war of Gog and Magog that will precede redemption. *Thanksgiving Hymns^a* includes about forty previously unknown psalms. The *Genesis Apocryphon,* written in Aramaic, provides a literary augmentation of the story told in the biblical book of Genesis.

During the excavation of Cave 1 by Harding and de Vaux in 1949, about seventy scroll fragments were discovered, some of them belonging to the seven scrolls found previously.[8] Meanwhile the Bedouin found additional scrolls in Cave 2, to the south of Cave 1. These comprised fragments of thirty-three scrolls, including part of the book of Sirach, which was written by Ben Sira, a Jerusalemite scribe of the early second century B.C.E. This book is typical of the more plebeian, anti-Sadducean approach of the Pharisaic sect. It also includes the use of a lunar calendar, in contrast to the solar calendar reflected in several of the Dead Sea Scrolls.[9] Another fragment discovered in Cave 2 is part of the book of *Jubilees,* a text apparently belonging to the elitist, priestly Sadducean faction, which advocated strict observance of the laws of the Torah, and supported the solar calendar.

As a result of the discoveries made by the Bedouin, Harding and de Vaux decided to conduct a systematic survey of the caves in the northwestern Dead Sea region. This survey, carried out in 1952, included about 250 caves, but scrolls were discovered in only one of them (Cave 3).[10] This cave contained fragments of fourteen scrolls, the most important of which is the *Copper Scroll,* the only one among the Dead Sea Scrolls that is made of copper (of the others, most are made of parchment and a few of papyrus). The scroll was deposited in a half-open state, with its two ends rolled up into rolls of equal size (fig. 12). Since the metal was very brittle, it was sent to Manchester, England, where it was sawed up into sections with a fine saw used in brain surgery. It was only four years after its discovery that the scroll was open and could be deciphered.[11]

The *Copper Scroll* turned out to be a list of the treasures of the temple. The copper sheets were inscribed with twelve columns containing sixty-four paragraphs describing the temple treasures deposited in various locations in Jerusalem, the Judean Desert, and the Dead Sea area. The quantities listed in the scroll are enormous; about forty-six

---

[8] On the discovery of Cave 1, see Harding 1949; 1955.

[9] On the calendars in the Dead Sea Scrolls, see VanderKam 1998; Glessmer and Abani 1999.

[10] On the discoveries in the caves near Qumran, see de Vaux 1962; Reed 1954.

[11] On the discovery of the *Copper Scroll* and its contents, see Milik 1962; Wolters 1994; 1998.

Figure 12. The *Copper Scroll* as found in Cave 3. (Courtesy of Israel Antiquities Authority.)

hundred talents of silver (a talent is equal to 24 kg), sixty-five gold ingots, six hundred jars of coins, the vestments of the high priests, and other treasures. Since the publication of the scroll, attempts to locate the treasures have been unsuccessful.

Among the geographical names appearing in the *Copper Scroll* are Secacah, Jericho, the Valley of Achor, Duq, Kohlat, the Cleft of Kidron, and Masada. Several scholars have identified Secacah with Qumran.[12] They argue that several features mentioned in connection with Secacah, such as a water conduit and a dam, appear at Qumran.[13] These features, however, also occur at other Judean Desert sites, such as Hyrcania, Cypros (Tel 'Aqaba west of Jericho), and 'En Boqeq. The identification of Qumran with Secacah is purely conjectural. On the other hand, the *Copper Scroll* notes that scrolls *(sefarim)* and writing *(ketab)* were buried near the treasures.[14] On the assumption that the information contained in the *Copper Scroll* is genuine, the only possible place of origin for the huge quantities of treasures, artifacts, and scrolls is Jerusalem.[15]

Concurrently with the discovery of the *Copper Scroll* in Cave 3, Bedouin found yet more scrolls in the marl caves around the site. In Cave 4, about 150 m southwest of the site, thousands of fragments in a poor state of preservation were found.[16] In this very rich cave, the hundreds of fragments of biblical scrolls include parts of all the books of the Old Testament (with the exception of Esther) and prayers such as Songs of the Sabbath Sacrifice and a prayer for the health of King Jonathan. Some scholars believe that this king is Alexander Jannaeus, who ruled 103–76 B.C.E. and whose Hebrew name was Jonathan.[17]

Another important discovery in Cave 4 was six copies of the composition known as *Miqṣat Maʿaśê ha-Torah*. This scroll is written in the form of a letter detailing twenty-two halakic rulings and reflecting the views of the priestly Sadducean faction in Jerusalem.[18] Some scholars date this composition to the beginning of Hasmonean rule in the mid-second century B.C.E., but others believe that it dates from the reign of Herod in the late first century B.C.E.

In the nearby Caves 5 and 6, the Bedouin found parts of fifteen scrolls, including several copies of the *Damascus Document*. This composition had been known since Solomon Schechter found two copies of it in the Cairo Genizah long before the discovery of the Dead Sea Scrolls.[19] The *Damascus Document* consists primarily of sectarian rules, which are less strict than those in the *Rule of the Community;* for instance, community members are allowed to marry and own private property. The *Rule* includes a short preface describ-

---

[12] John Allegro, who published the *Copper Scroll* in 1960, was the first to suggest this identification; see Allegro 1960, 68, 144. Eshel (1995) and Magness (2002, 24–25) accept this identification as a fact.

[13] Ilan and Amit 2002, 386.

[14] Milik 1962, 292, 298. Zissu (2001, 155) has recently identified the place called Kahelet, where another copy of the *Copper Scroll* is said to have been buried, at 'Ein Samiya in the Samarian Desert.

[15] See the discussion in Golb 1999, 841–44.

[16] On the archaeological discoveries in Cave 4, see de Vaux 1977; on the texts, see Allegro 1968.

[17] Eshel, Eshel, and Yardeni 1992.

[18] On the halakah at Qumran, see Schiffman 1975; 1990; 1993; Sussmann 1992, 108–16; Woude 1998, 23–24.

[19] The two medieval copies of the *Damascus Document* were discovered in the Ben Ezra synagogue in Old Cairo, Egypt. These manuscripts were published in Schechter 1910.

ing the foundation of the sect. The passing references to "the land of Damascus" and the "Damascus Covenant" show that the sect was formed outside Judea (in Damascus?) and that its members migrated to Judea in the early second century B.C.E.[20]

The last cave that yielded scrolls, Cave 11, contained the Temple Scroll (11Q19), which is the longest of Qumran's scrolls. Yadin acquired this scroll after 1967 from an American clergyman and deposited it in the Shrine of the Book in the Israel Museum.[21] At the center of this scroll stands the temple of Jerusalem. The *Temple Scroll* is outstanding in its conciliatory tone and lacks the hatred and hostility toward other groups that are generally found in some of the sectarian texts. In this scroll also, however, there is controversy between the author of the composition, a supporter of the Sadducean approach, and the Pharisaic faction. Yadin dated the Temple Scroll to the reign of John Hyrcanus I (134–104 B.C.E.) although other dates have been proposed.[22]

The importance of the contribution made to research by the Dead Sea Scrolls can hardly be overestimated. Suffice it to say that before 1947 the earliest known Hebrew manuscripts of the Bible, called the Masoretic texts, dated to the tenth century. The scrolls' discovery thus gave us a Hebrew text that was older than the Masoretic texts by more than a millennium.

The scrolls supply detailed information on the physical form of books in the Second Temple period and on other details of the scribe's craft.[23] Most of the scrolls are written on parchment and contain a single book. The most complete scroll, the Isaiah Scroll from Cave 1, is 7.34 m long when completely unrolled (from right to left), but not very wide (from the top to the bottom of each written column); most of the other scrolls are much shorter. The scrolls were prepared from sheets of parchment that were joined with glue and stitched with thread made from animal ligaments. The sheets vary in length between 26 and 90 cm, though their width is a fairly constant 22 cm; this width corresponds with the width of the reader's hand to ease the holding of a scroll when reading it. The columns are usually twenty lines long on average. Guidelines for the writing were scratched on the parchment with a sharp instrument and a ruler. Unlike the modern practice, the letters were "hung" from the guidelines rather than written above them.

In addition to the scrolls, the caves near Qumran also contained about thirty phylacteries (small pieces of parchment inscribed with biblical texts). Yadin published a complete phylactery case that is apparently from Cave 4.[24] The very small case (20 × 13 mm) is made of leather (fig. 13). It contained four compartments that held parchment sheets inscribed with verses from the books of Exodus and Deuteronomy. Study of the versions of the texts in this phylactery case reveals an interesting phenomenon. There are seven different versions, rather than the single version that we would expect had the phylacteries been deposited by members of a sect who lived at Qumran. It seems likely, therefore, that they

---

[20] For the text of the *Damascus Document*, see Baumgarten 1997. For its meaning, see Davies 1983.

[21] Yadin 1983. For the significance of the Temple Scroll, see Schiffman 1989; Burgmann 1989.

[22] Thiering (1989) suggests that the Temple Scroll should be dated to the time of Herod the Great.

[23] Tov 1998.

[24] Yadin 1969. For the phylacteries found in Cave 4, see Milik 1977, 78–79.

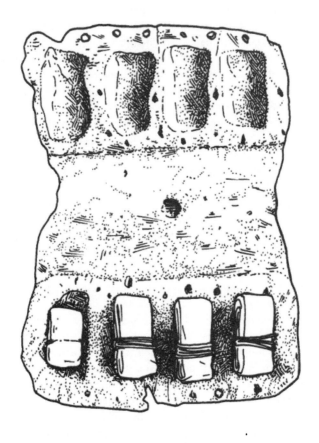

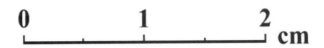

Figure 13. Reconstruction of phylactery found at Qumran.
(After Y. Yadin.)

were the personal property of individuals who arrived in the Judean Desert from different places in Judea during events connected with the First Revolt.[25]

2.2. The Archaeological Discoveries in the Caves

Excavating a cave is not a simple task. Breathing is difficult, space is cramped, the light is inadequate, and there is always a danger of collapse. Consequently, fieldwork in caves is not always well documented. Such was the case regarding the discoveries in the caves near Qumran, which consisted mostly of portable objects such as pottery vessels, baskets, mats, and metal tools as well as fragments of scrolls and the materials in which they were wrapped.

The best-documented excavation of the caves near Qumran is that of Cave 1, conducted by Harding in 1949.[26] The cave, in the cliff about two km north of Qumran, in maximum dimensions is 9 m long, 2 m wide, and 3 m high (fig. 14). According to Harding, the debris left by the clandestine excavations of the Bedouin in the cave yielded several hundred fragments of inscribed parchment, a few fragments of papyrus, and several linen wrappings. Above this was a thick layer, about 0.5 m deep, of animal dung that had decayed into gray dust, indicating that the cave had been used as a shelter by wild animals for a long period of time after the concealment of the scrolls. Harding admits that sieving was impossible because of the presence of many stones in the fill.

The gray layer in Cave 1 also revealed remains of human existence, such as olive and date stones, palm fibers, and pieces of wood eaten by rats. Objects of special interest included two tiny phylactery cases in leather, one of the type with four compartments worn on the head and the other of the type with one compartment worn on the arm. There were also two fragments of wooden combs. The pottery included six pottery jars with their lids, one cooking pot, several bowls, a juglet, and three wheelmade lamps. De Vaux claimed that the pottery found both at the site of Qumran and in the caves was unique and thus provided the best evidence for their connection.[27] Recent studies have shown, however, that the pottery of Qumran is not unique but is in fact typical of the Second Temple period in the Dead Sea region, and chemical analysis of the provenance of the pottery found at Qumran, including the "scroll jars," has indicated that some of it originated in Jerusalem.[28] The pottery assemblage is dated to the first century C.E.

The most interesting discovery in Cave 1 was the linen cloth used to wrap the scrolls. According to Harding, one scroll or part of a scroll was found still in its linen wrapper, stuck to the neck of a jar. One piece of linen was found folded, and when they opened it, the excavators found a black mass that was once a scroll. At least forty pieces of linen cloth were found. Their measurements varied between 0.6 × 1.57 m for the largest and 0.23 × 0.27 m for the smallest. More than half were of fine cloth decorated with indigo stripes.

---

[25] Golb 1999, 850.
[26] See above, chapter one, n. 59.
[27] de Vaux 1955, 11; 1959a, 91–92; 1973, 55–56.
[28] Yellin, Broshi, and Eshel 2001, 75–77; Gunneweg and Balla 2003, 26–27.

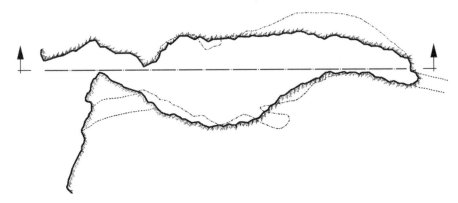

Plan-Cave 1

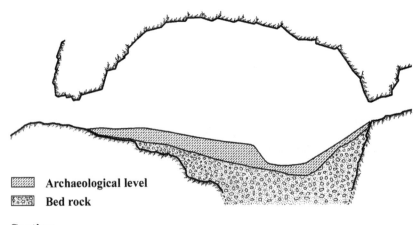

▨ **Archaeological level**

▨ **Bed rock**

Section

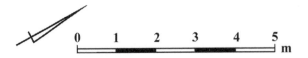

Figure 14. Plan and cross-section of Cave 1.
(After L. Harding.)

According to G. M. Crowfoot, the stripes are reminiscent of the fine linens of ancient Egypt, suggesting the possible origin of the cloth.[29]

Harding concluded that the scrolls and other objects were deposited for safety in Cave 1 during the First Revolt and were never recovered, probably because of the deaths of those who placed them there.[30] There are several signs, however, that the scroll deposits had already been thoroughly turned over in antiquity. As we shall see below, this accords with historical accounts about people who came to the caves from the third and the ninth centuries C.E.

Cave 4, cut into the marl cliff about 150 m southwest of Qumran and excavated by de Vaux in 1952,[31] is divided into two spaces. Cave 4a is the larger, in maximum dimensions 8 m long, 3.25 m wide, and 3 m high (fig. 92, color). It opens to the west, and a small window on the east provides ventilation. Cave 4b in maximum dimensions is 2 m long, 2.5 m wide, and 2 m high.

Excavation of Cave 4 proceeded both extremely rapidly and with minimal documentation—a "deadly combination" from an archaeological point of view. There are no photographs of the numerous scrolls in situ, and the descriptions of their location are very brief. Milik, who participated in the excavation, describes it as follows:

> The cave was accessible through a kind of tube. It was full of dust and dried mud that formed little mounds where they had encircled the scrolls. From one of these mounds I extracted the Book of Enoch, like a cork is extracted with a corkscrew. I understood immediately what we had here. The passage before me was from approximately Chapter XX. The cave was cleaned right down to ground level. . . . Not far from this den, we noticed a new irregularity in the side of the wadi. . . . Some manuscript fragments were there, soft and warm to the touch. In the air they dried quickly and crumbled to dust. There I was, watching them in utter despair. Using what things we had—in this case flat cardboard film boxes and toilet paper—I began to pack everything up.[32]

Thousands of scroll fragments were found in Cave 4, most of them buried under a thick accumulation of marl sediment, making it clear that this was a deposit concealed in an emergency. Apart from the inscribed parchment and papyrus items, de Vaux and his team uncovered about eight jars, several bowls, and a moldmade oil lamp. There was also a large number (over one hundred) of leather thongs (each 18 cm long) and tabs for fastening the scrolls.[33] The thongs were passed through the tabs, wound round the scrolls, and tied up on the outside (fig. 15).

As in Cave 1, remains of several phylactery cases were found in Cave 4. This time the compartments contained the actual phylacteries, which Milik studied.[34] A tiny mezuza (a rolled parchment inscribed with biblical verses that is affixed to the doorposts of Jewish homes) was found as well. As noted earlier, these are personal items that were most likely owned by the people who concealed the scrolls rather than by permanent cave dwellers.

---

[29] On the scroll wrappers, see Crowfoot 1955, 26; Schick 1993, 118–23; Bélis 2003, 207–22.
[30] Harding 1949, 114; 1952, 105.
[31] de Vaux 1973, 100; 1977, 9–21.
[32] For Milik's recollections of the fieldwork, see Mébarki 2000, 132.
[33] Carswell 1977; and Sussmann and Peled 1993, 114–15.
[34] Milik 1977.

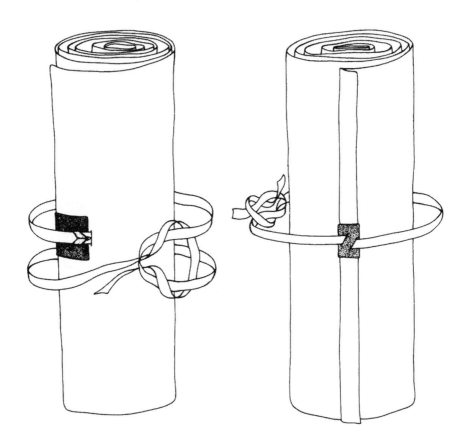

Figure 15. Reconstruction of scrolls' fastening with thongs and tabs.

In 1956 de Vaux excavated Cave 11, which lies to the north of Qumran. Just before his excavation, the Bedouin had found several documents in this cave. De Vaux would entirely clear the cave. The finds included a small amount of pottery (a jar and two lids), pieces of linen, basketry, ropes, and iron tools such as a small pick, a chisel, and a knife.[35]

Later surveys and excavations in the 1980s and 1990s made similar discoveries. Patrich and his team found archaeological remains in seventeen caves near Qumran, including caves in which scrolls had been found in the past.[36] The finds of the early Roman period included a rich collection of pottery (cylindrical and bag-shaped jars, cooking pots, bowls, and oil lamps). Some of the bowls are in the painted style typical of Jerusalem. Stone vessels of the type that is so widespread in Jerusalem were also found. From this evidence, Patrich concluded that the marl caves served as temporary dwellings for shepherds or refugees.

Broshi and Eshel have recently surveyed six collapsed artificial caves in the marl plateau north of Qumran.[37] The two caves that were excavated yielded the same type of finds, comprising the portable belongings of temporary dwellers. The pottery assemblage found by Broshi and Eshel included jars, cooking pots, bowls, and a complete wheelmade lamp of the first century C.E. The excavators argued that the manmade marl caves were permanent residences of the "Community of Qumran." (For more on this, see below.)

As we have seen, though most of the scrolls were wrapped in cloth, some were found inside cylindrical jars of a type that was also uncovered at the site of Qumran. These jars are perhaps the most distinctive object associated with Qumran. They contained the first scrolls discovered, in Cave 1, and are therefore called scroll jars.[38] This type of jar is cylindrical, about 35–78 cm tall and only about 25–28 cm in diameter. It has a large mouth with a low and plain vertical neck and a flat base. Some of the cylindrical jars have four small horizontal ledge handles on the shoulder. These jars were covered with bowl-shaped lids.

De Vaux believed that these scroll jars were produced expressly for the storage and concealment of the scrolls, but his excavation finds revealed a different picture. Storage jars including some of the cylindrical type, intentionally buried in the floors with only their mouths protruding, were found in several of the rooms exposed at Qumran (fig. 16).[39] This technique, known from many other sites, enables the storage of food in harsh climatic conditions.[40] From this it follows that the scroll jars were not produced solely for

---

[35] de Vaux 1956, 573–74.

[36] Patrich 1994a, 75–93.

[37] Broshi and Eshel 1999b.

[38] Magness 2002, 79–80; Gunneweg and Balla 2003, 7–8.

[39] A cylindrical jar of the scroll jar type, buried in the floor of the Qumran complex, is mentioned by Harding 1952, 105. Humbert and Chambon (1994) have published many examples of jars buried in floors, e.g., in the tower (locus 10, p. 23, photos 19–20), in the main building (Locus 34, p. 43, photos 66–68; Locus 13, p. 57, photos 104–7; Locus 2, p. 68, photo 142), and the best example in Locus 80 southwest of the main building (p. 171, photo 359).

[40] Magness 2002, 48; Gunneweg and Balla 2003, 29. In the excavations at En-Gedi that I have been conducting in recent years, jars and cooking pots have been found buried in the floors of dwellings from the late Roman and Byzantine periods, with their mouths facing upward (in some cases, the mouths of the vessels were still covered by lids). In the excavations of Roman-period Aqaba (Aila), jars containing remains of fish bones were found buried in the floor; see Parker 2000, 379–80.

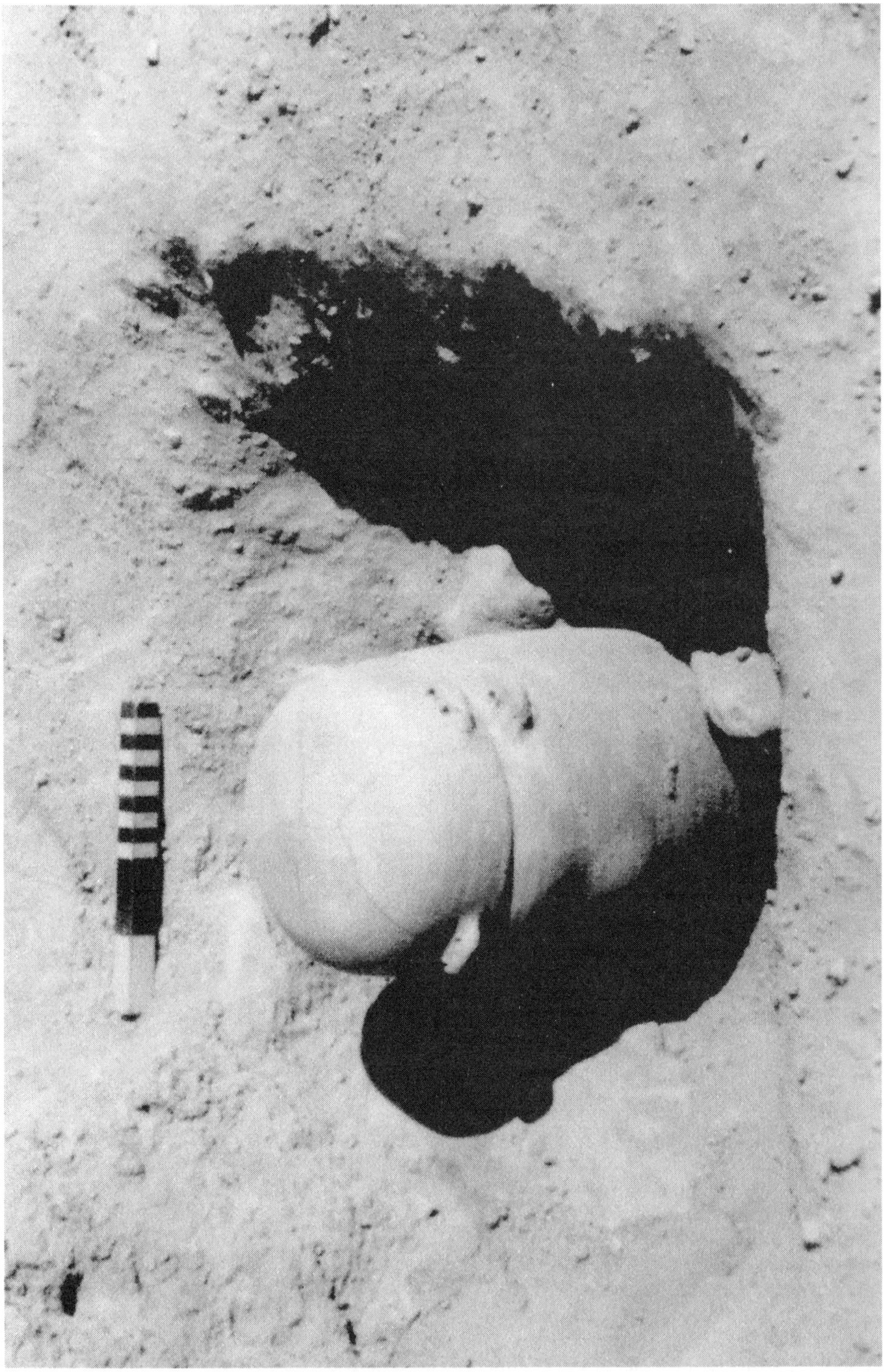

Figure 16. Cylindrical jar found under the floor at Qumran. (Courtesy of Ecole Biblique.)

the concealment of scrolls but were used to store the scrolls precisely because they were a common jar type at Qumran. Since some of the scrolls were found in jars that were probably produced at Qumran and because the caves in which the scrolls were hidden are located in the vicinity of the site, one can conclude that there was a close connection between those who deposited the scrolls and the inhabitants of Qumran, at least at the time of concealment. One can reasonably assume that, as Jews, the inhabitants of Qumran had an interest in helping to hide the scrolls from the approaching Romans and offered their aid. Any assumption beyond this is strictly conjectural.

In addition to scrolls, various manmade objects, such as pottery vessels, stone vessels, and organic items of various sorts (mats, cloth, and wooden poles), have been found in about fifty caves near Qumran. As noted, on the basis of these finds, de Vaux suggested that the caves served as the living quarters of the inhabitants of Qumran and that the complex itself served as a communal center.[41] The wooden poles found in one of the caves led him to assume that their living quarters were not confined to caves and that they also pitched tents on the surface close to the site.

In an attempt to substantiate de Vaux's claims, Broshi and Eshel conducted excavations in several caves cut in the marl north of Qumran (fig. 17), but their efforts were unsuccessful. Broshi and Eshel note that no floor was discerned in most of the caves that they excavated, and only two of them yielded sherds that might indicate that these caves served as living quarters at the end of the Second Temple period.[42] Sherds cannot serve as evidence of permanent living quarters in a cave. Broshi and Eshel attempt to convince us that the caves in the marl areas of Qumran are pleasant habitats, describing them as well ventilated, well lit, and cool. On the other hand, these scholars disregard the inconveniences of cave dwelling, such as excessive dampness, dust constantly falling from the ceiling, the lack of protection against wild animals, and so forth. Living quarters in caves are a last resort, and there is no reason to assume that the people who built the Qumran complex or acquired it from others preferred to dwell in caves rather than in the residential wings of the building.

As Patrich has shown, none of the caves excavated in the Qumran area, including those in the marl, have yielded remains, such as cooking and storage installations, sleeping couches, doorways, or windows, that might serve as evidence of permanent residence in them.[43] An instructive example of what such caves would contain is provided by some caves that did serve as the permanent living quarters of monks in the Byzantine period. At the site of 'Ein Abu Mahmud, about 5 km north of Qumran, Patrich discovered caves of a hermitage containing cooking installations, storage niches, benches, a prayer niche, doorways, windows, and crosses and inscriptions engraved on the walls.[44] No finds of this kind have been made in the caves excavated near Qumran.

---

[41] de Vaux 1959a, 92–94; 1973, 56–57.

[42] In 1978 I interviewed the head of a family that was living in a cave in the village of Deir Samit in the Hebron Hills who said he was obliged to live in a cave because of financial distress (Hirschfeld 1995, 151).

[43] Patrich 1994a, 93; 2000, 725–26.

[44] Patrich 1995, 128–32. Similar complexes of monks' caves have been found in the area of the laura of Gerasimus (Deir Hajla) north of the Dead Sea (Hirschfeld 1991).

Figure 17. One of the caves excavated by Broshi and Eshel.

From the finds in the caves, the conclusion is inevitable that they served only as temporary living quarters. As we shall see, Qumran was an economic center that must have drawn to its vicinity numerous people who were employed as laborers on the estate. These people—shepherds, hermits, and mere passersby—could have found temporary refuge in the caves or may have resided in tents, the meager remains of which were found by Broshi and Eshel, north of the site.

Broshi and Eshel present a system of ancient paths that supposedly linked the caves with the site.[45] Careful examination shows, however, that we are dealing here not with paved paths supported by retaining walls but with dirt tracks trodden by animals and chance passersby (including the team of laborers who worked in the caves during the excavation).

Along the main path leading to Qumran, Broshi and Eshel found sixty bronze sandal nails. Because all evidence points to the fact that the region's main roads, including the main road to En-Gedi and Masada, passed through Qumran, the discovery of the nails is not surprising. It seems likely that these belonged to sandals worn by Roman legionaries and not by inhabitants of Qumran, who probably wore simple leather sandals without the use of nails.[46] Two sandals of the simple type were found at Qumran. This is an example showing that attempts to comprehend the nature of the inhabitants of Qumran must be based on an analysis of the finds from the site itself rather than of those from the caves next to it.

2.3. The Origin of the Scrolls

In June 2002 a reception was held at the official residence of the president of Israel in Jerusalem to mark the completion of the publication of the Dead Sea Scrolls. Emanuel Tov of the Hebrew University of Jerusalem, who heads the publication project, announced that most of the scroll fragments found in the Judean Desert as a whole, and specifically those of Qumran, have now been published.[47] In his remarks he noted that the wide range of subjects reflected in the scrolls demonstrates the richness of the Jewish literature of the Second Temple period. Computer analysis has shown that the scrolls contain about five hundred different manuscripts, which indeed reflects literary activity of remarkable scope.[48] More and more scholars are convinced that a small sect such as the Essenes could not have been solely responsible for the huge literary scope of the scrolls discovered in the caves near Qumran and that the site itself cannot have been the place where such numerous and varied compositions were written and copied. As noted, many scholars have raised the possibility that the scrolls originated in Jerusalem and were brought to the site before the city was besieged by the Romans in 70 C.E.[49]

---

[45] Broshi and Eshel 1999b, 339–40; for a different interpretation, see Patrich 2000, 726.

[46] Sussmann and Peled 1993, 112–13.

[47] See an interview of Emanuel Tov by Hershel Shanks (2002).

[48] Cansdale 1997, 96; Golb 1999, 827.

[49] The best summaries are those of Golb (1999) and Hutchesson (2000).

These scholars point to a number of fundamental difficulties posed by the Essene-Qumran hypothesis. First of all, among the thousands of fragments found in the caves near Qumran, which reflect hundreds of manuscripts, there is not a single text that was indubitably composed at the site; all of them, with the exception of the *Copper Scroll,* are copies of compositions written many years before the scrolls were deposited. Second, there is no mention of the name of the site, or any detail connected with its history.[50] Third, the word "Essenes" does not appear in any of the scrolls. Fourth and most important, despite the thorough and comprehensive excavation of the site, not a single fragment of a parchment or papyrus scroll was found within it.

The Yahad Ostracon, published in 1997[51] and found the year before, as noted, by James Strange at the University of South Florida, aroused interest because the Hebrew word *yakhad* ("together") appears in several other scrolls and was presumed to be the name of the sectarians. The ostracon consists of two potsherds together measuring 6.3 × 17.2 cm and contains about fifteen truncated lines of script that comprise a contract. A person named Honi undertakes to give to Eleazar and Hisdai a house and crops or fig and olive groves belonging to the "Yahad," a sect that is mentioned in several scrolls found in the nearby caves. Reexamination of the ostracon, however, has revealed that the key word "Yahad" had been misread and in fact does not appear in the contract.[52] The ostracon does not therefore provide proof of the existence of a sectarian center at Qumran and at best attests to agricultural activity in the site and its surroundings.

Judging from the poor condition of the scroll fragments, we may assume that many more scrolls were deposited in the caves at the end of the Second Temple period. Indeed, there is historical evidence from two independent sources pointing to the existence of Hebrew scrolls in the Dead Sea area in antiquity. The first is the third-century church father Origen, who tells of the discovery of ancient manuscripts "in a pottery jar near Jericho."[53] The second is the account of Timothy I, patriarch of Seleucia in northern Syria from 779 to 823, reporting the discovery of ancient Hebrew manuscripts in caves near Jericho:

> We have learnt from trustworthy Jews who are being instructed as catechumens in the Christian religion that some books were found ten years ago in a rock-dwelling near Jericho. The story was that the dog of an Arab out hunting, while in pursuit of game, went into a cave and did not come out again; its owner went in after it and found a chamber, in which there were many books, in the rock. The hunter went off to Jerusalem and told this story to the Jews, who came out in great numbers and found books of the Old Testament and others in the Hebrew script.[54]

---

[50] The identification of Qumran with ancient Secacah, proposed by Eshel (1995) and enthusiastically adopted by Magness (2002, 24–25), is merely a conjecture.

[51] Cross and Eshel 1997; Roitman 1997, 39–40.

[52] Yardeni 1997.

[53] Driver 1951, 24. At the beginning of the fourth century, Eusebius (*Hist. eccl.* 6.16.1) repeated Origen's account and added that a Greek version of the Psalms and other Greek and Hebrew manuscripts had been found in a jar at Jericho during the reign of the Roman emperor Antonius (Caracalla, 211–217 C.E.).

[54] The translation of this letter from Timothy to Sergius is quoted from Driver 1951, 25–26. See Braun 1901.

Documents of the Second Temple period found in the cliffs west of Jericho help to confirm the historical data.[55] It is thus possible that the "Qumran library" was in fact part of a much larger library that was hidden in numerous cliff caves west of Jericho and the Dead Sea on the eve of the destruction of Jerusalem.

Yaacov Shavit of Tel Aviv University has shown that public libraries were a product of Hellenistic culture and were located in large cities.[56] The largest and best known was in Alexandria, but there were also public libraries in Rome, Athens, Pergamon, Ephesus, Antioch, Caesarea, and elsewhere. In his book on libraries in the ancient world, Lionel Casson of New York University points to two architectural features that characterized libraries: tall wall niches with bookshelves (Latin: *armaria*), and reading rooms or colonnades.[57] Not a trace of any of these elements was found at Qumran, and as mentioned above, no remains whatsoever of scrolls came to light during the excavations. In view of this, it is difficult to accept the assumption that the collection of books found in the caves near Qumran indeed came from this rural site. It stands to reason that the one place in Judea from which such a large library could have come is Jerusalem.

In terms of both extent and content, the Dead Sea Scrolls reflect the vigorous and varied literary activity that characterized Jerusalem in the Second Temple period. One of the centers of this activity was the royal palace in the Upper City. Herod's palace, like those of other Hellenistic kings, contained a large library. There was even a library in Herod's palace at remote Masada.[58]

Extensive literary work was one of the routine activities of the Second Temple priesthood. Books of the Bible were composed and copied by priests of the temple from its rebuilding in the days of Ezra and Nehemiah. It seems likely that this activity was not confined to the canonical scriptures but also included prayers, wisdom literature, and biblical commentaries. The Dead Sea Scrolls included many compositions of this kind, among them the books of *Jubilees* and Sirach, *Thanksgiving Hymns*[a] and *Songs of the Sabbath Sacrifice*[a]. Since the priests traditionally belonged to the Sadducean faction, it is not surprising that the religious law promoted in the scrolls generally reflects this trend in Judaism.[59] Indeed, most of the sectarian scrolls found in the caves reflect this trend despite their special content and style, and they are often interpreted as belonging to a separatist group that split off from the Sadducean faction.

Literary creation in the city, however, was not confined to the royal palace and the temple. Many groups and sects of various kinds were active in Jerusalem of the late Second Temple period. They focused on social and welfare activities and practiced communalism and the sharing of wealth to a certain degree.[60] We know of the "writers of books in Jerusalem" from the sayings of one of the sages of the period, Rabbi Eleazar ben Zadoq, who

---

[55] On the discoveries in the caves at Ketef Jericho, see Eshel and Zissu 2000.

[56] Shavit 1994, 302–3.

[57] Casson 2001, 49–52, 81–83.

[58] On the remains of the private library of King Herod at Masada, see Foerster 1995, 179; Hirschfeld 2004b. On the libraries founded by Herod, see Roller 1998, 55–56.

[59] For Schiffman's hypothesis, which strongly emphasizes the affinities between certain legal prescriptions found in the scrolls and the Sadducean halakah, see, e.g., Schiffman 1990.

[60] On the social activity in Jerusalem toward the end of the Second Temple period, see Oppenheimer 1980; Baumgarten 1998, 93–94.

lived in Jerusalem shortly before the destruction of the temple. He notes that it was the practice to leave scrolls half open, that is, as two rolls of equal size.[61] Each of these Jerusalemite groups probably had its own library.

The New Testament descriptions of the early Christian community in Jerusalem display great similarity to the lifestyle of the Yahad sect that is reflected in the scrolls. We may note, for example, the emphasis on the community *(yakhad),* the communal meals, and the sharing of wealth and property. The Christian community apparently had its own library, as we learn from the writings of Paul, who lived in the second half of the first century. In his epistle to Timothy of Jerusalem, Paul asks Timothy to bring him a cloak that he had left behind and "the books, especially the parchments" (2 Tim 4:13).[62] This early Christian library was similar in date to that of the collection represented by the Dead Sea Scrolls. The fact that Paul asked for the parchment books shows that they were of some importance; they were likely to have been Old Testament or other religious texts.

This is the background against which we should examine the partial library collection that was deposited in the caves of the Dead Sea. It reflects a wide range of literary activity on three main subjects: biblical texts, wisdom literature, and sectarian compositions. The sectarian texts do not necessarily represent a single sect or group; on the contrary, the varying tones of the texts give the impression that we are dealing with several groups. For example, *Pesher Habakkuk* reflects the deep antipathy of the members of the sect toward its opponents whereas *Miqṣat Maʿaśê ha-Torah* has a much more appeasing and moderate tone. The *Temple Scroll,* as mentioned, is outstanding in its conciliatory language and also in its moderate interpretations of religious law and lacks the aggressive approach of other sectarian compositions. Consequently, the sectarian texts cannot be seen as reflecting a homogenous approach but, rather, reflect the heterogeneity that characterized Jerusalem in the late Second Temple period. Though the Dead Sea Scrolls were indeed found near Qumran, they belong to Jerusalem in terms of their form and content and so detailed examination of them is beyond the scope of this book. In the next chapter, we will return to the site of Qumran to examine the nature of its remains in the framework of the general settlement picture of the Dead Sea Valley in the period under discussion.

---

[61] *b. B. Bat.* 14a. On Rabbi Eleazar ben Zadoq, see Oppenheimer 1980, 180.
[62] On early Christian libraries, see Elderen 1998.

CHAPTER 3

The Archaeology of Qumran

3.1. Stratigraphy and Chronology

Stratigraphy, the meticulous recording of remains, is essential to a proper excavation—it makes the difference between archaeological excavation and antiquities robbery. Jodi Magness points out the importance of this procedure: "During the course of excavations archaeologists destroy the evidence they dig up. This is because once a shovel of dirt or a stone is removed from the ground it can never be put back in the same way. For this reason, archaeologists record the excavation process using every means possible."[1]

Recording the precise origin of each excavated artifact and feature is of primary importance because it allows the archaeologist to date the site. Small artifacts such as coins, potsherds, and glass found above or below floors enable the dating of the floor levels and the walls attached to them. The function of a particular architectural space can sometimes be defined by the assemblage of artifacts found in it.

In 1994 Humbert and Chambon of the École Biblique in Jerusalem published the first volume in the projected series of Qumran excavation reports. This volume contains the raw data of the dig, including de Vaux's summary of each of the 144 loci that he excavated at the site. The publication of the report makes possible, for the first time, an analysis of de Vaux's working methods at Qumran. Careful examination reveals that the excavation was not conducted according to the customary stratigraphic rules. De Vaux gave each architectural space (room, hall, courtyard, or water installation) a separate locus number that in most cases was retained even when two or even three floors were revealed, one above the other, in the same space. For example, in the two rooms (Loci 1 and 2) south of the tower, two floors were found 0.5–0.6 m apart, one above the other, and above them another level 1.3 m higher. Despite this, the locus numbers of these rooms remained unchanged.[2] Other

---

[1] Magness 2002, 6–7.

[2] For Loci 1 and 2, de Vaux describes the levels from bottom to top (Humbert and Chambon 1994, 291–92). The two lower floors are close to one another, and the highest level is an occupation level above the destruction layer of 70 C.E.

49

spaces in which successive floors were revealed and whose numbers were not changed are Loci 4, 22, 33, and 35 (various rooms in the main building), Loci 28 and 29 (two rooms at the base of the tower), and Loci 38, 39, 41, and 47 (rooms to the east of the tower).[3] Even in a place where a clear ash layer was found, such as in Locus 27, de Vaux used the same locus number above and below it.[4]

Donceel and Donceel-Voûte cite the story of Locus 52 as a test case representing de Vaux's inadequate excavations methods at Qumran.[5] They observe that the excavation of the locus continued even when new levels of paving were encountered. We learn of this from a section drawing of the locus (fig. 18). To the best of my knowledge, this is the only section drawing from the Qumran excavations that has been published.

On the few occasions when de Vaux did change the locus numbers, it seems that this was done not because of the appearance of new occupation levels but because of the great thickness of the debris that he sought to remove. For example, the description of the remains in Locus 30 (the hall usually termed the "scriptorium") begins with the same debris that was attributed to the loci above it (15, 16, and 20); from this it follows that the changing of the locus number took place at some point during the removal of the layer of debris. In the further excavation of Locus 30, de Vaux reached a plaster floor, dug beneath it, and reached another floor with various installations, all listed under the same locus number.[6] Even the changing of the loci in the tower rooms was occasioned not by a significant stratigraphic change but by a change in the thickness of the walls; therefore, when de Vaux reached the base of the tower rooms, the locus numbers (28 and 29) were left unchanged even when two successive floors were uncovered.[7]

The conclusion to be drawn from this is that the excavation at Qumran was not stratigraphic, and therefore the basic principle of chronological distinction between archaeological strata according to datable finds (ceramic vessels, coins, etc.) above and below floors is generally not expressed. As a result, elevation measurements do not appear in the plans of Qumran (since there was obviously no separation of levels), and the walls of the buildings are not numbered (since no attempt was made to identify their stratigraphic contexts). It thus emerges that the locus numbers allocated by de Vaux at Qumran have only limited stratigraphic value, since they are merely inventory numbers for the various architectural spaces and installations that were excavated at the site.

---

[3] In Locus 4, de Vaux describes two plastered floors located 0.5 m apart (Humbert and Chambon 1994, 293). In Loci 22 (p. 300) and 33 (p. 303), he describes two floor levels, one above the other, that are 0.2 m apart. In two rooms of the tower (Loci 28 and 29), de Vaux records two floors that are 0.4 m apart (pp. 301–2). Two levels of paving were also found in the four rooms east of the tower (Loci 38–41; pp. 305–6).

[4] It can reasonably be assumed that the ash layer of Locus 27 was caused by a conflagration that occurred at the site during the destruction of 68 C.E. (Humbert and Chambon 1994, 301).

[5] Donceel and Donceel-Voûte 1994, 22, n 10.

[6] Humbert and Chambon 1994, 298 (Locus 16), 300 (Locus 22), 302 (Locus 30). Plastered elements interpreted as tables by de Vaux were found in the debris of two loci (16 and 30), indicating that the changing of the locus numbers in this case was arbitrary.

[7] The locus numbers within the tower were changed from 8 to 8A and from 9 to 9A, according to de Vaux, at a level at which the walls became thicker (ibid., 294–95). Although two levels of paving were found at the base of the tower rooms (Loci 28 and 29), it was not considered necessary to change the locus numbers (ibid., 302).

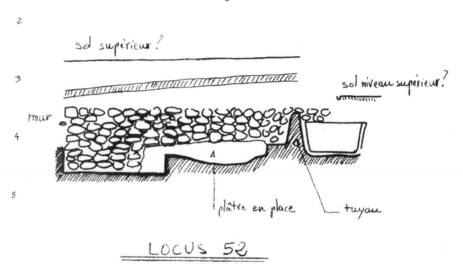

Figure 18. Cross-section of Locus 52 as drawn by de Vaux.
(Courtesy of R. Donceel and P. Donceel-Voûte. "The Archaeology of Khirbet Qumran"
in *Methods of Investigation of the Dead Sea Scrolls and the Khirbet Qumran Site*.
Edited by M. O. Wise et al. New York: New York Academy of Sciences, 1994, 23.)

To gain an idea of the nature of the excavation at Qumran, we will turn once again to the reminiscences of Milik, who took part in the dig from its beginning:

> At the beginning of our work on the site of Khirbet Qumran, we saw hardly anything of the walls, which were hidden under various kinds of debris. We cleaned out the structures with shovels, and the excavated material was taken out in railroad carts. I had taken a shovel and was positioned on an incline next to an Italian student who was shoveling without much concern about where he was, throwing things behind him. Suddenly in his shovel, I noticed a rather large fragment of pottery that he discarded with the rest. I picked up the fragment. It had an inscription! Later, Fr. de Vaux had a 5 meter long trench dug at this spot. But no other *ostracon* was found.[8]

Photographs of the dig provide further interesting evidence of de Vaux's unprofessional excavation methods. In them we can clearly see laborers working freely in areas that have not been divided into squares, as is customary in most archaeological digs.[9]

As a matter of fact, there is consensus regarding the inferior quality of de Vaux's excavation methods at Qumran. Jean-Baptiste Humbert, de Vaux's successor in processing the excavation finds, has also reached the conclusion that the excavations at Qumran were not carried out according to the stratigraphic conventions.[10] Donceel and Donceel-Voûte, who have studied the recording process of the dig at Qumran, write that de Vaux's diary is "a combination of both archaeological data and personal thoughts which Father de Vaux wrote down at important moments of the dig, often after a discovery he considered significant."[11] Even Magness, who endorses most of de Vaux's conclusions (including his archaeological conclusions), admits that de Vaux "used the same locus numbers to designate a single room from the beginning to the end of the excavation, instead of changing the number as he dug through different levels or distinguished different features in the rooms."[12] Magness justifies de Vaux's practices by pointing out that he worked according to the standard methods of the time. Thus, for example, she notes the fact that Yigael Yadin, who excavated Masada ten years later, used the same method, that is, the assignment of a single locus number throughout the excavation of a room.

In this matter Magness is probably right. There are many points of similarity between de Vaux and Yadin. Both came to the Judean Desert to dig sites of the classical period (the late Hellenistic and early Roman periods) after excavating biblical sites, Yadin at Hazor and de Vaux at ancient Tirzah (Tell el-Farʿah North, northeast of Shechem). Both had a preconceived historical concept of the site even before excavation began. Consequently, stratigraphic work, a careful process that is not only time-consuming but expensive, did not seem necessary to either of these excavators.[13]

---

[8] Milik as quoted in Mébarki 2000, 135.

[9] See, e.g., the photograph published by Roitman (1997, 17, Hebrew section) and also by Mébarki (2000, 135).

[10] Humbert 1994, 109.

[11] Donceel and Donceel-Voûte 1994, 15.

[12] Magness 2002, 7.

[13] From the final report of Masada published by Ehud Netzer (1991), it is clear that Yadin's excavations at Masada were not stratigraphic; see, e.g., p. IX. As a substitute for stratigraphy at Masada, Netzer marked the walls of the structures with graphic symbols to distinguish between the six different periods of the site's existence. It follows from this that the locus numbers at Masada, like those at Qumran, are lacking in stratigraphic value.

De Vaux proposed that the site's occupation should be divided into six chronological phases, as follows:

1. Israelite remains: First settlement at Qumran during the late Iron Age (eighth to seventh centuries B.C.E.).

2. Period Ia: Reoccupation of the Iron Age site in the second half of the second century B.C.E., in the reign of John Hyrcanus I (134–104).

3. Period Ib: Expansion of the site prior to the earthquake in the spring of 31 B.C.E. After the earthquake, the site remained abandoned for much of the reign of Herod the Great (37–4 B.C.E.).

4. Period II: Reoccupation of the site between 4 and 1 B.C.E., a date determined by de Vaux from a hoard of 561 silver coins found in Locus 120 at the site.[14] According to de Vaux, after an abandonment of about thirty years, life continued at the site along the same lines as before the earthquake, up to the First Revolt.

5. Period III: The site taken by a Roman detachment in June 68 C.E. during the First Revolt, resulting in destruction and fire. Some of the ruins were restored by a small garrison that may have been stationed at the site for five or six years, until the fall of Masada in 73 C.E., which signified the pacification of the whole region.

6. The Second Revolt: Traces of walls and some coins imply that what was left of the building was briefly reoccupied during the Second Jewish Revolt against Rome (132–135 C.E.).

The fact that the Qumran excavation was not conducted according to the standard stratigraphic conventions, however, pulls the rug out from under most of the chronological conclusions that de Vaux set out in successive publications.[15] Of his chronological proposals, only two are acceptable: Period II and Period III. The remains of Period II, dating from the reign of Herod until the First Revolt, had remained virtually frozen in time. The destruction of 68 C.E. acted rather like the volcanic ash at Pompeii, which buried buildings almost intact. The wings on the western and southeastern sides of the main building went out of use, and the Roman soldiers, who occupied the main building in Period III, leveled its debris and buried its contents under the new floors. The rich assemblage of artifacts discovered at the site and in the nearby caves (including the scrolls) reflect Period II and help us to reconstruct the site in this Period and to define its different spaces. The remains of Qumran after the destruction (Period III) were frozen also. This Period, which lasted for several decades, almost up to the Second Revolt, represents the last occupation at Qumran, and the site was never resettled.[16] Thus the architectural layout of Qumran during de Vaux's Period II and Period III can be traced with a fair degree of certainty.

---

[14] de Vaux 1973, 36.

[15] For summaries of de Vaux's chronological stages, see de Vaux 1993, 1236–40; Donceel 1997, 393.

[16] According to Harding (1958, 15), Roman soldiers remained at Qumran until the end of the first century.

On the other hand, de Vaux's view of the architectural layout of the site in the late Iron Age and in Period Ia and Period Ib is almost totally speculative and lacking in stratigraphic support. The fact that de Vaux did not separate the finds originating in the different levels beneath Period II makes his chronological conclusions almost meaningless. De Vaux admits that the fact that most of the rooms were cleared out by the inhabitants of Period II "deprived us [the archaeologists] of many pieces of evidence which would have been valuable for Period Ib."[17]

We must abandon two more of de Vaux's assumptions. The first of these is the idea of a thirty-year gap in settlement at Qumran. On the basis of the numismatic finds at Qumran, several scholars have already shown that the gap did not exceed a few years or did not exist at all. According to Broshi, Period II was longer than de Vaux had supposed and included most of Herod's reign.[18] Magness also rejects de Vaux's thirty-year gap, although she believes that the Hasmonean Period Ib should be extended to the end of Herod's reign.[19] This proposal, which stretches the Hasmonean Period Ib to the end of the Herodian period, is also illogical, since it ignores the changes that took place in Judea during the transition from Hasmonean rule to that of Herod and their possible influence on the site. In fact, there is no level of violent destruction under the remains of Period II. On the contrary, the remains of the Hasmonean and Herodian periods at the site are interconnected, as attested by the superimposition of the floors one above the other without interruption. It is reasonable to assume that the modification of the site took place at some time at the beginning of Herod's reign, which was a period of economic boom in Judea in general and in the Dead Sea Valley in particular.

The second assumption regards the effect of a 31 B.C.E. earthquake on the site. Although Josephus mentions an earthquake that struck Judea in 31 B.C.E.,[20] it can reasonably be assumed that at a site like Qumran, whose settlement started before the earthquake and continued thereafter, any damage was swiftly repaired and the building returned to normal. De Vaux's proposal to associate the geological fault line running across the site from north to south with the earthquake of 31 B.C.E. is a mere conjecture.[21] De Vaux surmised that those who returned to Qumran in Period II left in ruins some important elements that had been damaged by the earthquake, such as the stepped pool in the main building (Locus 48/49) and the vessel storeroom adjacent to the dining room (Loci 86 and 89). It seems unlikely that enclaves of destruction would have been left in a complex as bustling and active as that of Qumran in Period II. Some scholars, such as Magness, support de Vaux's interpretation without supplying a reasonable explanation.[22] It seems likely, rather,

---

[17] de Vaux 1973, 25. Magness (2002, 48) expresses a similar opinion: "Because the latest main occupation phase (Period II) is best preserved, it is often difficult to determine the plans and functions of buildings during the earlier phases (Periods Ia and Ib)."

[18] Broshi 1992, 111. The nonexistence of the "gap" in the reign of Herod at Qumran was already noted by Kenael 1958, 167.

[19] Magness 2002, 65–68; see also Magness 1995; 2000, 713–14.

[20] Josephus, *J.W.* 1.370–371; *Ant.* 15.121–122.

[21] de Vaux 1973, 20–21.

[22] According to Magness (2002, 57), "some of the damaged structures in the settlement [of Qumran] were strengthened, while others were left filled with collapse and abandoned." This sentence, which contradicts common sense, is left unexplained.

that the fault line that passes through Qumran from north to south should be attributed to tectonic activity that damaged the site some time after its final abandonment, perhaps during the earthquakes of 363 or 749 C.E. Magen and Peleg, during their excavations at Qumran, found two more north-south fault lines running parallel to the one discovered by de Vaux (fig. 19). Sections exposed in these cracks included artifacts of Period III.[23] This is stratigraphic proof of a late dating of the earthquake at Qumran.

The abundant archaeological material from Qumran can and should be used to re-examine de Vaux's chronological framework. More than twelve hundred coins, including several hoards, were recovered from all over the site.[24] From the coins, it appears that most of the site's structures were in use for more than two consecutive centuries, from the reign of John Hyrcanus I (134–104 B.C.E.) until the Second Revolt (132–135 C.E.).

For some contemporary archaeologists, such as Magness, de Vaux's Period Ia does not exist and Period Ib began no earlier than 100 B.C.E. or perhaps even later. Magness's claim, however, that "de Vaux found no coins associated with Period Ia" is misleading.[25] In fact, eleven coins minted by the Seleucids, who ruled the region before and after 130 B.C.E., were found in several locations in the site.[26]

Because each ruler minted his own new coins, the coins found in excavations usually represent a level of occupation relating to the period of the rulers shown on the coin. It is true that coins sometimes remained in circulation for long periods, but it is more likely that the people living in Qumran lost these Seleucid coins quite close to the time of their minting. This is one of several reasons to believe that Second Temple period Qumran was founded in the reign of John Hyrcanus I.

In 1994 Humbert published a long and important article analyzing the architectural components of Qumran and their chronological sequence. At the end of the article, Humbert suggests a new, improved, and simplified division of the different levels found at Qumran.[27] Table 1 is based on Humbert's chronology, with some minor modifications.

New Scheme of Qumran's Periods of Existence

Stratum	Period
I	Late Iron Age, late seventh to early sixth centuries B.C.E. (630–580 B.C.E.)
II	Hasmonean (130–37 B.C.E.)
III	Herod, Archaelaus, and Roman procurators (37 B.C.E.–68 C.E.)
IV	Post-68 C.E. Roman detachment (68–132 C.E.)

---

[23] This evidence was presented by the excavators at the Brown University conference of November 2002.

[24] According to Donceel and Donceel-Voûte (1994, 3), the total number of coins recorded at the Qumran excavations is 1,231; according to Murphy (2002, 305), it is 1,234. This is an impressive number in comparison with other sites. E.g., in my excavations at En-Gedi, the total yield of coins from seven seasons (1996–2002) is only 603.

[25] Magness 2002, 63.

[26] Laperrousaz 1976, 150.

[27] Humbert 1994, 209–10.

Figure 19. Fault line running east of the site, looking south. It contained remains of the last period of Qumran.

If this division is correct, Second Temple period Qumran underwent expansion and modification at some time in the thirties of the first century B.C.E., after the reign of Mattathias Antigonus (40–37 B.C.E.), the last Hasmonean king. One learns of the existence of two main stages at Qumran from an analysis of its plan. At the center of the site stands a square, right-angled precinct with a corner tower. This precinct, which de Vaux called the "main building," probably belongs to the first building stage during the Hasmonean period (Stratum II) whereas the additions in and around this structure should be attributed to the second building stage during the Herodian period (Stratum III).

What are the characteristics of each of the four strata at the site? The following discussion is devoted to this question and its implications.

3.2. The Late Iron Age (Stratum I)

The recycling of building materials was common in antiquity and down through the ages in premodern Palestine. Even the fellaḥin of the nineteenth and early twentieth centuries plundered ancient sites for building stones.[28] It may be assumed that the builders of Qumran in the Second Temple period made extensive use of the Iron Age remains that they must have found at the site. Since de Vaux and his team discovered large quantities of late Iron Age pottery, which they dated to the eighth to seventh centuries B.C.E., the existence of a settlement in this period is certain.[29] The excavations carried out by Magen and Peleg to the east and south of the site have also indicated that the Iron Age site was larger than previous estimates.[30]

De Vaux's reconstruction of the Iron Age settlement at Qumran as a rectangular building with an open courtyard containing a round cistern (Locus 110), however, is entirely speculative. All that we can say is that there was a settlement in this period and it probably had a reservoir. The walls of the well-preserved round cistern are coated with hydraulic plaster—high-quality plaster used in cisterns and other liquid containers—typical of the late Hellenistic and early Roman periods. It is conceivable, although this is merely a conjecture, that the settlers of the Hasmonean period made use of an abandoned Iron Age cistern and replastered it.

More interesting is the wall de Vaux called "le long mur," "the long wall." This wall ran southward from the site toward Wadi Qumran. It was built in the Iron Age and remained in use until the end of Period II, that is, until the end of the Second Temple period.[31] Down below in the plain of the 'Ein Feshkha oasis, beyond the riverbed of Wadi Qumran, de Vaux found the southward continuation of this wall, running parallel to the shoreline of the Dead Sea for several hundred meters. Traces of this wall can still be seen today (fig. 93, color). It is built of medium-sized fieldstones and is about 0.6 m thick. About 300 m to the south of Wadi Qumran, de Vaux discovered a casemate-walled compound (his "quadrilateral building"), which he dated to the Iron Age as well. If we accept this dating, it may

---

[28] Hirschfeld 1995, 221.
[29] de Vaux 1973, 1–3.
[30] For the new data on Iron Age pottery at Qumran , see Magen and Peleg 2002.
[31] de Vaux 1973, 3, 59–60.

well be that this wall is a boundary marker of the plantation in the oasis of 'Ein Feshkha, as de Vaux suggested. Lawrence Stager of Harvard University, who uncovered a similar wall in the Buqei'a Valley, suggests that the long wall of Qumran functioned as a barrier to enclose and protect the plantations of date palms that grew along the shore of the Dead Sea in the seventh century B.C.E.[32]

In my excavations at 'Ein Feshkha in April 2001, I uncovered the remains of a late Iron Age tower.[33] The square tower, measuring 4.7 × 4.7 m, is located about 50 m above the spring (elevation –336 m) on the slope to its west (fig. 94, color). This position gave a commanding view of the oasis and enabled eye contact with Qumran. Its strategic location, simple plan, and 1 m thick walls suggest that it was a watchtower guarding the plantations of the oasis (remains of which, however, have not yet been discovered) and the road leading south to En-Gedi.

De Vaux dated the Iron Age pottery from Qumran in general to the eighth–seventh centuries C.E. The recent study, however, of 270 diagnostic fragments (used in dating) of storage jars, jugs, decanters, cooking pots, kraters, bowls, plates, and lamps from Qumran by Mariusz Burdajewicz of the National Museum of Warsaw has shown that Iron Age Qumran should be redated to the late seventh and the beginning of the sixth century B.C.E.[34]

This is significant because it gives us a historical context—the reign of King Josiah of Judah, who ruled from 639 B.C.E. to 609 B.C.E. Josiah, best known for his religious reforms, enlarged the country and ruled an economically flourishing kingdom (2 Kgs 22:3, 2 Chr 35:7). According to Talmudic tradition, Josiah replaced the oil used to anoint kings with balsam oil (Hebrew: *afarsemon*); this connects his activities to the region and its balsam cultivation.[35]

The settlement of Qumran in the late Iron Age therefore fit into the general settlement picture of the Dead Sea region. According to Ephraim Stern of the Hebrew University of Jerusalem, recent archaeological research has uncovered a chain of settlements on the eastern border of the kingdom of Judah, between Jericho in the north and En-Gedi in the south.[36] Almost all of these settlements, and those in the Buqei'a Valley to the west, were established in the same period, between 630 and 580 B.C.E. In his surveys and excavations along the Dead Sea coast, Bar-Adon found Iron Age pottery at Rujum el-Bahr and Khirbet Mazin.[37] These finds indicate that the Dead Sea level was relatively low (under –395 m) and consequently that the road past Ras Feshkha to En-Gedi was open at the time. The occurrence of several sites along this road is indicative of its importance as a line of communication.[38]

---

[32] Stager 1976, 157. The sites of the Buqei'a Valley, which were first dated by Cross and Milik (1956) to the eighth–seventh centuries B.C.E., were redated by Stager to the late seventh–early sixth centuries.

[33] Hirschfeld 2004a, 66–68.

[34] Burdajewizc 2001.

[35] *b. Kritut* 5b; *y. Soṭah* 8.22. See Mazar, Dothan, and Dunayevsky 1966.

[36] Stern 1994.

[37] Bar-Adon 1989, 6–7 (Rujum el-Baḥr), 24 (Khirbet Mazin). Iron Age remains have been found at several other sites along the Dead Sea (Blake 1966).

[38] On the road that possibly connected Qumran and En-Gedi in the late Iron Age, see Dorsey 1991, 149.

According to Stern, the reasons for the sudden increase of settlements in the desert region of the Dead Sea were twofold: the fortification of Judah's eastern border against the expansion of the Edomites, and the economic advantage of the production of incense by the inhabitants of En-Gedi and probably also Jericho. The kingdom of Judah, which had achieved independence in the reign of Josiah, attempted to participate in the renewed incense trade with southern Arabia and at the same time become a producer of incense at the Dead Sea—the one region of the kingdom that was suitable for its cultivation.

We know nothing of the appearance of Iron Age Qumran, but its location at the most strategic site between Jericho and En-Gedi must have made it important. It may be assumed that it functioned as a military post on the main road from the southern part of the Dead Sea region to Jericho and Jerusalem. As we shall see, the same was true of Qumran in the Second Temple period.

Before proceeding to the next period, we should consider the identification of Iron Age Qumran. Modern scholars have suggested two main identifications: the City of Salt ('Ir Hamelah) and Secacah.[39] Both names appear in Josh 15:61–62, in a list of six "towns" in the wilderness of Judea: "Beth-arabah, Middin, Secacah, Nibshan, the City of Salt, and En-Gedi: six towns with their villages." Though the name Secacah is mentioned in the *Copper Scroll,* its identification with Qumran is merely conjectural. In my opinion, of the six "towns" in the list, only En-Gedi can be plausibly identified.

3.3. The Hasmonean Period (Stratum II)

After several centuries, the site of Qumran was reoccupied on a larger scale. As we shall see, construction during the Hasmonean period was large-scale; the builders probably reused Iron Age building stones that they found at the site. On the basis of the numismatic finds, de Vaux correctly dated the Hasmonean construction to the reign of John Hyrcanus I (134–104 B.C.E.). Six silver and five bronze Seleucid coins dating from the years around 130 B.C.E. were found at the site.[40] Although there is no way of ascertaining how long these coins had been in circulation, they give the *terminus post quem,* that is, the earliest possible date, for the Hasmonean construction.

Pottery is a sensitive indicator of date because it is breakable and therefore has a short life span. Since the pottery assemblage of Qumran contains several vessel types that are typical of the late Hellenistic period (after 150 B.C.E.), it supports the conclusion drawn from the coins. Andrea Berlin of the University of Minnesota has published an inventory of the Hellenistic pottery of Palestine,[41] where she notes that many of the storage jars,

---

[39] For a long discussion of the identification of Qumran, see Cansdale 1997, 101–6. For the proposed identification of Qumran with Secacah, see Eshel 1995, 38; Ofer 1998; Magness 2002, 24–25.

[40] de Vaux 1973, 18–19; Laperrousaz 1976, 150; Cansdale 1997, 161–62. According to Kenael (1958, 165–66), fifteen coins of John Hyrcanus I were found at Qumran, but their identification is not certain.

[41] Berlin 1997, 44–47. This article is the most comprehensive archaeological discussion so far published of the Hellenistic period in ancient Palestine. The plates presented by Berlin may be compared with those published by de Vaux in several places, such as de Vaux 1961, Planche XLII.

cooking pots, bowls, and lamps of the late Hellenistic period (i.e., after 150 B.C.E.) found at Jerusalem, Beth Zur, and Gezer are similar in shape and design to vessels found at Qumran. Decorated lamps with a ray motif of the type called delphiniform were found in different locations at the site; this type is dated to the second half of the second century and the first half of the first century B.C.E. Loop-handled lamps that display the influence of late Hellenistic lamps of the second century B.C.E. were also found.[42]

John Hyrcanus I also built other sites in the area: the winter palace at Jericho and the fortress named Hyrcania after him, on the route from Jerusalem to Qumran and the Dead Sea. In addition to the numismatic and pottery evidence linking him to the site, his building these palaces gives us good reason to believe that during his thirty-year reign, Qumran was also built.

De Vaux attributed to his Period Ia only a few rooms around the round reservoir and the potter's kilns (Locus 84) in the southeastern part of the site.[43] He later claimed that the settlement acquired most of its elements, including the water supply system, in Period Ib. This reconstruction, however, lacks a stratigraphic basis. Indeed, the only way to understand the two stages of Second Temple period Qumran (our Strata II and III) is to analyze its architectural remains.

Looking at the layout of the site, one is immediately struck by the square structure, right in the center, that de Vaux called the "main building" (fig. 20). The main building is notable for its straight walls forming a square built around an inner courtyard and for its corner tower surrounded by a massive stone revetment.

The exterior walls of the building on the north and west emerge from the northwestern corner of the tower. The northern wall is 37 m long and preserved to a height of 2.1 m (fig. 21). Close to its eastern end, one can discern a seam line separating it from a building addition from the later Herodian phase (fig. 22). The northeastern corner is notable for its relatively large building stones, which are laid on top of one another as headers and stretchers (fig. 23). The eastern awall extends from this corner for 37 m. According to these data, one can reconstruct the building as a square structure, each side of which measured 37 m. The area of the building, including the tower, whose walls project outward slightly, is approximately 1,400 m².

Judging from its simple, roughly square plan, its fortification (the tower), and its strategic location, Hasmonean Qumran seems to have been a fortress. Humbert, recently suggesting a different interpretation, proposes a similar though not identical reconstruction.[44] He, too, isolates the main building of Qumran, dates it to the Hasmonean period (his Stratum II), and compares its plan to farm buildings of the Second Temple period that were found adjacent to the Dead Sea, for example, at 'Ein Feshkha and 'En Boqeq. On the basis of these data, Humbert suggests that Hasmonean Qumran should be regarded as the center of an agricultural estate, or *villa rustica*. Humbert, however, overlooks the existence

---

[42] Donceel 1998, 90–93, figs. 1–2 (delphiniform type), figs. 9–10 (loop-handled type). For further information on the lamps of the period, see Lapp 1961, 194– 96; Smith 1964, 123–24; Rosenthal and Sivan 1978, 13. Parallels have been found in the winter palace at Jericho; see Bar-Nathan 2002, 106–7.

[43] de Vaux 1973, 3–24.

[44] Humbert 1994, 170–74; 1999, 194–96.

Figure 20. Aerial view of the main building at Qumran, looking south.

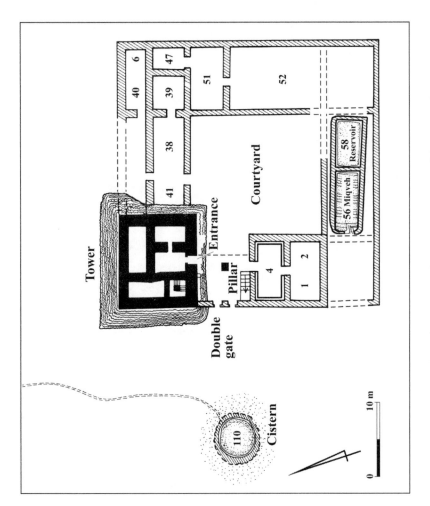

Figure 21. Plan of Qumran in the Hasmonean period (Stratum II).

Figure 22. The seam line separating the northern wall of the main building (on right) from later additions (on left), looking east.

Figure 23. The northeastern corner of the original building, looking west.
Note the seam line separating it from the later additions.

of the tower and the strategic location of the site, elements that lead to the inescapable conclusion that Qumran had a military function during this period.

The main building is the best-preserved part of the site: the walls of the tower rise to a height of 4.5 m above ground level, and the walls of the rooms to its east and south reach a height of 2–3.5 m (fig. 24). The facade wall of the main building faces west. In its center is a double doorway with a frame constructed of ashlars with dressed margins, in contrast to the other parts of the building, which are built from fieldstones (fig. 25). The combination of ashlars and fieldstones is a building technique typical of the late Hellenistic and early Roman sites in the Dead Sea, including Masada, Jericho, and the sites along the shoreline. The ashlars are made from sandstone of the Samra formation (the stone is called *hajar samra* in Arabic), which comes from the quarries at Khirbet Samra.[45] These huge quarries supplied ashlars for openings (doorways and windows) and for architectural decorations such as columns and cornices. Khirbet Samra is about 5 km north of Jericho and about 20 km north of Qumran, and although the transport of such stone was expensive, the ancient builders of Qumran, like those of the winter palace at Jericho and other royal complexes, made extensive use of it. Most parts of the building, however, were built of unhewn or roughly hewn local stones, bonded with lime plaster and aligned with small stones.

Most of the internal fittings at Qumran, such as benches and raised platforms, together with the upper parts of the walls, were made of sun-dried mud bricks. The ceilings and the presumably flat roofs (since no tiles were found at the site) were constructed from wooden beams—probably from local trees such as date palm and acacia—covered with layers of reeds, palm branches, and mud. The floors were usually of packed earth and were sometimes plastered or cobbled. Jars sunk into the floors were used for storage of food.[46] It thus seems that the builders of Qumran were familiar with the common building techniques of their period.

An estimate of the population of Qumran in the Hasmonean period can be made on the basis of its area (ca. 1,400 m²). Population estimates of ancient settlement sites are usually based on a factor of fifteen to twenty-five people per 1,000 m² (one dunam, or one-tenth of a hectare).[47] If we use the lower value of fifteen people per dunam, it emerges that in the Hasmonean period only about twenty people occupied the site of Qumran. They may have comprised a small military unit, its associates, and perhaps a transient population of travelers.

The dominant component of the building is the tower, located in its northwestern corner. This is a large tower (measuring ca. 11 × 13 m), surrounded on all sides by a sloping stone revetment (fig. 26). From the considerable thickness of the walls (1.3–1.4 m), it appears that the original tower was three or four stories high. If the height of a story is taken to be 3 m, the height of the tower may be estimated at 9–12 m. The incorporation of

---

[45] On the building techniques of Qumran and other sites in the Dead Sea region, see Donceel 1997, 394; Bar-Adon 1981, 349–50; Magness 2002, 47–48. The quarries of Khirbet Samra are described by Conder and Kitchener 1883, 212–13.

[46] Magness 2002, 48.

[47] On estimates of population in ancient sites, see Finkelstein 1990, 49, and Broshi 1980, 3–5, for a higher factor of twenty to twenty-five people per dunam; Sumner 1979, 165, for a lower factor of fifteen people per dunam. Zorn (1994, 340) gives an average factor of twenty people per dunam.

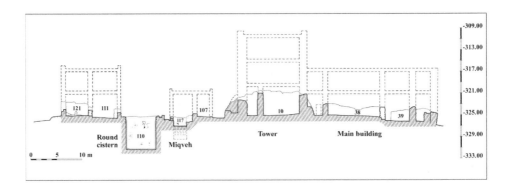

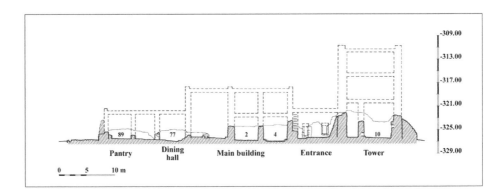

Figure 24. Cross-sections of the architectural complex of Qumran, through the tower in the main building and the wings to its west and south. Scale is meters below sea level.

Figure 25. Entrance doorways of the main building, looking southeast. Note the doorways' dressed stones.

Figure 26. The stone revetment surrounding the tower, looking southwest.

towers is characteristic of fortresses, as well as palaces and even rural estates, in the Hellenistic-Roman world.[48] The fortified tower could be used to store equipment and accommodate defenders. The location of Qumran's tower near the entrance indicates that it also served as a watchtower. As we shall see below, the tower was still part of the complex of Qumran in the Herodian period, when it became the center of a rural estate.

On the ground floor, the tower's interior was divided into five rooms that are equal in size, apart from a smaller corner room that must have been a stairwell, in view of the pillar located at its center.[49] Since no doorway was found in the exterior walls of the ground floor, it follows that access to these rooms was from the tower's second story by means of a stairway and a wooden gallery or a bridge leading from the south (see below). Remains of stucco plaster were preserved on the walls of the second-story rooms, but this may belong to the use of the tower in the Herodian period (fig. 27). A crenellated parapet probably surrounded the roof of the tower, as was customary in fortified buildings.

An important component of the tower is the revetment, or defense wall, surrounding it on all sides. It is built of a mass of medium-sized and large fieldstones, bound together by lime mortar. In a few places, the revetment is fully preserved to a height of 4 m above ground level (fig. 28). The thickness at the base of the revetment reaches about 4 m on the northern and western sides, double the thickness of the inner sides facing the courtyard. Of similar revetments at various sites in Judea, one of the best examples is that in front of the Northern Palace at Masada.[50]

In Hellenistic literature, this element is called a *proteichisma*, "forewall," and always has defensive connotations. Its function was to reinforce the tower walls and to prevent the undermining of the wall by enemy diggers and battering rams. Lawrence describes the *proteichisma*.[51] Sometimes it is squarish, like the one I found at Horvat 'Eleq at Ramat Hanadiv northeast of Caesarea, and sometimes it is pyramid-shaped with inclined walls, as at Qumran and Masada. In the Crimea, in Hellenistic sites near Chersonesos, examples of inclined forewalls are also found.[52]

De Vaux proposed a later date, that is, the third stage of occupation at the site (his Period II), for the construction of the revetment. In his view, the tower was originally built as an independent structure, and the revetment was added for reinforcement after the earthquake of 31 B.C.E.[53] If this theory were correct, the front of the tower behind the revetment would have been vertical and finished like the other walls of the structure. In a probe performed on the western side of the tower, however, it became clear that this was not

---

[48] On towers in Hellenistic fortifications, see McNicholl 1997, 178–81. On the incorporation of towers in domiciles of the classical period, see Nowicka 1975. In the Ramat Hanadiv excavation report, I presented examples of towers at various sites in and beyond Judea that attained a height of ca. 20 m or more (Hirschfeld 2000a, 692–97).

[49] On stairwells in Hellenistic and early Roman architecture in Judea, see Kloner 1996, 484–89.

[50] Netzer 1991, 106, photo 174. Similar revetments appear at other Judean sites of the Second Temple period, such as Rujum el-Hamiri, Horvat Salit, and Khirbet el-Muraq (Hilkiya's palace) (Hirschfeld 1998, 168–71; 2000c, 681).

[51] Lawrence 1979, 277–88.

[52] On fortified towers in the Crimea, see Nowicka 1975, 112–17.

[53] de Vaux 1954, 210–11; 1973, 25.

Figure 27. Remains of stucco plaster in the tower's second story.

Figure 28. The revetment on the tower's western side, looking north.

the case.[54] A section of the revetment was removed to expose the exterior wall of the tower that was hidden behind it. Examination of the wall face demonstrated that it was crudely built and deviated from the vertical (fig. 29). This indicates that the builders knew that the revetment would be built and therefore did not waste any effort on the finish of the tower wall. Thus, the revetment was clearly designed and built as an integral part of the tower. And since the function of the revetment was clearly defensive, its presence at Qumran is an indication that its inhabitants were far from being pacifists, as were the Essenes.

In Stratum II, the tower guarded the entrance of the fortress. Those entering through one of the doorways proceeded eastward through a passage (Loci 12 and 13) at the foot of the tower's southern side (fig. 30). This gave access to the inner courtyard, which was probably large and spacious. It was surrounded on four sides by residential and storage wings, two of which, to the west and north of the courtyard, were about 10 m wide. If, as seems likely, the other wings were of equal width, the courtyard measured about 17 × 17 m and its overall area was approximately 290 m².

The best-preserved wing is that on the west side of the courtyard. It contained three rooms, a vestibule (Locus 4) and two smaller rooms (Loci 1 and 2) behind it (fig. 31). These were entered from the passage to the south of the tower. In the next period (Stratum III), the vestibule was used as a storeroom. A flight of stairs (1 m wide) that led up to the rooms of the second floor is preserved in front of the vestibule. The staircase probably gave access to the tower via a wooden gallery[55] built over the passage leading to the inner courtyard. The gallery also had the advantage of shading the ground floor passageway. Though nothing of the gallery was preserved, a square pillar measuring 1 × 1 m that may have supported it was uncovered in the center of the passage. Figure 32 presents a reconstruction of the approach via the staircase and the gangway to the entrance in the second story of the tower.

In addition to providing access to the tower, the staircase in front of the vestibule led to the second-story rooms. The rooms in the second story around the courtyard were most likely living quarters whereas the ground floor rooms were used for services and storage.[56] Later, in the Herodian period, rooms were added in the courtyard and another staircase was built in its southeastern corner.

The water supply during Stratum II at Qumran was probably based on two reservoirs: a rectangular one (Loci 56 and 58) under the foundations of the southern side of the main building, and the round cistern (Locus 110) located about 15 m west of the main building.

Although the rectangular reservoir was part of the water system of the Herodian period (see below), its origins may well date back to the Hasmonean building period, judging by the correlation between the sides of the reservoir and the walls of the large two-story hall directly above it (fig. 33). The reservoir is long and narrow, 18 m long and 4.5 m wide (fig. 34). The relatively narrow width of the reservoir is deliberate, to enable it to be

---

54 Two excavations were conducted at Qumran after de Vaux, one under the direction of R. W. Dajjani and the other by S. H. Steckoll. The probe in the revetment was presumably carried out during one of these digs. For further details, see Donceel and Donceel-Voûte 1994, 20–21, n. 73.

55 Magness (2002, 50–51) calls it a gangway.

56 On the functional separation between the upper residential floor and the ground floor used for services, see Hirschfeld 1995, 264; Ellis 2000, 17.

Figure 29. The wall of the tower behind the revetment (on right).
Note that the stones are unfinished because they were intended to remain unseen.

Figure 30. The passageway into the main building, looking west.

Figure 31. The three rooms (Loci 4, 1, and 2) to the south of the tower, looking south.
Note the stairway to the right of the entrance doorway.

Figure 32. Proposed reconstruction of the wooden gallery leading to the second story of the tower.

Figure 33. The reservoir in the main building of Qumran (Loci 56 and 58), looking west.

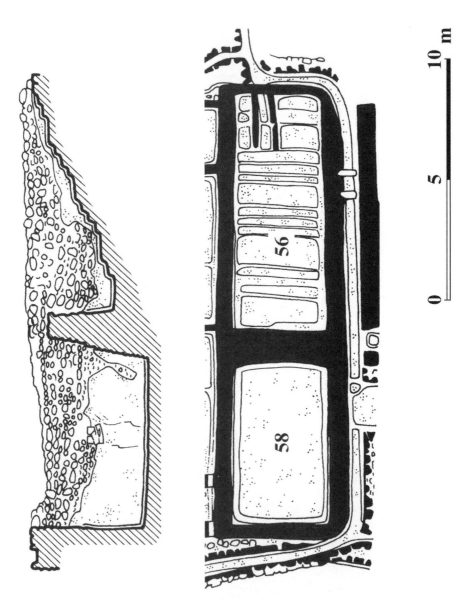

Figure 34. Plan and cross-section of the reservoir and *miqveh* (Loci 56 and 58) below the main building.

roofed with local date palm beams. Its interior was divided into two by a cross-wall that was probably built to serve as the foundation of the wall above it. The wall is well built and coated with the same plaster as the other parts of the reservoir, indicating that it was part of the original structure rather than a later addition, as suggested by de Vaux.[57] The cross-wall created a stepped pool to its west and a pool without steps to its east. According to my survey at the site, the capacity of the western pool is 50 m³, and that of the eastern pool 123 m³. The combined volume of both parts of the reservoir is thus 173 m³.[58]

Both parts of the reservoir received runoff water from the roofs of the structure and its courtyard, probably via ceramic gutters and pipes. (Later, in the Herodian stage, a conduit that drained floodwaters from nearby Wadi Qumran conveyed the water.) The water filled the two parts of the reservoir by means of a narrow passage (now missing) in the upper part of the dividing wall. A broad stairway in the western half of the reservoir led down to its floor, enabling easy access to the water even when its level dropped during the dry season (fig. 35). It is likely that the inhabitants of Qumran used this part of the reservoir as a mikveh. Stepped pools were widespread in Judea in the Hasmonean and Herodian periods, when it became the custom to dig such pools in the ground to hold water for ritual purification.[59] The bathers descended into the water by means of the staircase. Consequently, the ceiling above the steps had to be high enough to permit access. Figure 36 shows a proposed reconstruction of the mikveh in Locus 56. In contrast, the ceiling of the eastern part of the reservoir was low and was presumably no more than the floor of the story above. Its water was most likely drawn with a bucket and rope through an opening in the floor of the room above.

The round cistern (Locus 110) located to the west of the main building is well preserved; it is 5.2 m in diameter and 6.3 m deep (figs. 37 and 95 color). Its volume can be estimated at approximately 120 m³.[60] The proposal to link the round cistern with the Hasmonean stage at Qumran is based on two considerations: its round shape, which differs from that of the reservoirs and ritual baths built during the Herodian stage, and its location directly opposite the entrance doorways of the main building. As noted above, de Vaux's proposal that the round cistern dates from the Iron Age is unfounded. The walls of this cistern are coated with white hydraulic plaster containing fine stone grit, which is typical of the late Hellenistic period. Similar plaster was found at sites such as Hyrcania and Khirbet Mazin, which are dated to the Hasmonean period.[61] The round cistern at Qumran

---

[57] de Vaux 1973, 27; see also Magness 2002, 61; Galor 2002, 42.

[58] The data given here on Qumran's water reservoirs and ritual baths are based on measurements that we took at the site in 1999. In her paper on the water systems at the site, Galor (2003, 171) states that Loci 56 and 58 could hold 196 m³ of water altogether, ca. 23 m³ more than the capacity that we measured. Wood (1984, 57) gives similar figures to Galor's.

[59] On the definition of the mikveh, see Magness 2002, 142–43.

[60] According to Galor (2003, 293), the round reservoir (Locus 110) could hold 110 m³ of water.

[61] Though Bar-Adon (1989, 18–19) dates the site of Khirbet Mazin to Iron Age II, its main construction seems to have taken place during the reign of Alexander Jannaeus (103–76 B.C.E.). In a section of the shore opposite the site, I recently found more than two thousand coins of the anchor-and-star type minted during the reign of Jannaeus (Hirschfeld 2002). On the hydraulic plaster at Hyrcania, see Patrich 2002, 351. This evidence joins other considerations that cast doubt on de Vaux's proposal that the round cistern should be dated to the Iron Age.

Figure 35. The stepped pool *(miqveh)* under the main building, looking east.

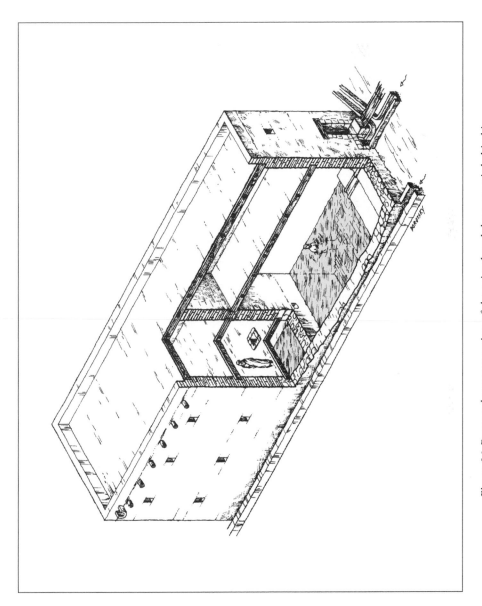

Figure 36. Proposed reconstruction of the *miqveh* and the reservoir behind it.

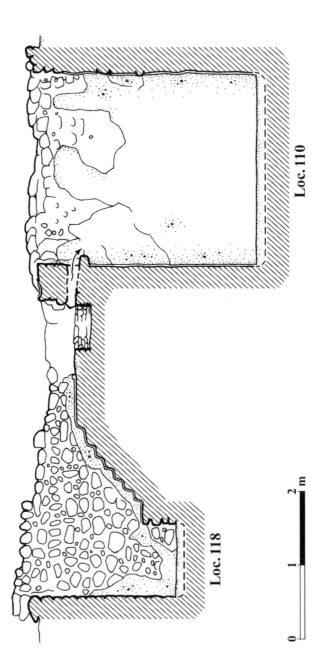

Figure 37. Cross-section of the round cistern and the *miqveh* adjacent to it.

Loc. 110

Loc. 118

0   1   2
         m

lacks steps, implying that the water was drawn by means of a bucket and rope. In order to prevent evaporation of the water, it is possible that the opening of the cistern was covered with perishable materials such as mats and ropes. The cistern was probably fed by one or more channels that drained runoff water from the surface of the surrounding area. The location of the cistern outside the building indicates that the complex was used not only for military purposes, as one might surmise from its fortifications, but also to meet the needs of passersby and caravans that halted there.

A cemetery containing about 820 graves is located 30 m east of the site (fig. 38). I will discuss the cemetery below in the context of the Herodian period at Qumran. It seems self-evident, however, that the use of the cemetery began in the Hasmonean period. The graves, which are arranged in neat rows on the plateau, are marked by heaps of stones on the surface (fig. 39). Most of them are oriented north-south. Other graves are located at the cemetery's edges, on low hills to the north, south, and east of the plateau. It stands to reason that the graves were dug parallel and fairly close to the long wall separating the site from the cemetery. It thus seems that in the Hasmonean period the inhabitants of Qumran were already meticulous in their observance of the religious law calling for the separation of an inhabited area from a place reserved for the dead (*m. B. Bat.* 2:9). On the assumption that Hasmonean Qumran was a fortress, one may speculate that the first burials were those of soldiers who died either from accidental causes (broken bones, a scorpion sting, or a venomous snake bite) or from illness. This might explain the fact that most of the excavated graves on the plateau contained the remains of adult males whereas some of those in the extensions were of women and children (see below).

To conclude, the architectural data at our disposal make it possible to reconstruct Qumran during the Hasmonean period as a fortified, right-angled, two-storied building equipped with a large, impressive corner tower (fig. 40). Analysis of the architectural remains permits the assumption that the building was erected as a fortress and not as a villa (as suggested by Humbert) or as a sectarian settlement (as maintained by de Vaux).

On the basis of the excavation finds, it is customary to assign the construction of the main building at Qumran to the days of John Hyrcanus I (134–104 B.C.E.). In support of this assumption, one can point to the architectural similarity between Qumran in Stratum II and the fortified palace built by Hyrcanus to the west of Jericho. The palace is square and is built around a courtyard surrounded by rooms; it, too, has a corner tower built of ashlars.[62] According to the excavator, Ehud Netzer, the palace was intended to ensure the safety of the king and his entourage. In view of the high status of the palace's builder and owner, the structure may well have served as a model not only for the building at Qumran but also for numerous similar fortified structures elsewhere in Judea.[63] For example, the fortress of Hyrcania was also a square fortified building equipped with a massive tower in

---

[62] On the palace (the "Buried Palace") built by John Hyrcanus I to the west of Jericho, see Netzer 2001a, 2–3; 2001b, 13–70; Nielsen 1994, 155–56. On the central role played by Hyrcanus in the initiation of building projects in the area of Jericho and the Dead Sea, see Bar-Adon 1981, 351–52.

[63] About ten other sites of the Qumran type in the Hebron Hills alone are listed by Barouch 1996; for a review of other parallels, see Hirschfeld 1998, 162–71; 2000a, 712–20.

Figure 38. Aerial view of the cemetery of Qumran, looking south.

Figure 39. Stone heaps marking the graves, looking south.

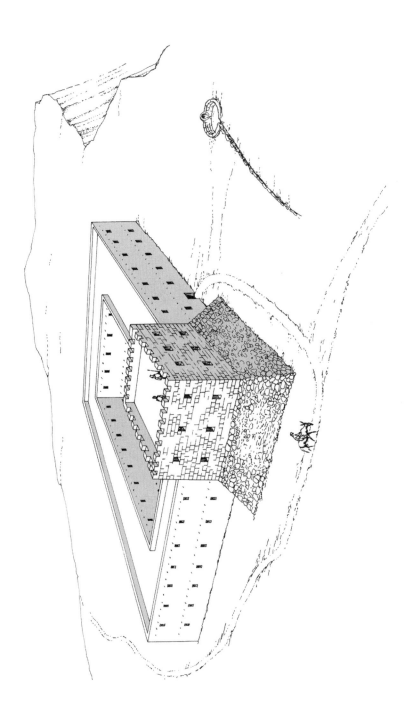

Figure 40. Proposed reconstruction of the Hasmonean fortress at Qumran.

one of its corners.[64] It may be assumed that John Hyrcanus I built both Qumran and Hyrcania, which are located along the shortest route between Jerusalem and the Dead Sea, to complement one another.

In view of Qumran's position as a strategic Judean crossroads and its proximity to the eastern frontier of the kingdom of Judea, bordering on the Nabatean kingdom, Cansdale's interpretation of Hasmonean Qumran as a combined complex consisting of a field fort and road-station seems to be the closest to reality.[65] The site's hilltop position ensured control of the road leading from Jerusalem to the southeastern part of the kingdom of Judea (fig. 96, color). Its fortified building offered the inhabitants the possibility of defending themselves when the need arose. All the Hasmonean rulers were diligent in enhancing the fortifications of Judea and maintaining garrisons. Josephus mentions twenty-two fortresses (Greek: *ta chōria,* "fortified places") that were built by the Hasmonean rulers and were controlled by their loyalists.[66] In his comprehensive study of the fortresses of the Second Temple period in Hasmonean and Herodian Judea, Israel Shatzman[67] of the Hebrew University of Jerusalem distinguishes between three types of fortification: city fortresses, in which most of the military forces were stationed; fortified palaces, built by the kings for their private needs; and field forts erected close to the frontier of the kingdom and along the main roads. One of the latter was the complex at Qumran. The long wars of John Hyrcanus I and his son Alexander Jannaeus against the Nabateans dictated the fortified, military form of the complex.[68] Later on, during the reign of Herod the Great, the kingdom achieved stability, and the inhabitants of Qumran also benefited from the long period of economic prosperity that ensued.

3.4. The Herodian Period (Stratum III)

What I consider to be the third and main stage in the history of Qumran lasted from Herod's reign (37–4 B.C.E.) until its complete devastation during the First Revolt in 68 C.E. As a result of the destruction, the remains of the building were buried beneath the debris of its superstructure. Thanks to this fact and, as noted, to the dry desert climate and de Vaux's comprehensive excavations, we have a better knowledge of Qumran in its final form than of other sites of this type.[69]

The layout of the site has thus been revealed in its entirety. The great wealth of finds, including architectural elements, that came to light during the excavation may be of

---

[64] On Hyrcania, see Patrich 1993; 2002, 345, fig. 17 (a reconstruction of the site).

[65] Cansdale 1997, 123.

[66] Josephus, *Ant.* 13.422, 427. Josephus provides this account in the context of the attempt by Aristobulus II (67–63 B.C.E.) to secure his accession to the throne.

[67] Shatzman 1991, 266–67.

[68] On the conquests of John Hyrcanus I in Transjordan, see Foerster 1981; on Alexander Jannaeus and his wars against the Nabateans, see Kasher 1993.

[69] According to Donceel and Donceel-Voûte (1994, 21), "the site of Qumran can be considered as totally excavated." According to Wood (1984, 53–54), fifty laborers were employed at de Vaux's large-scale dig. Fairly advanced mechanical equipment (trolleys and railway lines) was used to remove the excavation waste to the banks of the nearby streams.

assistance in understanding the site's function and identifying its inhabitants. Most of the finds in the nearby caves, including the scrolls hidden on the eve of the destruction of the site, can be attributed to this period at Qumran.

Expansion in almost every direction characterizes the Herodian building stage at Qumran. The main building additions (i.e., the west wing) are on the west of the main building, but other additions are discernible to the southeast and north of this structure and also within it (fig. 41). The construction at Qumran in this stratum is characterized by less rigid planning than in the previous one. This is evident both in the orientation of the walls, which are not precisely parallel or at right angles to one another, and in the adaptation of the building additions to the site's topographical conditions (e.g., on the southwestern side, which is bounded by the ravine that descends steeply to the riverbed of Wadi Qumran). The organic development of the Herodian complex at Qumran implies that it was now not a military but a civilian site. The large number of entrances enabling easy access from all directions support this assumption. The many agricultural installations and workshops indicate that most of the occupants of the site in this stage were engaged in the production of agricultural and industrial products (food, perfumes, etc.). Qumran was now not a fortress but the center of a rural estate.

The modifications of Stratum III are often attributed to the destruction and rebuilding of the site as a result of either the Parthian invasion in the days of Mattathias Antigonus (40–37 B.C.E.) or the earthquake that ravaged Judea, according to Josephus, in 31 B.C.E. There is, however, no level attesting to a violent destruction between Strata II and III, and the differences between the two strata show evidence of organic growth and intentional change.

The builders of Stratum III greatly enlarged the area of the site. Its maximum extent on the east-west axis was about 80 m and on the north-south axis about 60 m; its overall built-up area was 4,800 m², more than three times the size of the site in Stratum II.[70] De Vaux, and many other scholars after him, claimed that the complex at Qumran was used not for habitation but rather as a community center. Thus he states that the remains of the site "include very few rooms that would have been suitable as living quarters."[71] Magness, too, asserts, "The rooms in the settlement [i.e., the complex of Qumran] seem to have been used mostly if not entirely for communal purposes."[72] These are generalizations that lack a basis in fact. The complex of Qumran contains dozens of rooms and halls with installations and artifacts attesting to residence at the site. There is no reason to assume that the inhabitants of Qumran did not lead a routine existence there, including sleeping, eating, and other mundane activities typical of humans. Three staircases, two in the main building and one in the west wing, are evidence that there was a floor above, which could have been used as living quarters. Magness herself notes that in the houses of ancient Palestine the living and sleeping quarters were often in the second story to escape the dirt and noise of the ground floor.[73]

---

[70] De Vaux erroneously states that the dimensions of the building at Qumran are 100 × 80 m, i.e., 8,000 m² in overall area (de Vaux 1973, 1). Broshi (1992, 104) has perpetuated the mistake.

[71] de Vaux 1973, 56.

[72] Magness 2002, 70. Broshi and Eshel (1999b, 330) state categorically that "indeed no residential quarters were found at Qumran."

[73] Magness 2002, 221–22. On domestic architecture in Roman Palestine, see Hirschfeld 1995, 264–65.

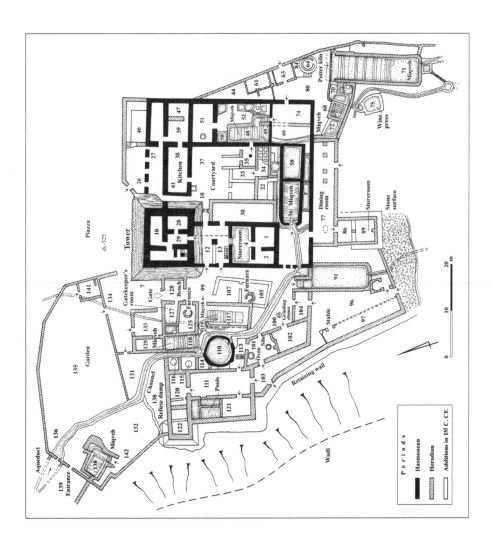

Figure 41. Plan of the complex of Qumran in the Herodian period (Stratum III).
Note that the walls in black are from the Hasmonean period (Stratum II).

One of the many debates surrounding Herodian Qumran concerns the number of its inhabitants, on which scholars differ very markedly. Laperrousaz, for example, believes that 350–400 people resided in the caves around the site, whereas Humbert estimates the group residing permanently at Qumran itself at only 10–15 people.[74] Patrich suggested that the permanent population was 50–70, but later he reduced his estimate to 30–50.[75] Broshi proposes that Qumran's inhabitants numbered no more than 150, since the dining room could accommodate this number.[76] On the basis of a calculation of water consumption, Bryant Wood has arrives at a number of 312 occupants in "Period II."[77] In my opinion, however, the only objective method of estimating population in ancient sites is the density formula mentioned above. Using a factor of 15 people per dunam, we arrive at a population of 72 permanent residents of Herodian Qumran (15 people × 4.8 dunams). The number of transient occupants of the caves near Qumran cannot be estimated.

Architectural Layout

The new construction at Qumran, particularly the addition of the west wing, changed the architectural layout of the site. The main gate now faced a square (Locus 7) to the northwest of the tower. This was because most people approaching Qumran in antiquity, like today, would have come from the direction of Jerusalem and Jericho to the north. This meeting point was dominated by the tower and could be inspected by the guards from above (fig. 42).

From the square, the visitor could enter the complex through the main gate. The gate, 1.8 m wide, was well built from sandstone ashlars. The gate led through a vestibule (Locus 128) to a spacious open space (Locus 99), separating the west wing from the main building. The vestibule is almost square (4.3 × 5 m). A bench, 5 m long, is preserved along the vestibule's eastern wall, along the lower edge of the tower's revetment. The shady vestibule would have been a pleasant place, since the doorways on a north-south axis enabled the prevailing local breeze to freshen the air. A small room (Locus 127, 2.5 × 4 m) may have been for a porter.

The open space (Locus 99) separating the west wing from the main building measures 8 × 27 m (fig. 43). In country houses of the Roman period, like that at Qumran, the living quarters, known as the *pars urbana* in Latin, and the farm's outbuildings, called the *pars rustica*, were usually closely associated.[78] Another name for this area was the *pars fructaria*, indicating a garden where botanical and horticultural experiments were also carried out. A striking similarity from the modern era may be found at the estate of George Washington in Mount Vernon, Virginia, with its division between the residence of the owner, his family, and guests and the two wings of outbuildings—one housing workshops and the other serving as living quarters for the overseer and dozens of slaves.

---

[74] Laperrousaz 1976, 109; Humbert 1994, 175.

[75] Patrich 1994a, 95–96; 2000, 726. Stegemann (1998, 38) has published an assessment similar to Patrich 2000.

[76] Broshi 1992, 114; see also Broshi and Eshel (1999b, 330), where the number given is 115–200.

[77] Wood 1984, 58. Golb (1995, 9) suggests that during a siege more than 750 people could have survived on the water contained in Qumran's reservoirs.

[78] On country houses in the Roman period, see Percival 1996, 66–67; Ellis 2000, 13–17.

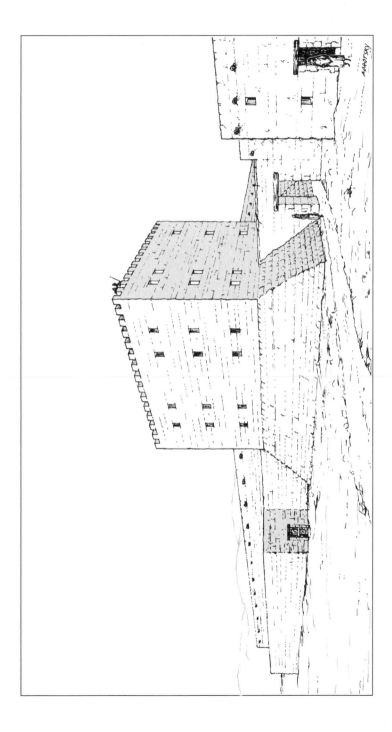

Figure 42. Proposed reconstruction of the gate to the Herodian complex.

Figure 43. The open space between the main building (on the left) and the western wing (on the right), looking south. (Courtesy of Israel Antiquities Authority.)

At most ancient sites, the industrial workshops were detached physically from the rest of the house, as they were at Qumran, not only to keep offensive odors away from the living quarters but also because of the risk of fire (the flat roofs at Qumran were made of highly flammable wooden beams, branches, and reeds). At some later time, probably during the first century C.E., two rooms (one of which contained an oven) were built within the open space, giving it the narrow, winding character of a rustic lane.

The creation of the new gate made the approach to the main building longer and more complex. The main building and tower, which were the quarters of the complex's owner, were now more isolated. A similar process can be discerned at Horvat 'Eleq at Ramat Hanadiv, where I uncovered a palatial complex with a tower in the center.[79] Another such site is the winter palace of Jericho, which during the reign of Herod expanded to become a huge complex with several wings, surrounded by gardens.[80] This development is the architectural expression of a social trend toward greater segregation in the reigns of Herod and his successors.

The main building at Qumran probably served as the *pars urbana*, that is, the residential part of the site. The architectural details and small finds from the main building show a degree of luxury. Several column bases and capitals made from high-quality local sandstone, still visible at the site, probably originated in the main building (fig. 44). De Vaux suggested that some of these elements came from a colonnade that stood in the inner courtyard of the main building, between Loci 35 and 49.[81] Among the utilitarian local pottery and glass, many examples of fine wares were found, as were beautiful stone vessels, demonstrating the high economic status of Qumran's owners.[82]

Halls and rooms, including the long, narrow hall (Locus 30) interpreted by de Vaux as a scriptorium (fig. 45), surrounded the inner courtyard.[83] From the debris and finds, it is clear that this was a high-quality, well-equipped, two-story hall. The second story could be accessed by two staircases, the old one near the main entrance (in Locus 13), constructed during the Hasmonean period, and a new one (Locus 35), probably constructed in this phase, in the southeastern corner of the inner courtyard.[84] The new staircase, with a square central pillar, provided convenient access to the living quarters on the second-story level on the southern and eastern sides of the inner courtyard.

Locus 30 (the so-called scriptorium) was filled with the debris of the collapsed second story, which yielded the remains of "plastered elements," as de Vaux called them in his excavation logs.[85] Later on he called these long, narrow mud-brick objects "tables." One piece is approximately 5 m long and 0.5 m high; it is concave and well plastered on the front whereas the back is straight and unfinished. But it seems likely that these were wall

---

[79] Hirschfeld 2000a, 687–96.

[80] Netzer 2001b.

[81] See Magness 2002, 69. For updated information on the architectural details found at Qumran, see Humbert 2003, 445.

[82] Donceel and Donceel-Voûte 1994, 7–14. For discussion of the pottery, see pp. 146–49 below.

[83] de Vaux 1954, 212; 1973, 29–33; Magness 2002, 60–61.

[84] On the construction of this staircase, see Magness 2002, 122–23.

[85] "Les éléments plâtrés"; see Humbert and Chambon 1994, 302. A photograph appears in Roitman 1997, 15.

Figure 44. Two column bases found in the west wing at Qumran, looking east.

Figure 45. The hall known as the "scriptorium" (Locus 30) in the main building, looking south.

benches rather than tables.[86] These benches could have been part of the furniture of a *triclinium,* a private dining room for the use of the estate's owner, his family, and his guests.

Two inkwells, one of pottery and the other of bronze, were found at the ground floor level of the hall, beneath the debris of the upper story.[87] An additional clay inkwell was found in another room (fig. 46). De Vaux regarded these inkwells as evidence of literary activity, but they could equally well have been used by the owner or his staff for commercial business. The fact that they were found under the debris indicates that they should be attributed to the economic activity that took place on the ground floor. Inkwells of this kind are not an unusual find; for instance, two inkwells similar to those from Qumran were found in the "Burnt House" in Jerusalem, which was a fairly ordinary upper-class domicile.[88]

In addition to the "scriptorium," various rooms and installations connected with the daily life and mundane activities of the site's inhabitants were arranged around the courtyard of the main building. On the north side of the courtyard, a large room measuring 4.4 × 10 m (Loci 38 and 41) was uncovered. This room had a paved floor and several fireplaces, making it likely that, at least in the Herodian period, it was a kitchen.[89] The food could have been carried by slaves to the owner's dining room or to the laborers' dining room (Locus 77) outside the main building (see below).

The three rooms to the south of the tower—the vestibule (Locus 4) and the two rooms behind it (Loci 1 and 2)—have suffered, like the "scriptorium," from over-interpretation. Along the walls of the vestibule were low, plastered benchlike surfaces about 20 cm high (fig. 47). De Vaux suggested that these features were benches and that the room served as the assembly room of the religious community's leaders.[90] He also proposed that a small basin or niche built into the wall to the east of its entrance (fig. 48) was a receptacle through which food or water could be served to members of the community in closed session in the assembly room without disturbing them. Stegemann, on the other hand, has offered a different interpretation: in his opinion, Loci 1, 2, and 4 were the rooms of a library: the vestibule (Locus 4) was a reading room, and the other two rooms (Loci 1 and 2) were used to store scrolls.[91] But he overlooks the absence of two essential elements

---

[86] Donceel-Voûte 1992; Donceel and Donceel-Voûte 1994, 27–30. De Vaux's interpretation of this room as a "scriptorium" has been challenged by Metzger 1959. Reich (1995) has shown that the benches are too narrow for reclining.

[87] Donceel and Donceel Voûte 1994, 31; Cansdale 1997, 148. See also Gorenson 1992; 1994. For inkwells made of stone, see Magen 2002, 175.

[88] Avigad 1983, 127. For a different opinion, see Magness 2002, 61. On inkwells found in Jordan, see Khairy 1980.

[89] de Vaux 1973, 7. A photograph of the kitchen appears in Laperrousaz 1976, pl. V.14.

[90] de Vaux 1973, 10–11; Magness 2002, 51. Recently Rapuano (2001) has suggested that Loci 1, 2, and 4 at Qumran should be compared with similar rooms in the synagogue of the Herodian winter palace in Jericho. This suggestion cannot withstand critical examination for two reasons: 1) the identification of the structure in Jericho as a synagogue is not certain; 2) in the structure at Jericho, the rooms are far from the entrance whereas those at Qumran are adjacent to it. It is possible that the similarity between the buildings stems from the use of date palm beams, which were of a standard length.

[91] Stegemann 1998, 39–40. It should be noted that Stegemann's book contains many curious assumptions, at least from an archaeological point of view.

Figure 46. The three inkwells from Qumran. (Courtesy of Israel Antiquities Authority.)

Figure 47. The vestibule (Locus 4) looking west.
Note the bench-like surfaces built along the walls.

Figure 48. A niche (cupboard) in the western wall of the vestibule (Locus 4).

of ancient libraries: large wall niches for the storage of scrolls and a well-lit peristyle court-yard or colonnade in which the scrolls could be read.[92] In my opinion, the plastered "benches" in Locus 4, at only 20 cm high, were too low to provide a comfortable seat; rather, they served as stands for vessels whose contents were intended for storage or sale (fig. 49).[93] The "benches" and floor of the room were coated with a thick layer of imper-vious plaster, lending support to the idea that the room, at least in its Herodian stage, was used for the storage of valuable liquids, such as fragrant oils and perfumes, that may have been produced at the site. The other two rooms were probably also storerooms.

Various rooms and installations connected with the daily life of the site's inhabitants were built in the inner courtyard and rooms of the main building. Thus, for example, two tublike structures and small basins used as bathtubs were built in Locus 34 in the southeast-ern corner of the courtyard.[94] A new mikveh (Locus 48/49) was constructed on the eastern side of the courtyard (see p. 121 below). Locus 52 served, according to de Vaux, as a laun-dry.[95] He interpreted as a toilet a pit with a clay pipe in the east wing of the main building (Locus 51). Magness ascribes great significance to this "toilet."[96] This proposal is intrinsically implausible, however, since the device is a fixed installation lacking the water channels needed for flushing. It seems unlikely that the occupants of the main building would have tolerated the nuisance caused by the location of such a toilet within the structure. It is more likely that they used chamber pots, as was the usual custom in antiquity.[97] No convincing ex-planation has yet been offered for the function of this pit. All these installations, however, show that the main building at Qumran continued to function as living quarters.

If the main building at Qumran was the *pars urbana*, the surrounding wings were the *pars rustica*, that is, the industrial area of the site. This conclusion is based on the remains of numerous industrial installations and workshops that were found in these wings. For example, in the wing to the east of the main building, a large kiln (Locus 64) was discov-ered; it was probably used in the production of the local pottery wares found at the site. South of the main building, the remains of a storeroom and a winepress were found.[98] The storeroom, which contained large numbers of vessels, was connected to a hall that could have been a dining room. This was a large, long, and narrow hall with internal dimensions of 4.5 × 22 m and an area of about 100 m[2] (fig. 50). It has three doorways; one is in the long northern wall and connects the hall with the main building, and the other two are in the long southern wall, one leading to the plateau to the south and the other leading into the storeroom (Loci 86 and 89, fig. 51). The more than one thousand pottery vessels that

---

[92] For public and private libraries in antiquity, see Casson 2001, 74–75, 80–82. A beautiful ex-ample of a library with a set of five large niches and a colonnaded building has been preserved in the Northern Palace at Masada (Foerster 1995, 179). I am grateful to Gideon Foerster for drawing my attention to this important find. Nothing like it has been uncovered at Qumran.

[93] On the placing of vessels on stands built against the walls of ancient dwellings, see Hirschfeld 1995, 139.

[94] Galor 2003, 304. De Vaux's suggestion that this was a dyeing installation is unfounded.

[95] de Vaux 1973, 7.

[96] Magness 2002, 52, 105–7.

[97] The use of chamber pots is recorded for the desert monasteries of Byzantine Palestine; Hirschfeld 1992, 96–97.

[98] Pfann (1994) suggested this.

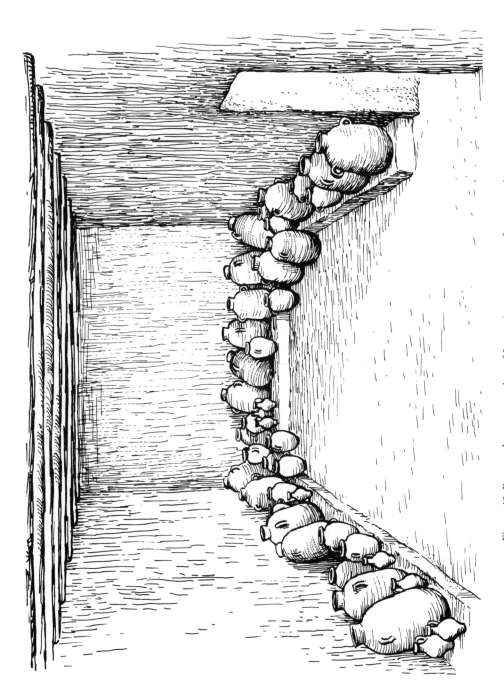

Figure 49. Proposed reconstruction of Locus 4 as a storeroom for storage jars.

Figure 50. The dining room (Locus 77) in the south wing, looking east.

Figure 51. The storeroom (Loci 86/89) south of the dining room, looking northeast.

were found in it indicate this room's function. They were unearthed beneath the layers of debris resulting from the destruction of the site during the First Revolt, invalidating de Vaux's claim that the vessels belong to a period preceding the earthquake of 31 B.C.E.[99] Most of the vessels are typical tableware (plates, cups, and bowls), implying that the large hall adjacent to the storeroom served as the main dining room of Qumran during this period. In view of the large numbers of vessels found, however, it is possible that at least some of them were kept there for commercial purposes.

The storeroom is relatively large (5 × 8.4 m). In the center of the room was a pillarlike structure about 0.8 m high, and a kind of pilaster abutted the southern wall. These features may have been added during the first century C.E. to support the ceiling. Similar pillars were found in a row in the eastern part of the dining room. It has been suggested that these supported not only the ceiling but also a story above.[100] No sign of a staircase that would attest to the existence of an upper floor, however, has been found. These pillars, like those in the storeroom, probably supported only the ceiling of the ground floor.

The dining room at Qumran probably served the laborers and slaves who lived and worked at the site. The food could have been carried from the kitchen in the main building. Similar halls have been uncovered at several late Hellenistic and early Roman sites in Judea, including, among others, Beth Zur, Khirbet el-Muraq, Horvat Salit, Kalandiya, and Mount Gerizim.[101] The fact that Qumran was located on the important road from the southern Dead Sea region to Jerusalem makes it likely that the dining hall also served pilgrims and other travelers.

The most significant addition to the site was the west wing, which almost doubled its area (fig. 52).[102] This wing, about 2,400 m² in area, includes a stable in the south; industrial installations, workshops, and storerooms around the round cistern in the center; an immersion pool (Locus 138); and an open space (Loci 132 and 135), which was probably a garden, in the north. A boundary wall surrounded the pool and garden.

The west wing was built along the bank of a small watercourse that slopes steeply from north to south. In order to reinforce the exterior western wall, a stone revetment 1.5–2 m wide was built along its foundations. The narrow surface of the revetment wall gave access to an open space (Locus 103), from which one could enter the different buildings of the west wing. One doorway in the north led to Locus 111, a second doorway in the east led to Locus 101, and an open space in the south led to the courtyard (Locus 96) in front of the stable (Locus 97). Another doorway enabled separate approach to the courtyard from the plateau to the south.

The stable was a long, narrow structure (ca. 3 × 18 m) with an entrance near its northeastern corner. Its walls are thin; it was probably a light construction that provided shelter to about a dozen beasts of burden (mules and donkeys) and perhaps one or two cows. From the courtyard in front of the stable one could go through a doorway into a small

---

[99] A C[14] test of ceiling beams found in the debris of Locus 86 showed that the vessel storeroom was destroyed in the mid-first century C.E. (Taylor and Higham 1998).

[100] Magness (2002, 122–23) writes that the staircase in the main building (Locus 35) "must have provided access to a second-story level above . . . L77." The dining room (Locus 77), however, is outside the main building, separated by some distance from the staircase in the main building.

[101] For these sites, see Berlin 1997; Hirschfeld 1995.

[102] Magness (2002, 53) calls this area "the western sector."

Figure 52. Aerial view of the west wing, looking east.

room (Locus 104), which led to the open space between the west wing and the main building. As noted, the large number of openings indicates that Qumran in the Herodian stage was a civilian establishment rather than a fortress.

The rooms of the west wing, centered on the round cistern (Locus 110), included living quarters, storerooms, industrial installations, and workshops. The cistern itself was in the center of an open courtyard (9 × 10 m). The main channel of the water supply system crossed the courtyard to the west of the cistern. On its northwest, a small storeroom full of pottery vessels (Locus 114) was found. In Locus 113, south of the round cistern, a well-preserved staircase (fig. 53) led to the living quarters on the upper floor of the west wing.[103]

A large, well-built structure measuring approximately 12 × 20 m on the outside occupied the western part of the west wing. The building contained four rooms, two oriented north-south and two east-west. De Vaux considered (for no good reason) one of the north-south rooms (Locus 111) to be a courtyard.[104] This large room (5 × 13.5 m) gave access on the north and west to two rooms, Loci 120 and 121. Beneath the floor of Locus 120 a hoard of silver Tyrian tetradrachms was discovered (see below), and in Locus 121 three shallow pools were found. The room in the northwest corner (Locus 122) does not have a door and was probably entered by a ladder from the second story above. Magness's assumption that there must have been another dining room in the second story above Locus 111 is unfounded. She claims that "the ceramic assemblage in Locus 114 must be associated with a communal dining room located nearby."[105] The large numbers of pottery vessels found in Locus 114 may be equally indicative, however, of a storeroom. The staircase in Locus 113 indicates that the four-room structure was a two-story building. The upper story may have been living quarters; because of the long, narrow shape of the room, it may be that these were slaves' dormitories.

The open area to the north of the west wing included the garden (Loci 130, 132, and 135), an immersion pool (Locus 138), and additional rooms, such as Loci 133, 129, 140, and 141. A boundary wall surrounded this large area, which extends over at least 1,000 m². We learn of the existence of the garden from de Vaux. According to him, this area of the site had been flooded during the earthquake of 31 B.C.E., and silt had accumulated to a depth of 75 cm as a result of the neglect of the water system during the supposed 30-year gap.[106] This silt had overflowed and spread into the northwestern corner of the site, overlying a deposit of ash, which de Vaux related to fire damage caused by the earthquake of 31 B.C.E. As noted above, however, there is no evidence of either earthquake damage or abandonment, and as also noted, Stratum III followed Stratum II without interruption.

On the other hand, de Vaux's description of his finds here accords very well with what we know about ancient gardens. Recycling was an important part of life for the ancients. The ash, found together with other organic material, is waste and refuse from the daily activity at

---

[103] Though nothing now remains of this staircase, it is clearly visible in the photographs of the excavation (Humbert and Chambon 1994, photos 227, 231, 236). On the basis of its discovery, de Vaux (de Vaux 1973, 28) suggested correctly that there was an upper, residential story in the west wing. These data are given no mention in the discussion by Broshi (2001, 168) of the living quarters at the site of Qumran.

[104] de Vaux 1973, 8. Magness (2002, 53) follows de Vaux.

[105] Magness 2002, 125.

[106] de Vaux 1973, 23; see also Magness 2002, 56–57; Rohrhirsch and Röhner 2001, 169.

Figure 53. Stairway leading to second story in the west wing. (Courtesy of École Biblique.)

the site, and the silt came from accumulations from the reservoir settling tanks. The many terraces that we have excavated at En-Gedi also include layers of ash or other organic material, overlaid by silt. Both materials were intentionally applied as fertilizer. It seems likely, therefore, that the boundary wall enclosed a garden that the inhabitants of Qumran cultivated.

In the south part of the garden, in Loci 130 and 132, to the north of the four-room structure, de Vaux found clusters of pottery, some intact vessels, broken vessels, and animal bones mixed together and buried in the ground with ash (fig. 54).[107] The species represented were mainly sheep and goats, but cattle or oxen were found as well.[108] De Vaux and other advocates of the Qumran-Essene hypothesis attach great significance to the animal bones found in various parts of the site, particularly the garden. According to de Vaux, these bones were found in "deposits," indicating that the meals "had a religious significance."[109]

Magness claims that the animal bones were the remains of ritual meals that were "analogous to the Temple sacrifices."[110] But this is not necessarily the case. The photograph from the excavation gives the impression of a refuse dump. Some of the pots were buried intentionally. For instance, a cooking pot was found with the lid on it. Animal bones were found piled into the lower halves of more than thirty pottery jars, which the inhabitants of Qumran buried in the soft silt of their garden (fig. 55). Another, smaller container of animal bones and pottery was found in the eastern part of the site, in the triangular area between the main building and the long wall (Loci 44 and 80). In their recent excavation of the long wall, Magen and Peleg found about eight first-century C.E. intact jars buried intentionally at a depth of about 1 m.[111] In their excavations, Broshi and Eshel also found buried, intact pottery vessels near the caves north of Qumran.[112]

What is the meaning of this phenomenon? In my opinion, it is connected to the "craze" of the Jewish people at this time regarding ritual purity. The sages of the Talmud gently mocked this obsession when they said, "purity broke out in Israel."[113] The discussion of the issue of purity and the transmission of impurity to vessels and materials begins in the Bible (Lev 11:32–33; Num 31:22–23). Because it was believed that pottery could acquire irreversible impurity, a solution had to be found to dispose of the large number of impure vessels. Stone vessels were perceived to be impervious to impurity, which is why these vessels are found in most Second Temple sites, including Qumran. This was a subject of concern for the entire Jewish population of Second Temple period Judea, not only for sectarian groups. Only because Qumran was so extensively excavated over the years was such a large amount of buried pottery discovered.

And what about the bones? According to Magness, the animal bones were left over after communal meat meals, designed to mimic the temple sacrifices: "They *carefully* [my emphasis] deposited the remains of the animals in or under potsherds or pots."[114] Can this

---

[107] de Vaux 1973, 12–14.

[108] On the animal bones from Qumran, see Zeuner 1960, 28–30.

[109] de Vaux 1973, 27.

[110] Magness 2002, 119.

[111] These jars were published in Magen 2002, 139.

[112] Broshi and Eshel (1999b, 336) found the complete vessels with a metal detector right under the surface of bedrock. It seems to me that the vessels had been buried intentionally because of impurity.

[113] *t. Šabb.* 1:14; *y. Šabb.* 1:3b. See a comprehensive study in Magen 2002, 138–47.

[114] Magness 2002, 121.

Figure 54. Pottery vessels, ash, and animal bones found in the garden area. (Courtesy of École Biblique.)

Figure 55. An animal bone deposit (Locus 130) at the time of de Vaux's excavations. (Courtesy of École Biblique.)

be the case when photographs show the piles of bones at the site as if in a garbage dump? It is more likely that the inhabitants of Qumran buried the remains of the meat meals to prevent wild animals from being attracted to the site by the scent. And research on the gardens of the winter palace complex at Jericho and the agricultural terraces of En-Gedi has shown that bones were often used for the improvement of soil.[115] At Pompeii, too, the leftovers of ordinary meals were found buried in the gardens of private houses.[116] Another important point concerns the presence of animal bones at what is purported to be an Essene site. Josephus (*Ant.* 15.371) says that the Essenes lived a "Pythagorean way of life," which was ascetic and characterized mainly by vegetarianism. It is absurd to think that the inhabitants of Qumran, who were obviously meat eaters, could also have been Essenes. We can only conclude that if the bones were deposited, it was for a prosaic reason, for fertilizing the soil the inhabitants were cultivating.

The immersion pool (Locus 138) at the western end of the garden was an isolated structure (fig. 56). A small entrance (Locus 139) was found nearby; it was probably a service gate for the gardeners. The mikveh would have enabled them to purify themselves before and after their work, thus ensuring that their produce would be considered ritually pure. The proximity of agricultural installations near mikvehs is a well-known phenomenon in other Jewish sites of this period. The location of a mikveh near the entrance to the site would have also enabled visitors to purify themselves, if necessary, before entering the compound.

Figure 57 presents a proposed reconstruction of the complex's appearance during the Herodian period. At its center stood the main building, with its tower rising to a height of three or four stories, and around it were various wings that served as dwellings and workshops. Analysis of the remains shows that the complex was civilian in character and most likely served as the center of a rural estate, like similar sites in Judea during the Herodian period.[117]

The Water Supply System

As part of the expansion of Qumran, major additions were made to the water supply system. This system consists of a series of mikvehs and reservoirs connected by a central channel (fig. 58) that drained winter floodwaters by means of a conduit that started in the nearby Wadi Qumran.[118] A calculation of the capacity of all the mikvehs and reservoirs (including the round cistern) shows that it was possible to store the considerable quantity of about 1,200 m³ of water at Qumran. This quantity was not exceptional when compared with the water storage capacity of other fortresses of the Judean Desert.[119] For example, in

---

[115] Gleason 1993, 159–167 (for Jericho); Hadas 2002, 23 (for En-Gedi)

[116] Jashemski 1979, 95–96, 211–18; 1987, 70.

[117] Hirschfeld 1998, 161–64.

[118] For descriptions of Qumran's water conduit, see Humbert and Chambon 1994, 342; Ilan and Amit 2002. Although Ilan and Amit (p. 385) date the beginning of the conduit to the Iron Age and the Hasmonean period, Humbert's (1994, 182–83) dating of the conduit to the site's Herodian stage (Stratum III) is preferable, in my view. For a detailed description of Qumran's water system, see Galor 2002; 2003.

[119] Hidiroglou 2000, 139. According to Wood (1984, 57, table 1), the water storage capacity at Qumran was 1,127 m³ (including small pools and settling tanks whose capacity was only 3–5 m³). My measurements at the site indicate that the capacity was ca. 1,200 m³.

Figure 56. The *miqveh* (Locus 138) at the western edge of the garden, looking southeast.

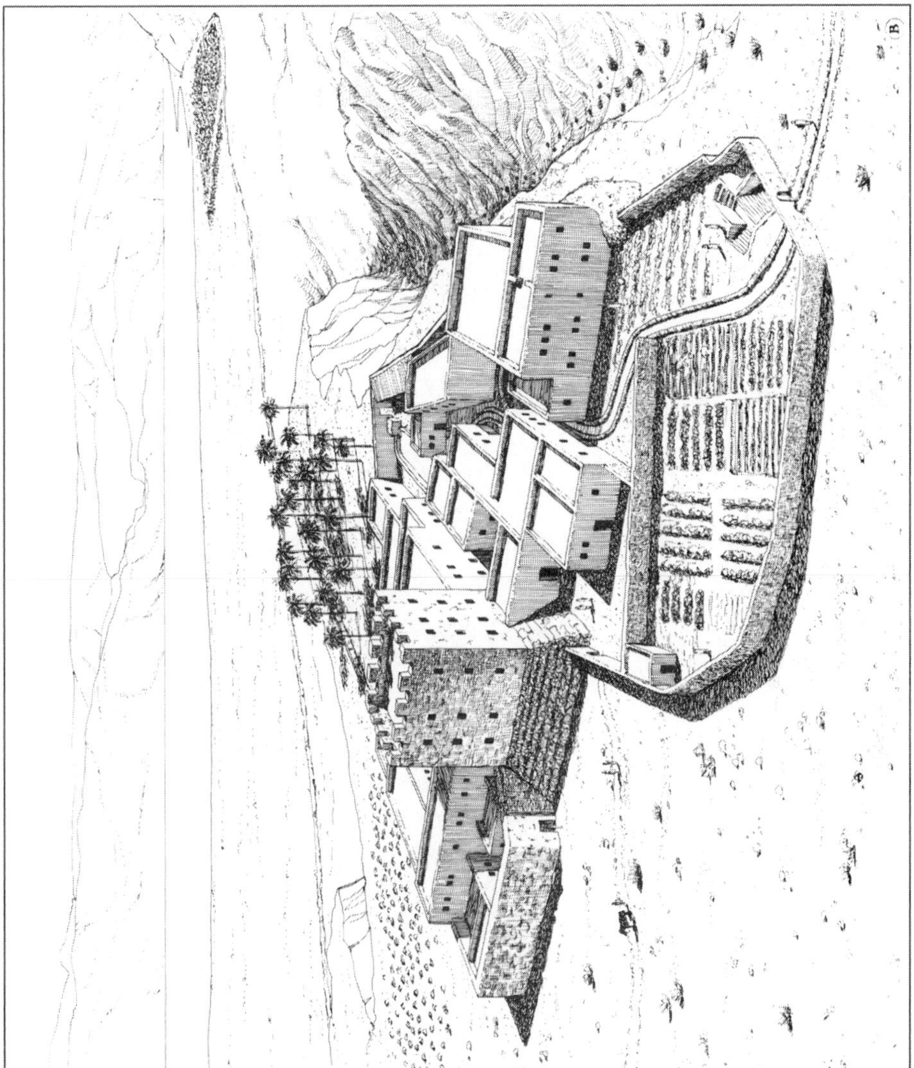

Figure 57. Proposed reconstruction of Qumran during the Herodian period (Stratum III).

Figure 58. Qumran's main water channel, looking northwest.

the relatively small palace-fortresses of Dok and Cypros (to the west of Jericho), the capacity was 2,100 m³ and 6,000 m³ respectively, and at larger sites such as Hyrcania and Masada, the capacity was 16,000 m³ and 46,500 m³ respectively.[120]

The water supply system at Qumran, like those of Hyrcania and Masada, was based on the infrequent and sudden winter floods that occur in the desert almost every year. This system must be able to receive large quantities of water in a very short time. Special devices had to be installed to catch the water in the riverbeds, and each reservoir and pool had to have a settling tank to catch the dirt, and an overflow arrangement. The construction of such a system demanded both extensive hydrological knowledge and a large budget; this points to the affluence of Qumran's owner.[121] Because of the strength of the floods, the system required constant maintenance and repair.

Today the water system of Qumran is exposed and immediately attracts our attention when we visit the site. In antiquity, however, the system was mainly hidden below the floors and walls of the buildings, and the water was invisible apart from the few hours per year during which it flowed to the site through the conduits.

Where the conduit reached the northwestern corner of the west wing (Locus 136), the water passed through a sluice gate.[122] This device, which consisted of three stones standing 0.2 m apart, was intended to trap flood debris (fig. 59). The water channel winds around the first mikveh (Locus 138), crosses the garden (Loci 130, 132, 135), and reaches the northern end of the round cistern (Locus 110). The channel was plastered with the hydraulic plaster used in the pools and reservoirs. Some of the stone slabs that capped the channel still remain in situ.

As the channel circumscribes the eastern half of the round cistern, it opens onto two similar mikvehs, Loci 117 and 118. The people who lived in the west wing probably used these mikvehs. To the south of the round cistern, the channel continues in a southeasterly direction to connect with the large reservoir (Locus 91) in the south of the site. A small settling tank (Locus 83) cleaned the water before it entered the reservoir.

The main channel continues in an easterly direction toward the large rectangular reservoir (Loci 56 and 58). As we have seen, this combination of a mikveh and a reservoir was installed in the foundations of the building in the Hasmonean phase. Shortly before it reaches the mikveh of Locus 56, the channel forks, with a branch leading to three basins (Loci 55, 57, and 59) built along the southern wall of the mikveh.

The main channel winds around the northeastern corner of Locus 58 and continues southward to connect consecutively with four small pools (Loci 68, 69, 70, and 72) and the largest mikveh at the site, Locus 71, at the site's southeastern end. From the northeastern corner of Locus 58, a secondary channel branches off to the north, supplying the mikveh (Locus 48/49) built in the foundations of the east wing of the main building. The fact that the main water channel connects all the components indicates that the entire water supply system was constructed at one time, that is, in the Herodian period.[123]

---

[120] On the water systems of the Judean Desert fortresses, see Garbrecht and Peleg 1994, esp. the table on p. 169.

[121] On the hydrological knowledge of the Qumran's builders, see Humbert 1994, 182–83.

[122] In this I have followed Galor's 2003 description.

[123] As shown above, de Vaux's dating of the water installations in the different occupation levels is unacceptable because of the lack of stratigraphic data; see Galor 2003, 307–8.

Figure 59. A sluice gate of the aqueduct entering Qumran.

A distinction must be made between reservoirs intended for the supply of drinking water and mikvehs intended for immersion purposes. Various scholars have interpreted all the reservoirs and stepped water installations of Qumran as mikvehs.[124] In view of Qumran's desert location and its size, which is indicative of a large permanent population, however, it is difficult to accept this interpretation. The round cistern, whose capacity is about 120 m³, could not have met the drinking-water needs of at least seventy people for a whole year.

It seems that Herodian Qumran had two large reservoirs that served, together with the round cistern, for the storage of drinking water for human beings and animals, and perhaps also for irrigation. One of them (Locus 58) is the reservoir that was installed below the south wing of the main building during the Hasmonean period.[125] Its capacity was 123 m³. The second reservoir (Locus 91) is the largest of Qumran's reservoirs, with a capacity of 345 m³ (fig. 60). The combined capacity of these two reservoirs, together with that of the round cistern, was about 588 m³, that is, 49 percent of the overall amount of water that could be stored at Qumran. The large reservoir (Locus 91) in the southern part of the site has a long, narrow, rectangular plan like that of the reservoir under the main building (fig. 61). Although their length is variable, their width is similar at 4–5 m. This narrow width implies that the reservoirs were roofed with wooden beams, probably made out of date palm trunks. When exposed, Locus 91 was found to be filled with masses of masonry, which can still be seen today, from the destruction of the building above during the First Revolt. We know this because the Roman soldiers who lived in Qumran after the revolt built their water supply channel around this masonry. The channel can also be seen today. From the amount of debris, one can reasonably assume that above the reservoir there was a large hall of the same shape as the reservoir below it. This building method conferred a double advantage: it shielded the water from the sun and the heat of the desert, and it significantly increased the space available for living quarters. The efficiency of this method is demonstrated to this day in the desert monasteries, in which large reservoirs are located under the living quarters of the ground floor. A good example of this practical architectural solution is the reservoir of Saint Anthony's Monastery (Deir Mar Antonius) in the Eastern Desert of Egypt (fig. 97, color). Built above the reservoir, which is roofed with wooden beams, are rooms and halls that form part of the monastery building.

The evaporation rate in the Dead Sea region is the highest in Israel, reaching up to 3 m per annum.[126] Consequently, at a site such as Qumran, which lacks a permanent water source, it was essential to provide the water installations with substantial roofing to insulate them. Roofing the reservoirs with light, perishable materials, as has been suggested,

---

[124] Reich (2000) enumerates ten mikvehs for immersion purposes at Qumran, six for humans and four for vessels, leaving only the round cistern as a source of drinking water. See also Reich 1990, 306–18; Galor 2002, 43–44. It is hard to accept Galor's conclusion "to refrain from making clear distinctions between the pools that were used as cisterns and those that were used as ritual baths." High-quality drinking water was an important issue for people in antiquity, as it is for us today. In case of severe drought, the inhabitants of Qumran could bring water from the springs near 'Ein Feshkha.

[125] According to Wood (1984, 52), the water installation (Locus 56/58) was originally built as a mikveh, and the decision to construct a partition wall across it was made later. The wall dividing Locus 56 from Locus 58, however, appears to have been built in the original stage of construction.

[126] Gat and Karni 1998, 261.

Figure 60. The largest reservoir (Locus 91) at Qumran, looking north.
Note the column drum at the base of the debris.

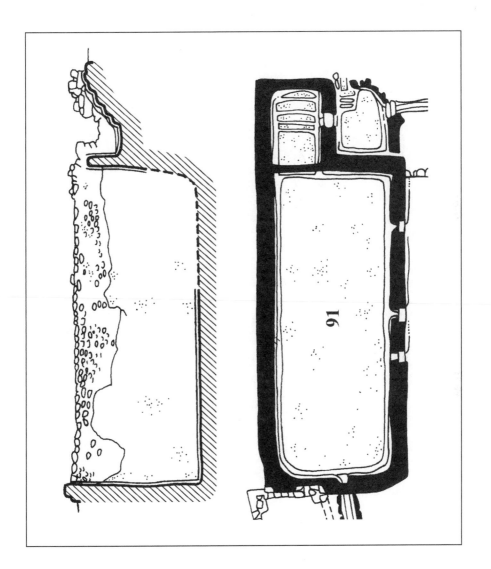

Figure 61. Plan and cross-section of the reservoir (Locus 91).

would not have been effective.[127] The stepped pools and reservoirs at Qumran were enclosed with walls and roofed, like the other structures in the complex, with wooden beams covered with layers of rushes, reeds, and mud plaster. The reservoirs and mikvehs found at contemporary sites, such of those in the basements of the houses in Jerusalem, were enclosed in roofed structures.[128]

In addition to the reservoirs that provided Qumran with drinking water, there were at least ten stepped pools. Four of these (Loci 48/49, 56, 117, and 118) are very similar in plan, architectural details, and workmanship to stepped water installations found in Jerusalem and in other Jewish sites in Judea and Galilee—Sepphoris and Gamla, for example—that served as mikvehs. Some of the differences between the mikvehs of Qumran and those of other sites reflect local geological conditions. In Jerusalem, for instance, the mikvehs were hewn into the hard limestone beneath the houses. These installations tend to be smaller and narrower than those of Qumran, which were dug into the soft marl of the plateau. Most of the mikvehs of Qumran have a volume of about 50 m³, twice as much as the larger mikvehs of Jerusalem. This is due to the fact that Qumran's water installations were located in the desert and quickly filled with muddy floodwaters. The silt settled at the bottom of the mikveh without disturbing the users, who, when the mikveh was full, needed to descend only two or three steps for total immersion.[129]

Although the mikvehs of Qumran in Stratum III are scattered throughout the site, their distribution does not appear to be random. They seem, rather, to be associated with the living quarters in the main building and the west wing and with workshop areas. Thus, for example, the largest mikveh (Locus 71), at the southeastern end of the complex probably served the potter's workshop and was also used by those entering the site from the east, where the cemetery is located.[130] The mikveh in the northwest (Locus 138) was probably for the use of the gardeners and those entering the complex through the northwestern entrance.

The mikvehs of Qumran resemble the Jerusalem type, in which the staircase occupies the entire width of the pool, rather than the type that is common in nearby Jericho, in which a narrow staircase is built against one or two of the pool's sides.[131] Several other technical details, such as the design and workmanship, link the Qumran installations with the architectural tradition of Jerusalem rather than Jericho.

Some of Qumran's mikvehs have a single, double, or even triple partition built in the middle of the staircase, separating the entrance from the exit. The intention was probably to avoid contact between impure persons entering the mikveh and pure persons leaving it.[132] Mikvehs with partitions occur mainly in the Jerusalem area. It has been suggested that mikvehs with partitions (and sometimes also with double doorways) were intended

---

[127] See, e.g., the proposed reconstructions of the site in Humbert 2000, 141; or Ilan and Amit, 2002, 386.

[128] Magness 2002, 152–53.

[129] Reich 2000, 728–30.

[130] Magness 2002, 127.

[131] Reich 2000, 729. On the mikvehs of Qumran, see also Murphy 2002, 297–99. According to Wood (1984, 49–51), the wide staircases at Qumran were intended to facilitate entry and exit, from which it follows that they were used for immersion.

[132] Magness 2002, 145.

for the use of priests, who were obliged to maintain a higher level of purity.[133] If this is the case, the numerous mikvehs with partitions at Qumran should be understood in light of the priestly orientation of the owners.

Four mikvehs at Qumran are located in the residential areas of the complex, two (Loci 56, 48, and 49) in the main building and two (Loci 117 and 118) in the west wing (fig. 62). Bathing in the mikveh was an intimate activity, and consequently it was built in an enclosed space, probably without windows (fig. 63). The ceiling had to be high enough to enable a person to enter the mikveh without stooping.

The mikveh on the southern side of the main building (Locus 56), which was constructed in the previous period, continued in use unchanged. The approach to this mikveh, which has a capacity of about 50 m³, was from the west. The mikveh on the eastern side of the main building (Locus 48/49) has a capacity of 47 m³ (fig. 64).[134] Its broad steps, which are accessed from the south, were damaged by earthquake activity at some time after the abandonment of the site (and not during the earthquake of 31 B.C.E., as suggested by de Vaux). In the southeastern corner, close to the entrance, is a bathtub (Locus 34), which enabled users of the mikveh to wash themselves before ritual purification. The close association of a bathtub and a mikveh is known from other Jewish sites in Judea.[135]

The two mikvehs in the west wing (Loci 117 and 118) are well preserved. They are located close together, and it is clear from their similarity that they were built at the same time (fig. 65). Their capacity is 56 m³ and 50 m³ respectively.[136] Locus 117 lies to the east of the round cistern, and Locus 118 is adjacent to it on the north. Locus 118 was entered from Locus 117.[137] Pairs of mikvehs are common in Jerusalem. It has been suggested that they were used for immersion by different groups, such as men versus women or family versus servants. Magness, however, has suggested that when mikvehs occurred in pairs, they were not used simultaneously.[138] During the long, dry summer at Qumran, the second mikveh would be opened when the water in the first one dropped to an unacceptable level or became too dirty for use.

Two or three mikvehs were uncovered in the industrial zone at the southeastern end of the site. One of them is Locus 68. This is fairly small (with a capacity of 8.4 m³) and has two stairways opposite one another (fig. 66). It is close to the area in which the processing of agricultural products took place and to a winepress (Locus 75).

The location of the mikveh next to the winepress implies that it enabled people to purify themselves before they started work.[139] Next to it is the largest of Qumran's mikvehs, Locus 71 (fig. 67). From its size (its capacity is 283 m³), it seems likely that it was used,

---

[133] Regev 1996b; Reich 2000, 731.

[134] Galor (2003, 293, table 1) presents data on the capacity of all the pools at Qumran.

[135] Reich 1990, 129–30. This combination was found, e.g., at Ramat Hanadiv; Hirschfeld 2000a, 22–24.

[136] According to Galor (2003, 293, table 1), the capacity of Locus 117 is 39 m³ and that of Locus 118 45.6 m³.

[137] Contra Magness (2002, 148), who assumes that the entrance was through what de Vaux assigned Locus 119 *bis.*

[138] Ibid., 149. Netzer (2002b) has recently suggested the same idea.

[139] On the connection between mikvehs and installations of agricultural industries (wine and oil presses, etc.), see Reich 1990, 52; 1988.

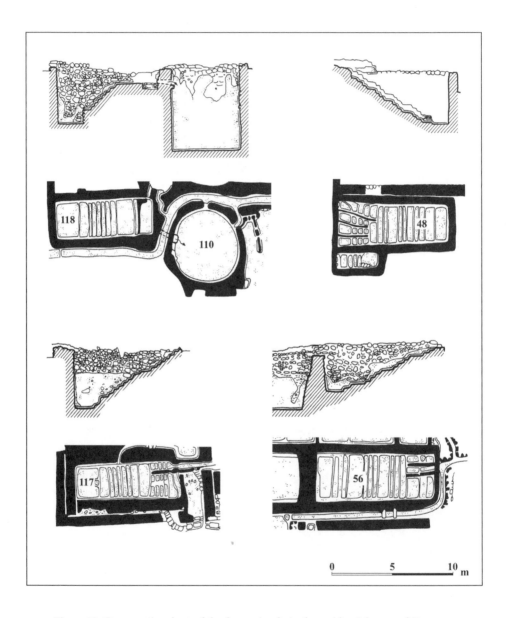

Figure 62. Comparative chart of the four *miqvehs* in the residential areas of Qumran.

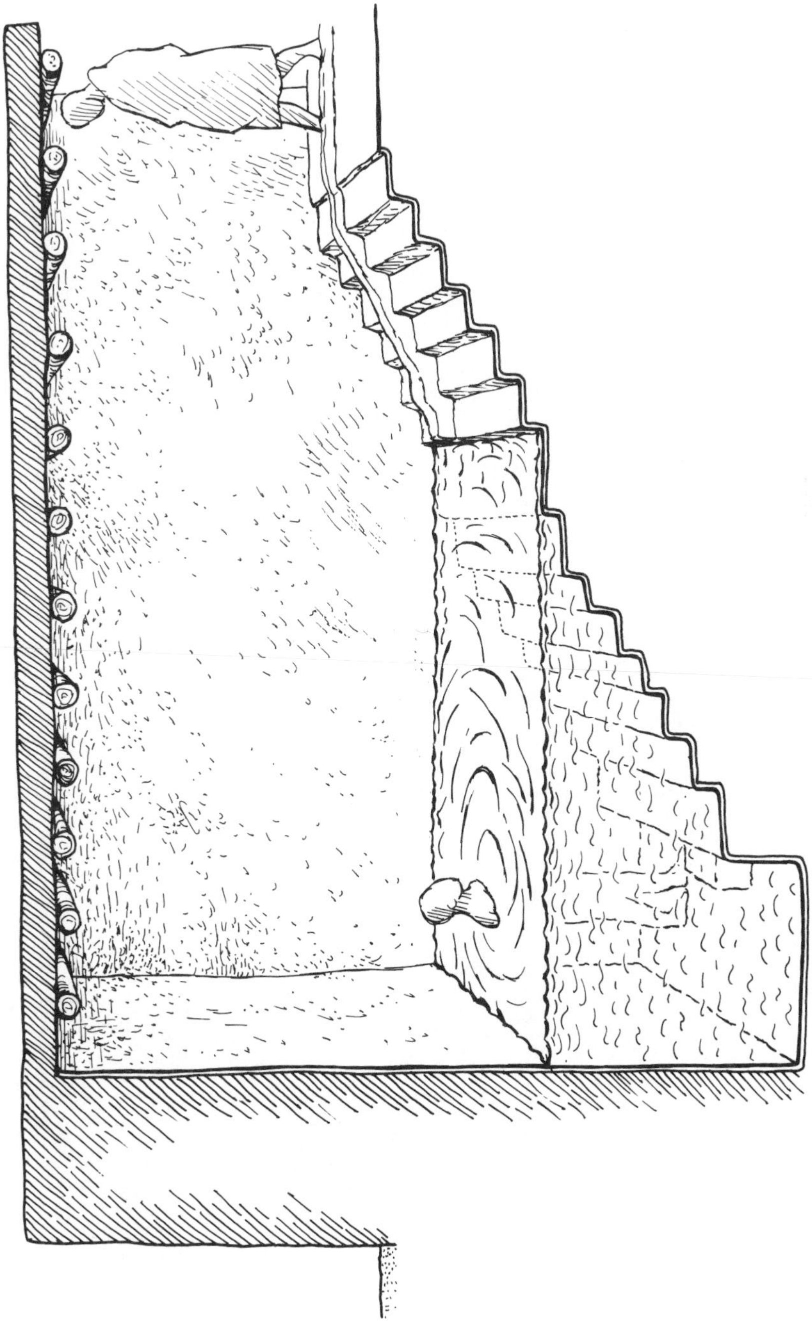

Figure 63. Proposed reconstruction of a *miqveh* at Qumran.

Figure 64. The *miqveh* on the east side of the main building (Locus 48/49), looking south.
Note the geological fault line, bottom left, dating from after the abandonment of the site

Figure 65. The two *miqvehs* (Locus 117 on the right and Locus 118 on the left) in the west wing.

Figure 66. The small *miqveh* with two stairways in the industrial zone (Locus 68), looking southwest.

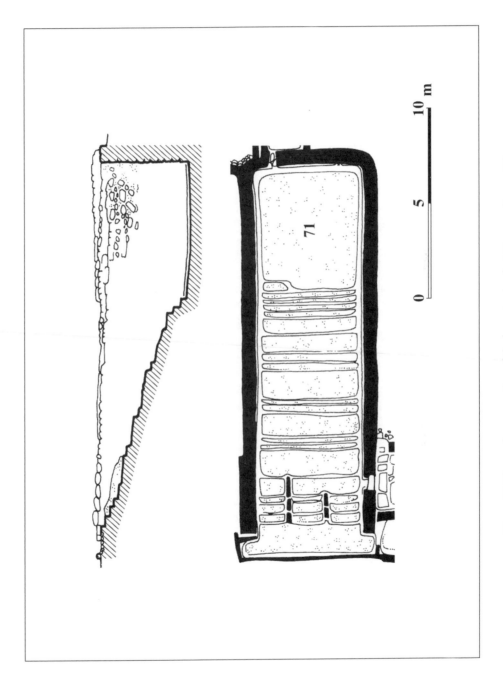

Figure 67. Plan and cross-section of the largest *miqveh* at Qumran (Locus 71).

inter alia, for the immersion of large pottery vessels,[140] a custom noted in Mark 7:4: "there are also many other traditions that they [the Pharisees and all the Jews] observe, the washing of cups, pots, and bronze kettles." The exceptional size of this mikveh and its location outside the main building may suggest that it was intended to serve travelers and pilgrims on their way to or from Jerusalem. Extremely large mikvehs have recently been found along the pilgrim routes from the Hebron Hills to Jerusalem.[141]

Scholars who endorse the Essene-Qumran hypothesis frequently point to the multiplicity of mikvehs at Qumran as indicative of the exceptional piety of its inhabitants. Broshi, for example, determines that the mikvehs at Qumran are "the strongest argument for defining Qumran as a religious site. Nowhere in Palestine . . . do we have such density of these religious installations."[142] Magness, like de Vaux, claims that the stepped pools are "Qumran's most striking feature" and that they "should be understood within the context of the community's concern with purity,"[143] At the time of de Vaux's excavation, the number of mikvehs at Qumran was indeed considered exceptional. After numerous excavations and studies have been carried out at various Second Temple period sites in the country, however, it can be concluded that their number is large but not exceptional. For example, a complex of the early Roman period was exposed near Shoham on the coastal plain. Smaller than the complex at Qumran, with an area of 2,800 m³, it contains four mikvehs of various sizes.[144] During his studies in the Hebron Hills, David Amit discovered several sites with two or three mikvehs as well as huge public mikvehs that he believes were intended for pilgrims journeying to Jerusalem.[145] During the late Hellenistic and early Roman periods, Hyrcania had three mikvehs, Masada at least fifteen, and the palace complex at Jericho more than thirty.[146] It is now clear that the number of mikvehs at Qumran is not exceptional but is close to the norm in houses owned by affluent Judean Jews of the period.[147]

---

[140] According to Galor (2003, 171, table 1), the capacity of Locus 71 is 204 m³.

[141] Amit 1993.

[142] Broshi 1998, 24.

[143] Magness's comparison (2002, 156–57) of Qumran to Nabatean sites such as Petra and Mampsis is curious, since she recognizes that the stepped pools of Qumran "are not paralleled at Mampsis."

[144] Dahari and Ad 1998, 80. Another Second Temple period settlement, with an area of four dunams and featuring four rock-cut mikvehs, was found at the site of Nahal Yarmuth in the southern coastal plain (Eisenberg 2001, 92). A Second Temple period farmhouse with three mikvehs was discovered at Khirbet Ka'kul northeast of Jerusalem (Seligman 1995, 69). These are only some of the examples of Second Temple period buildings that contain numerous mikvehs.

[145] Amit 1993, 185.

[146] At Hyrcania, Patrich (2002) surveyed three stepped water installations that he interprets as mikvehs. This is in addition to about fifteen cisterns and two large pools on the saddle to the west of the site. In the final report on Masada (Netzer 1991), the remains of at least fifteen different mikvehs are described. Among them one can mention the one in Building 7 (Netzer 1991, 13–14); the two in the large bathhouse (pp. 81–86); the three at the entrance to the Northern Palace and in the palace itself (pp. 127–29, 158–67); the one to the south of the storeroom complex (p. 183); the two in Building 9 (pp. 221–27); the three in the Western Palace (p. 259) and the small palaces next to it (p. 320); the large mikveh (which perhaps served as a public bath) to the west of the small palaces (pp. 329–31); and another three in the southern part of the site (pp. 499, 507–10, 513). On the mikvehs at Jericho, see Netzer 1978; Reich 1990, 270–75.

[147] Reich (2000, 730) has established that the number of mikvehs at Qumran is close to the norm in contemporary domiciles in Jerusalem.

Industrial Installations

To my mind, the most striking feature of Herodian Qumran is the numerous industrial installations found in various parts of the site.[148] The large number of these installations is particularly notable in the west wing. This wing, which centered on the round cistern, contained storerooms, industrial installations, and workshops. A large furnace associated with a plastered platform was uncovered close to the gate in Locus 125 (fig. 68). The entrance faced the passage between the main building and the west wing. Still visible on the furnace's plastered rim at the time of the excavations was the imprint of a large vessel, possibly made of bronze, that once stood there (fig. 69).

Two rooms (Loci 105 and 107) were added in the center of the passage that divided the site. One of these (Locus 105) contained a furnace that held metal slag (fig. 70), indicating that it was used for blacksmithing.[149]

The small courtyard to the south of the round cistern (Locus 100) contained a well-preserved bakery oven made of brick (fig. 71). A mill for grinding grain was discovered a little farther to the south. It contained a circular platform with a flour mill known as a "Pompeian donkey mill" on top of it (fig. 72). This type of mill was introduced to Judea during the early Roman period.[150] Two silos for grain storage were discovered in Loci 115 and 116 to the north of the round cistern (fig. 73).[151]

In addition to the furnaces and ovens, three adjacent pools were revealed in a room west of the round cistern (Locus 121). The pools are well preserved (fig. 74). They are uniform in size (ca. 2 × 4 m), and their relatively thin walls (20 cm) may attest that they were soaking pools used in balsam production. Soaking the pruned branches of the balsam shrub was an important stage in the production of balsam perfume; placement of the soaking pools inside a solid and roofed building may have controlled evaporation.[152] In the room west of Locus 121 (Locus 111), a pair of jars were found imbedded in the floor. Jars sunk into the floors of rooms were used for storage, mostly of food items such as grain.[153] My excavations at En-Gedi have also uncovered jars imbedded in floors, associated with installations that we have related to the balsam industry on the basis of historical accounts describing En-Gedi as a center of balsam production.

In the industrial area at the southeastern end of the Qumran site, a potter's workshop (Loci 64 and 84) and a winepress (Locus 75) were unearthed. The potter's workshop includes two circular kilns (Locus 64) and the smaller (Locus 84) to its north (fig. 75).[154] The discovery of the potter's workshop is unusual but not unique. At the late Roman site northeast of Ashkelon called by its excavator the "Third Mile Estate," two large and

---

148 On the industrial installations at Qumran, see Donceel and Donceel-Voûte 1994, 25–27.

149 Humbert and Chambon (1994, 325, photo 274) describe and illustrate the oven in Locus 105. According to Magness (2002, 59), this was a bakery oven.

150 For further discussion, see Frankel 2003, 19–20.

151 Magness (2002, 53) suggests that Loci 115 and 116 were used in an industry requiring water. Elsewhere (p. 59), however, she suggests that they were silos.

152 On the balsam industry in the Dead Sea region, see Donceel-Voûte 1998. A very interesting and precise description of a soaking pool appears in b. Kritut 5a.

153 Magness 2002, 48.

154 For a description of the potter's workshop, see Magness 2002, 52–53.

Figure 68. The industrial furnace (Locus 125), looking west.

Figure 69. Proposed reconstruction of the industrial furnace.

Figure 70. A large industrial furnace (Locus 105), looking north. Note the basalt mortar in the foreground.

Figure 71. A bakery oven in the west wing (Locus 100), looking north.

Figure 72. A donkey-powered mill as found and as a proposed reconstruction.
(Photo courtesy of École Biblique.)

Figure 73. Two silos, as found (Loci 115 and 116), looking south. (Courtesy of École Biblique.)

Figure 74. Shallow pools in the west wing, looking north.

Figure 75. The potter's kiln in the southeastern industrial wing, looking south. (Courtesy of Israel Antiquities Authority.)

well-preserved potter's kilns were discovered.[155] This appears to indicate that the owners of such estates sometimes produced their own pottery for local use as well as for marketing of their produce.

The winepress (Locus 75) is fairly small and consists of a treading surface and a collecting vat (fig. 76).[156] Grapes have been grown in the Dead Sea area up to the present day, though not in large quantities,[157] and the people of Qumran may have cultivated a small vineyard at 'Ein Feshkha. From the small dimensions of the winepress, it seems likely that it produced wine for the private consumption of the people of Qumran.

A recent discovery at Qumran should be included among the industrial installations. This is a large stone surface with an estimated area of about 200 m^2, exposed to the south of Qumran (fig. 77). Hundreds of date pits were found in the excavations carried out by Magen and Peleg in the vicinity, leading to the conclusion that the surface may have been used for the drying of dates and the removal of their pits.[158]

It is obvious from the numerous industrial installations at Qumran that in the late stage of its existence its inhabitants subsisted mainly on agriculture. Further evidence of this assumption is supplied by the agricultural tools, such as a hoe, sheep shears, knives, and sickles (fig. 78) that were unearthed in the excavations.[159] Remains of irrigation systems and cultivated plots were found on the plateau on which Qumran is located and in the oasis of 'Ein Feshkha to the south of Wadi Qumran.[160] Besides growing field crops, the inhabitants of Qumran probably also kept livestock, as indicated by the discovery of animal bones, mainly those of sheep, in various parts of the site.[161] Animals for local consumption could have been grazed in the oasis of 'Ein Feshkha.

It is most likely that many of the installations at Qumran were connected with the processing of the unique resources of the region, the valuable perfumes and ointments produced from balsam. The Herodian juglet found in one of the caves near the site and still containing remnants of oil—possibly balsam oil—hints at a perfume industry.[162] The red material and ash found in another cave have been interpreted as a cleansing product manufactured by the inhabitants of Qumran.[163] In sum, the complex of Qumran

---

[155] Israel 1993.

[156] On the winepress in Locus 75, see Pfann 1994. Magness (2002, 52) follows de Vaux, who interprets the installation in Locus 75 as a basin in which clay for the potter's workshop was soaked. This is a strange interpretation for an installation that looks like any other winepress all over the country. For soaking clay, potters used a simple pit in the ground.

[157] Conder and Kitchener (1883, 189) describe Jericho as a village surrounded by vines trained on low trellises. A small winepress was found in the excavations at En-Gedi (Hadas 2002, 144). This evidence contradicts the assertion of Netzer (2002a, 69) that vines were not grown in the Dead Sea region in antiquity.

[158] Magen and Peleg presented this information at the archaeological conference at Brown University. For further discussion, see Murphy 2002, 301.

[159] Murphy 2002, 329–30; Magness 2002, 184. Photographs of these tools appear in Roitman 1997, 33, Hebrew section; 34, English section.

[160] On the agricultural remains on the plateau, see Rohrhirsch and Röhrer-Ertl 2001, 169; on those to the south of Wadi Qumran, see Porath 1998.

[161] Zeuner 1960, 28.

[162] Patrich and Arubas 1989.

[163] Amar 1998b.

Figure 76. The winepress (Locus 75) in the industrial zone, looking south. (Courtesy of Israel Antiquities Authority.)

Figure 77. The cobbled stone surface for the processing of agricultural produce located south of the site, looking east.

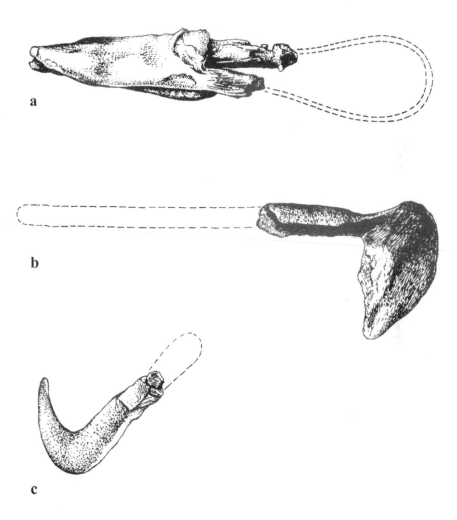

Figure 78. Drawings of sheep shears (a), hoe (b), and sickle (c) found at Qumran.

was a production center for commodities of commercial value, and the owners profited from their sale.

Evidence of Wealth: The Excavation Finds

The theory that Qumran was the center of a rural estate, a local version of the Roman *villa rustica*, was first proposed by Donceel and Donceel-Voûte. Closer examination of the small artifacts from the excavations has revealed numerous lamps, juglets, lathe-turned stoneware, and glass vessels.[164] This evidence, almost totally ignored by de Vaux in his publications, demonstrates the wealth of the residents of Qumran and their engagement in the regional economy.

The discovery of interior decoration such as architectural details, geometric tiles, and stucco also supports the interpretation of Qumran as a villa or manor house. Magness lists the architectural elements found in various places at the site of Qumran. Among these, she mentions a number of column drums and bases, several voussoirs (stones from an arch or vault), a console (the springing stone of an arch), a frieze fragment found south of Locus 34 in the main building, and a cornice in addition to flagstone and flooring in the *opus sectile* technique (large, smooth, triangular colored stone tiles carefully cut and set in geometric patterns).[165] Similar floors were found at 'Ein Feshkha (see below, ch. 4), in the residences of the wealthy in Jerusalem, and in Herodian palaces such as those of Herodium and Jericho. In addition, a beautiful cornice fragment decorated with the classical egg-and-dart motif was found in Locus 42 in the south wing of the main building.[166] Even today one can see at the site five column drums, three sections of engaged columns (half-columns attached to a wall), three column bases, and one Doric capital (see above, fig. 44). All the architectural details were made of sandstone brought from the quarries at Khirbet Samra. Similar details have been found at various sites in Herodian Judea, such as the palaces at Jericho and Masada, in Jerusalem, and in the so-called Governor's House at Tel Goded northeast of Bet Guvrin.[167]

Most of the architectural details at Qumran date from the Herodian period.[168] These elements were probably incorporated in the facade of the complex or in the inner courtyard of the main building. All of these finds are of great importance, since they are another manifestation of the considerable financial means of the owner of the complex and his desire to follow the fashionable taste of the time.[169]

---

[164] Donceel-Voûte 1994, 34; Donceel and Donceel-Voûte 1994.

[165] Magness 2002, 69, 99–100. This list is based on Humbert 1994, 193–94; 1999, 194.

[166] Humbert 1999, 194; Chambon 2003.

[167] In the Governor's House, column bases and capitals were found in situ as part of the peristyle courtyard that was added to the building during Herod's reign (Gibson 1994, 214–16, figs. 13–14). For Jericho and Masada, see Netzer 2001a, 176–77.

[168] According to research carried out by Orit Peleg of the Hebrew University of Jerusalem (verbal personal communication to author).

[169] It is hard to understand how Magness (2002, 99), who lists the abundant evidence of decoration at the site, can write, "The strongest argument against the identification of Qumran as a villa or manor house lies in its almost complete absence of interior decoration."

On the other hand, some indications of wealth, such as frescoes, mosaic pavements, or a bathhouse, are lacking at Qumran. These elements frequently occur in patrician dwellings in Jerusalem and in royal palaces such as those of Jericho and Masada. The comparison made by Magness between Qumran and such residences, however, is invalid: Qumran was clearly not an urban dwelling, and it has never been suggested that it was a palace.[170] In my view, this was the country estate of a wealthy city dweller, probably a permanent resident of Jerusalem. Only parts of the complex were decorated, and the rest of it retained its rustic character as a working farm. As for the lack of a bathhouse, the springs of nearby ʿEin Feshkha, where temperatures are higher, could have provided an acceptable substitute.

Many other finds attest to the wealth of the landowner at Qumran. For example, there is the hoard of 561 silver coins, mostly the Tyrian tetradrachms noted above, found intentionally buried under the floor in three pots in Locus 120 (fig. 79). The hoard was probably hidden during the riots that broke out in Judea after the death of Herod the Great. Tyrian tetradrachms were used for the annual half-shekel tax paid by Jews to the temple in Jerusalem in the Second Temple period and are mentioned in many ancient sources, including Matt 17:27. These coins have been interpreted as the collected wealth of a community that lived at Qumran, which they were keeping to give to the temple.[171] But it is possible that the hoard has no connection with the temple tax and represents the private wealth of the site's owner or one of his associates, consisting as it does of the silver coins in common circulation at the time. Baruch Kenael suggests that the hoard was a monetary gift that, according to Josephus, Herod gave to his favorites and members of his family while he lay on his sickbed in Jericho.[172] If this assumption is correct, the owner of Qumran had a close relationship with Herod. In any event, it is clear that the person who concealed the hoard hoped to return some day and retrieve it, but for some reason was unable to do so.

Besides the hoard, 673 bronze and silver coins were found in the excavations,[173] mostly near the gate (in Loci 7, 130, and 134) and in the main building.[174] This is a large number in comparison with other sites and reflects lively commercial activity and extensive external contacts. It is a far cry from Pliny's description of the Essenes as living "without money" and keeping company only with palm trees.

In fact, here, as in other digs, coins are an indication of an economic life; not finding them would be an indication of a lack thereof. For example, in the large monastery excavated at Khirbet ed-Deir in the Judean Desert, only two coins were found (in the hospice), since the monks did not have any economic activity. We should remember that people frequently lost coins in antiquity. They simply dropped out of poorly sewn pockets and rolled into inaccessible corners or cracks. The New Testament parable of the woman who lost a coin and searches until she finds it is an example of this sort of mishap (Luke 15:8–9). These lost coins are the ones later discovered by archaeologists.

---

[170] Magness (ibid., 93) admits that a comparison between Qumran and sites such as Jericho and Masada is invalid, "since these sites were royal palaces."

[171] Ibid., 188–91.

[172] Kenael 1958, 167–68; Josephus, *J.W.* 1.658; *Ant.* 17.173–175. On the hoard of silver coins from Qumran, see Sharabani 1989; Ariel 1993.

[173] On the total number of coins found at Qumran, see Murphy 2002, 305–6, table 12.

[174] Ibid., 309.

Figure 79. The hoard of silver coins found under the floor (Locus 120) in the west wing. (Courtesy of Israel Antiquities Authority.)

A rich collection of about two hundred fragments of stone vessels originating in Jerusalem was found in the excavations at Qumran.[175] Vessels made from soft limestone or chalk are common at Jewish sites throughout Judea from the first century B.C.E. to the second century C.E. They range in size and shape from large lathe-turned vases to small, crudely made "measuring cups" (fig. 98, color). As noted, according to Jewish religious law, unlike pottery and glass, stone vessels could not be contaminated by contact with impure objects. Consequently, they were popular among observant Jews who could afford them. (Stone vessels were more expensive than pottery.) In addition to the simple stone vessels found at Qumran, there are also large and splendid urns of the type known as *kallal*. The vessel has a high pedestal and was carved from a single block of soft limestone.[176] Vessels of this type have been found in patrician residences in Jerusalem. The "stone water jar" mentioned in John 2:6 was probably also this type of vessel.

Among the most striking discoveries at Qumran are the rich assemblages of glass vessels and jewelry.[177] Some of the vessels were imported from the Phoenician coast, whereas others resemble glassware that was produced in Italy. Moreover, there are traces of a local glass industry at Qumran, where raw material of a light green glass has been found.[178] The presence of a large collection of glassware at the site (never mentioned by the excavators) is an indication of industrial and commercial, rather than religious, activity.

According to Donceel's report, 150 fragments of glass vessels were recorded at Qumran; 89 of them were identified as belonging to mold-blown cups, goblets, flasks, and ampullae.[179] Five glass beads were found as well. Almost all the glass fragments were found in the main building, which was the living quarters of the owners (the *pars urbana*). Goblet fragments are the most numerous at the site, and fifteen to seventeen complete vessels have been identified; their closest parallels are at Pompeii and Herculaneum. Cup fragments are the second most numerous group, comprising about thirty vessels; most of them came from different locations in the tower. The third most important group is what Donceel calls "ointment bottles."[180] Thirteen to fifteen examples were found in the main building, particularly in the courtyard and the tower. A few fragments of glass flasks and bottles were also discovered. Some of the glass finds, however, belong to Stratum IV (de Vaux's Period III), representing the occupation of the site by Roman troops after 68 C.E.

The ceramic finds at Qumran present a similar picture. In addition to local pottery vessels of simple and everyday character, there are imported vessels, albeit few, such as eastern terra sigillata (fine tableware, usually imported from the big cities near the coast, such as Antioch, and easy to recognize because of its shining color), and molded oil lamps.[181] Recent

---

[175] On the stone vessels of Qumran, see Donceel and Donceel-Voûte 1994, 10–11; Murphy 2002, 328. Stone quarries where these vessels were manufactured on the spot have been discovered in Jerusalem; Gibson 1983, 177–81; Amit, Zeligman, and Zilberbod 2001; Magen 2002.

[176] Donceel and Donceel-Voûte (1994, 31–33) published fragments of these stone vessels.

[177] On the glass finds at Qumran, see ibid., 7–8; Murphy 2002, 329; Donceel 2002. For the jewelry found in the cemetery, see Clamer 2003.

[178] Donceel and Donceel-Voûte 1994, 8–9.

[179] Donceeel 2002, 13–18.

[180] Ibid., 17.

[181] On the ceramic finds at Qumran, see Donceel and Donceel-Voûte 1994, 9–10. The richness of Qumran's pottery is demonstrated by Sussmann and Peled 1993, 90–105; Donceel-Voûte 1994,

excavations at Qumran have recovered some beautiful eastern terra sigillata and a number of painted "pseudo-Nabatean" vessels.[182]

The pottery repertoire is exceptional in its quantity. According to Mariusz Burdajewicz, who is studying the material, it includes hundreds of intact vessels as well as almost four thousand diagnostic sherds (used to identify archaeological periods).[183] Most of the pottery (ca. 60 percent) consists of tableware (plates, dishes, bowls, and goblets). This group includes the 1,020 vessels found in the storeroom (Locus 89) near the dining hall (see above). Another large group (ca. 22 percent) consists of utilitarian kitchen vessels used for the preparation or serving of food. This group includes cooking pots, storage jars, jugs (including cooking jugs), large bowls, casseroles, and kraters. Among the storage jars, two main types occur: ovoid bag-shaped jars and the cylindrical jars known as "scroll jars" (fig. 99, color). At different places within the site (particularly in the main building), jars of both types were found sunk in the floor. This was a common method of storing food in antiquity, especially in dry areas.

A small but significant group (3.7 percent) comprises personal wares such as unguentaria,[184] perfume bottles. Miniature vessels and juglets were also found. Within this group, the most popular vessel type (77 percent) is the globular juglet, probably a container for balsam. In a photograph published by Donceel-Voûte, about thirty juglets of this type from Qumran can be counted (fig. 100, color).[185] The juglet found in a cave near Qumran and still containing traces perhaps of balsam oil was similar in shape. Many of these globular Herodian juglets have been found at different sites in the Dead Sea Valley, such as 'Ein Feshkha, 'En Boqeq, and the winter palace at Jericho. The shape of these juglets, with a narrow neck and mouth that limited evaporation, allowed the contents to be poured out in a thin trickle, and was easy to seal, implies that they contained precious liquids. The shape accords with the Talmudic description of the *tslokhit ha-bosem* ("perfume bottle").[186] This might also have been the appearance of the "alabaster jar of perfume" of Luke 7:38.

Most of the local vessels from Qumran are made from a pink, light red, or gray clay, often covered with whitish slip. The presence of the potter's workshop at the site implies that at least some of the vessels were locally manufactured. The pottery from the caves is identical to that from the site except that the repertoire is more limited.

The clay from which some of the Qumran vessels were manufactured has been subjected to neutron activation analysis (NAA), used to determine their origin, with interesting results.[187] Half of the vessels, including the ceramic inkwell from Locus 30 (the "scriptorium") and four cylindrical jars of the type known as "scroll jars," were made of Je-

---

32–33; and Gunneweg and Balla 2003. Magness (2002, 76–77) mentions sherds of eastern terra sigillata and a "pseudo-Nabatean" jug and unguentarium, probably made in Jerusalem, in contradiction of her claim (p. 75) that imported wares are completely absent from the site.

[182] Magen and Peleg 2002.

[183] Burdajewicz 2001.

[184] The unguentaria of the Second Temple period had a type with a unique, spindle-like shape that makes them easy to identify.

[185] Donceel-Voûte 1994, 33.

[186] On the use and distribution of this type of juglet at Jericho, see Bar-Nathan 2002, 49–51.

[187] Yellin, Broshi, and Eshel 2001; Gunneweg and Balla 2003.

rusalem clay whereas the rest were made from a clay that is not from Jerusalem and may be assumed to be local to Qumran (fig. 80). These results reflect a pattern of trade that was not unusual, especially for sites, such as Qumran and Jerusalem, that are not far from one another. For Magness, however, the results of the NAA analysis are "surprising."[188] This is because the advocates of the Qumran-Essene hypothesis view the "scroll jar" as the most distinctive object associated with Qumran and the scrolls. These jars, according to de Vaux, "are not found outside the area of Qumran."[189] In order to explain the contradiction, Magness suggests that the clay was brought from Jerusalem and used by the potters of Qumran to manufacture the vessels at the site.[190] In support of this claim, Magness makes two points: first, the complete absence of cylindrical jars in Jerusalem and, second, the high cost of transportation of finished vessels.

The absence of a certain vessel is an argument *ex silentio*. As a matter of fact, cylindrical jars were also found at Herodium, not far from Jerusalem.[191] The high cost of transportation in antiquity is the very reason that potter's workshops used local clay for manufacture. Clay was never brought from a distance whereas trade in pottery vessels, particularly jars and amphorae, as containers of commodities for sale was common.

The results of the NAA analysis simply demonstrate that some of the cylindrical jars, like the ovoid jars, originated in places such as Jerusalem, Herodium, and Jericho. As noted, recent studies have shown that the pottery of Qumran, including the "scroll jars," is not unique but is typical of Second Temple period sites in the Dead Sea Valley and beyond.[192] All one can say on the basis of the pottery is that there was a connection of some kind between the deposition of the scrolls and the inhabitants of Qumran. Any further conclusions are purely speculative.

The recent publication of pottery from contemporary sites along the Dead Sea places the Qumran corpus in a different light. The assemblages from Callirrhoe and 'En Boqeq consist largely of local types. The only fine wares found at the first-century C.E. villa at Callirrhoe are a few sherds of painted Nabatean bowls and eastern terra sigillata.[193] Likewise at the contemporary farmhouse at 'En Boqeq, the fine wares consisted mainly of painted Nabatean wares and only a few sherds of eastern terra sigillata.[194] I agree with Magness that this represents a regional phenomenon.[195] In the Dead Sea region, eastern terra sigillata and imported amphorae seem to be restricted almost entirely to royal palatial sites such as Jericho and Masada. Because of the high cost of overland transport, only residents of the region's palaces could afford to purchase fine red-slipped dining services or expensive wines and luxury foods. Herod and his associates were consumers of these products, and the Jerusalem aristocracy, including priestly families, adopted the practice. Although the inhabitants of the *villa rustica* at Qumran, like those at Callirrhoe and 'En

---

[188] Magness 2002, 74.

[189] de Vaux 1973, 54–55. Magness (2002, 81) claims that "the cylindrical jars are rare or unattested at other sites in the region."

[190] Magness 2002, 74.

[191] On the presence of "scroll jars" at Herodium, see Bar-Nathan 1981, 56–57.

[192] Bar-Nathan 2002, 9; Gunneweg and Balla 2003, 26.

[193] On the pottery of Callirrhoe, see Clamer 1997, 63–80.

[194] On the pottery of 'En Boqeq, see Fischer and Tal 2000, 23–44.

[195] Magness 2002, 78.

Figure 80. A cylindrical jar with a lid ("scroll jar") and other vessels from Qumran.
(Courtesy of Israel Antiquities Authority.)

Boqeq, aspired to this lifestyle (as indicated by the design and decoration of the villa), the purchase of imported wine and fine pottery was apparently beyond their means, as were the heated bathhouses, frescoes, and mosaic pavements that we find in the royal palaces of the region. The pottery of Qumran is another reflection of the rustic nature of the site and reinforces the impression that the owner had his permanent home elsewhere.

Oil lamps also provide evidence for regionalism in pottery types.[196] During the Herodian period, the inhabitants of Qumran used a wheelmade type of pottery known as the "Herodian lamp," which has a short, splayed nozzle and a rounded body. This lamp type is characteristic of Judea in the first century C.E. Molded lamps that originated in Jerusalem were found as well. Mainly members of the upper class used these decorated lamps.

Among the metal objects found at Qumran, in addition to tools, were bronze fibulae used to pin togas and similar garments. The toga was a prestigious item, and the discovery of fibulae at Qumran could indicate that the site was frequented by people of high social standing.[197] On the other hand, it is not impossible that some of the fibulae reached Qumran in de Vaux's Period III, that is, after 68 C.E., when there was a Roman presence at the site. In the absence of stratigraphic data, it is difficult to establish the provenance and date of these important objects. De Vaux's field notes list five needles, all of bronze.[198] Another needle was found in Cave 24. These provide evidence for the manufacture or mending of clothing or the sewing of other materials, such as leather.

Such activities are normally associated with women. Other finds, such as cosmetic vessels, spindle whorls, and combs, may also indicate the presence of women at the site (fig. 101, color). According to Joan Taylor, the spindle whorl is one of the most striking objects for engendered archaeology to be found at Qumran.[199] The spindle was a wooden stick at the end of which was the whorl—a cone-shaped object made of stone, bone, or wood and pierced for attachment to the spindle to provide weight. At least six spindle whorls were found at Qumran (fig. 81).[200] This discovery complements the excavations in the nearby cemetery, in which the skeletons of women were found (see below). Granted, each of these finds in isolation cannot make a statement; combs, for instance, are not exclusively female equipment. Still, the sources do indicate that spinning was done by women, and the sum total of such finds is a strong indication of the presence of women at Qumran.

A large limestone disk, 14.5 cm in diameter, with a slightly concave upper surface and a small depression in the center, decorated on its face with concentric circles and radial marks (fig. 82), was discovered at Qumran. Some scholars have defined it as an "astronomical instrument" or a "special kind of sundial."[201] But I believe that this object has suffered

---

[196] On the oil lamps of Qumran, see Smith 1966, 3–4; Donceel and Donceel-Voûte 1994, 6–7; Donceel 1998; Magness 2002, 79; Gunneweg and Balla 2003, 16–17.

[197] Magen and Peleg (2002) have recently found early Roman fibulae at Qumran; see also Donceel and Donceel-Voûte 1994, 13. Similar fibulae were revealed, e.g., in the Herodian palace complex at Ramat Hanadiv (Kol-Yaakov 2000, 497–99). On the toga as the official garment of a Roman citizen, see Adkins and Adkins 1994, 344–45.

[198] Magness 2002, 200; Murphy 2002, 330.

[199] On finds indicative of the presence of women at Qumran, see Taylor 1999, 318–23.

[200] Donceel and Donceel-Voûte 1994, 14; Magness 2002, 176–77.

[201] Albani, Glessmer, and Grasehoff 1997; Glessmer and Abani 1999, 408; Glessmer 1998. For different interpretations see Hollenback 2003 and Levy 1998.

Figure 81. Six spindle-whorls found at Qumran.
(Courtesy of Israel Antiquities Authority.)

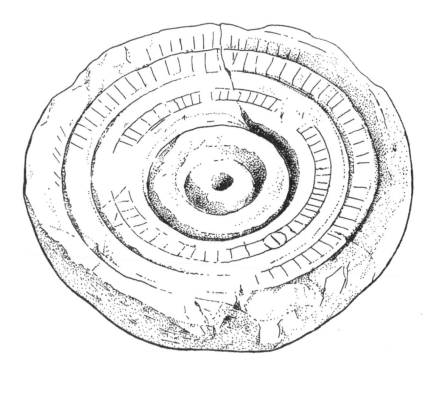

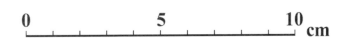

Figure 82. Drawing of a potter's wheel from Qumran, previously interpreted as a sundial or a spindle-whorl.

from overinterpretation, as is the usual practice at Qumran. A disk of similar size and identical shape from ancient Crete is on display at the British Museum and labelled as a potter's wheel. This latter identification is reasonable in the context of Qumran given the existence of a pottery workshop.[202]

Not a single fragment of a scroll was brought to light at the site despite the fact that much organic material of various kinds, such as beams and fibers of date palms, mats, wickerwork baskets, date pits, and animal bones, was uncovered.[203] The only written material found at the site of Qumran itself are ostraca bearing Jewish names such as Yohanan, El'azar, Pinhas, and Shim'on, proving that the site was indeed inhabited by Jews.[204] The striking absence of scrolls from the site of Qumran, especially notable in light of the discovery of scrolls and other documents at neighboring sites such as Masada and Hyrcania,[205] is, as noted, perhaps the most cogent argument against the prevailing belief that the Dead Sea Scrolls originated at the site of Qumran.

The Cemetery of Qumran

Jews living in Judea in the first century B.C.E. and the first century C.E. practiced two basic methods of burial. Many Jews buried their dead in rock-cut burial caves, consisting of one or more rooms, which were used by an extended family over several generations. Rock-cut burial caves are found both at Jericho and En-Gedi.[206] By the first century C.E., burial caves in Jerusalem and Jericho had *loculi* ("recesses") cut into the walls of the cave to accommodate individual bodies, which were wrapped in a shroud and sometimes placed in a wooden coffin. After the body was placed in the *loculus,* the opening was sealed with a stone slab. The entrances of burial caves were closed with a large stone slab or sometimes a rolling stone. According to the New Testament, Jesus was laid to rest in a burial cave belonging to Joseph of Arimathea (Matt 27:60).

The shaft graves at Qumran represent the second method of burial that was practiced in Second Temple period Judea.[207] First a rectangular shaft was dug to a depth of about 1.2–2 m, and then a recess was created at the bottom to make a narrow *loculus* for the body.

---

[202] The Cretan object can be seen in the Department of Greek and Roman Antiquities within the context of the Life in Ancient Greece and Rome exhibit in Room 69. Taylor's (1999, 318 fn. 117) suggestion to identify the object as a spindle whorle is problematic since the small depression in the center does not pierce the disk. See, for example, Figure 95. The identification of the disk as a unique sundial is completely unfounded. As far as I know, there is no existing parallel.

[203] On the organic finds at Qumran, see Zeuner 1960, 30–37. For photographs of the organic material, such as ropes, a basket, a wickerwork mat, date pits, and wooden combs, see Roitman 1997. For the wooden artifacts and leather objects from Qumran, see Sussmann and Peled 1993, 110–13.

[204] On the ostraca of Qumran, see Vaux 1973, 103; 1956, 564–65; Lemaire 2003, 344–57.

[205] On the documents from Masada, see Cotton and Geiger 1989. In the excavations conducted at Hyrcania in 1952, papyri from the seventh–eighth centuries C.E. were discovered (Milik 1959, 15–16).

[206] For the burial caves of Jericho, see Hachlili and Killebrew 1999; for En-Gedi, see Hadas 1994.

[207] There is an extensive literature on the cemetery of Qumran. The most recent publications are Kapera 1994; 1995; Hachlili 1993; 2000; Taylor 1999; Zangenberg 2000b; Donceel 2002; Magness 2002, 168–75; Murphy 2002, 333–43; Norton 2003.

The body was normally laid supine with the head to the south and feet to the north, although east-west orientations are also found. Sun-baked bricks or flagstones were placed over the body to seal the *loculus,* and the graves were then filled in with soil (fig. 83). Most of the excavated burials are of individuals, although at times two bodies were buried together. Remnants of wood or brown dust are indicative of the use of wooden coffins, not common at the time, suggesting that at least some of the individuals were transported to Qumran for burial or reburial.

The shaft grave is a modest form of burial, much less elaborate than the family sepulchers that were carved from stone in contemporary Judea. But because burials in rock-cut tombs are usually better preserved than interments in the ground, we may have a biased picture of burial norms in Judea. As Taylor has suggested, the cemetery at Qumran represents the burial customs of the poor.[208]

The cemetery of Qumran extends over an area of at least 20,000 m³ (fig. 84), with the graves marked by heaps of stones on the surface. Because of the site's total abandonment after the Roman period and its lack of suitability for cultivation, the stone heaps marking the graves were not put to secondary use or moved. As a result, most of the graves are fully preserved and readily visible on the surface (fig. 85).

In my opinion, the unique element of the Qumran cemetery is its very existence, since cemeteries of this type have not been found at most Second Temple period sites located in more intensively settled parts of the country. For example, Herodian building complexes larger than that at Qumran were discovered during my recent excavations at the sites of Ramat Hanadiv, but no burials whatsoever were found in their vicinity.[209] On the assumption that the people who lived at these sites were buried in their close vicinity, one may conjecture that their graves were dug in the ground, like those at Qumran, and that the heaps of stones that once marked them were removed over time. It is not a coincidence that most of the known graves from the Second Temple period were found either at sites such as Beit Safafa near Jerusalem, which was discovered by chance, or at remote desert sites such as 'Ein el-Ghuweir south of Qumran.[210]

The Qumran graves find their closest parallel in a Nabatean cemetery of thirty-five hundred graves recently discovered at Khirbet Qazone on the Lisan Peninsula east of the Dead Sea.[211] At both sites the graves share a common form, are oriented north-south, and contain a single skeleton with the head to the south.

Because the Qumran cemetery is so exceptionally well preserved, we can trace its development. It stands to reason that the first graves, dating from as early as the Hasmonean period, were dug parallel and fairly close to the wall separating the site from the burial place; from there the cemetery began to expand eastward, initially on the elevated, flat part and later along three extensions that spread eastward from it. A small, isolated group of burials is preserved about 60 m to the northeast of the main cemetery. The graves are distributed in accordance with the topography of the area. For this reason, the supposed

---

[208] Taylor 1999, 312–13. See also Norton 2003, 123–24.

[209] For the final excavation report on Ramat Hanadiv, see Hirschfeld 2000a.

[210] For the Beit Safafa cemetery, see Zissu 1998; for 'Ein el-Ghuweir, see Bar-Adon 1977, 16–17.

[211] For Khirbet Qazone, see Politis 1998a; 1999.

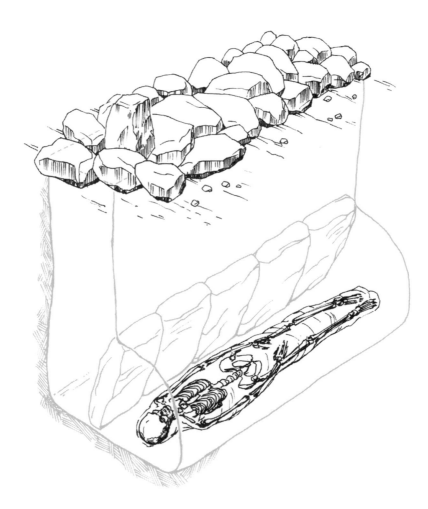

Figure 83. Reconstruction of a typical shaft grave at Qumran.

Figure 84. Plan for the cemetery east of Qumran.

Figure 85. Stone heaps preserved in the cemetery, looking south.

distinction between the central part of the cemetery and the extensions, as suggested by de Vaux, is doubtful.[212]

The north-south orientation of most of the graves was not dictated, as claimed by Émile Puech, by religious law[213] but, rather, by the architectural layout of the site itself. The Nabatean graves at Khirbet Qazone had a similar orientation, which may suggest that this was a regional phenomenon, perhaps inspired by the geographical layout of the Dead Sea valley (fig. 86).

The number of graves preserved at Qumran is a controversial subject. Clermont-Ganneau, who visited Qumran in 1874, assessed the number of graves as being roughly one thousand.[214] On the other hand, Conder and Kitchener, who had reached the site a year earlier, estimated the number as only seven hundred to seven hundred fifty.[215] On the basis of Clermont-Ganneau's estimate, de Vaux proposed that there were eleven hundred to twelve hundred graves in the cemetery.[216] According to a count made by Zdzislaw Kapera with the aid of aerial photographs, the number of graves at Qumran was only 711.[217] On the basis of their recent survey of the cemetery, Eshel and Broshi estimate the number of graves as approximately twelve hundred.[218]

In order to clarify the question of the grave count at Qumran, I carried out a survey of the cemetery during which each heap of stones marking a grave was marked on a map (fig. 87).[219] The total number of graves surveyed was 823, of which 596 are in the main elevated area and 227 are located in the extensions. In the southern extension we counted 69 graves, in the central extension 88, and in the northern extension 33. In the small cemetery to the northeast of the main cemetery, we counted 37 graves. Two passages divide the main body of graves in the flat, elevated area. There are 126 graves in the southern plot, 352 in the central plot, and 117 in the northern plot. One grave with an east-west orientation was unexpectedly found in the middle of the northern passage; its existence is inexplicable.

Remains of a rectangular building (exterior measurements 5 × 6.5 m) were found at the eastern end of the central extension, on top of a small hill (fig. 88). Broshi and Eshel, who recently excavated it, date it to the late Second Temple period (first century B.C.E. to first century C.E.).[220] About 1.2 m below the floor of the building, a skeleton in primary

---

[212] de Vaux 1973, 45–47.

[213] Puech 1998. On the orientation of the graves at Qumran, see Donceel 2002, 20–22.

[214] Clermont-Ganneau 1899, 15–16.

[215] Conder and Kitchener 1883, 183.

[216] de Vaux (1973, 43) initially estimated the number of graves at eleven hundred but later in the same publication increased it to twelve hundred (p. 128). Many scholars, such as Broshi (1992, 111) and Hachlili (1993, 247; 2000, 661), have simply adopted de Vaux's estimate. Hachlili (2000) reports de Vaux's higher estimate of twelve hundred whereas Hachlili (1993) mentions his lower figure of eleven hundred graves.

[217] Kapera 2000, 143.

[218] Broshi and Eshel 2003, 31.

[219] A team of surveyors led by Israel Vatkin of the Israel Antiquities Authority carried out the survey. The discrepancy between the results of the two surveys (more than twelve hundred versus 823) can only be explained as being due to an error on the part of one of the two teams. A new survey carried out by an objective team of surveyors would thus be desirable. The small cemetery south of Wadi Qumran was not included in my survey.

[220] Broshi and Eshel 2003.

Figure 86. The Nabatean cemetery at Khirbet Qazone on the Lisan peninsula, looking south.

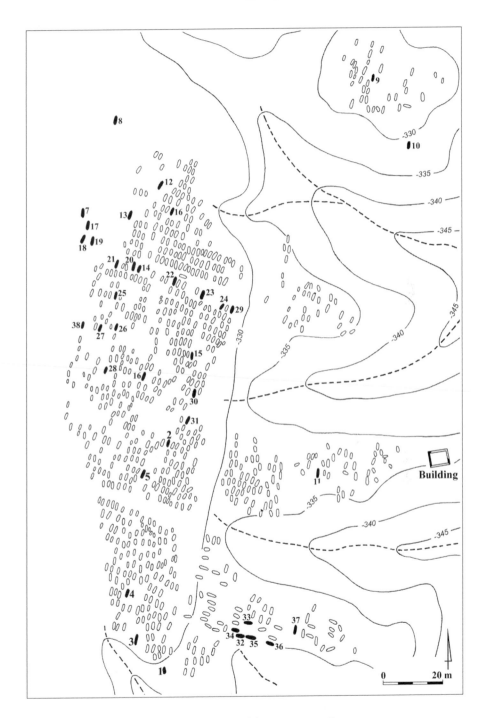

Figure 87. Detailed plan of the cemetery at Qumran.
(Surveyor: I. Vatkin.)

Figure 88. The central extension of the cemetery at Qumran, looking east.

burial was found. The skeleton was oriented east-west, with its head toward the Dead Sea in the east. The orientation is not unusual; more than fifty of the graves in the cemetery are oriented in this direction (see below).

The structure is very poorly built without mortar, resembling an enclosure more than a building. On the other hand, its location indicates that the person buried inside was important. The excavators claim that the structure was a mourning enclosure *(beth misped)*. As adherents to the Essene-Qumran hypothesis, they suggest, as noted, that the skeleton may be one of the descendents of the Teacher of Righteousness.[221] This specific an identification is purely speculative, but in my view, the structure may be a *nefesh* ("memorial") that commemorates an important person who lived at Qumran. It is probably not the owner, however, who would have been able to afford a more impressive tomb.

The internal organization of the cemetery displays several striking features. In the flat part there are two passages, 1.5–3 m wide, probably intended to facilitate movement within the cemetery. Almost all the graves in this area have a north-south orientation. On the other hand, the graves are more freely arranged in the extensions, and some have a different orientation. For example, in the southernmost extension only 33 of the 69 graves have a north-south orientation, while the other 36 have an east-west orientation.[222]

The shaft graves at Qumran are dated to the end of the early Roman period (first century B.C.E. to first century C.E.) by their few grave goods, found mainly in the graves of women and children.[223] An example of such goods is a beautiful chain of different kinds of beads that was found in one of the women's graves at Qumran (fig. 102, color).

To date, only 49 of the hundreds of the graves at Qumran have been excavated, from which the bones of 60 deceased have been identified with certainty as being those of 33 men and 23 women and children. This ratio rules out the identification of the inhabitants of Qumran as Essenes, since, according to Pliny, they shunned the company of women.[224] A similar ratio of males to females was also noted in the cemetery excavated by Bar-Adon at 'Ein el-Ghuweir and in that excavated by Zissu at Beit Safafa southwest of Jerusalem.[225] The cemetery of Qumran is therefore not unique, as certain scholars have claimed.

---

[221] The burial under the building was numbered "1000" by the excavators, Broshi and Eshel (2003). Their approach may be considered part of the general tendency among supporters of the Essene-Qumran hypothesis to overinterpret the evidence.

[222] From his all-too-brief look at the bones in Munich, Zias (2000) claims that the graves in the southern extension that have an east-west orientation are recent Bedouin graves. But Zangenberg (2000b) and Norton (2003, 118) have systematically refuted his claims.

[223] On the basis of Kapera 1994; 1995. The fact that the deceased were buried in individual shaft graves at Qumran is in line with the use of ossuaries for individual burials in this period (Regev 2001).

[224] On the ratio between the graves of men and those of women, see Norton 2003, 123, and Elder 1994, 224. From the data yielded by the excavation in the Qumran cemetery, it is evident that women's graves were found not only in the extensions but also in the flat, elevated area of the site (Taylor 1999, 303; Kapera 2000, 144–47; Zangenberg 2000b, 74–75; Rohrhirsch and Röhrer-Ertl 2001, 166).

[225] Kapera 1995, 130. According to Bar-Adon (1977, 16), the ratio of men to women in the 'Ein el-Ghuweir cemetery is 2:1. In the Beit Safafa cemetery, the ratio is 3:2 (Zissu 1998, 160). From these data and Zeev Weiss's study of Jewish burial practices in Galilee in the period of the Mishnah and the Talmud, it seems that the inhumation graves at Qumran represent the common method of burial among simple folk (Weiss 1989, 64–66; see also Patrich 1994b, 191–92).

The simplicity of the Qumran graves does indicate that those buried in them were simple folk. The absence of remains of mausolea is another indication that the owner of the Qumran estate, who was a wealthy man according to the excavation finds, did not permanently reside at the site but was based in one of the Judean towns, such as Jericho or Jerusalem. The large number of graves at Qumran teaches us that the cemetery served a far larger population than that living permanently at the site. From this it follows that the Qumran cemetery served for the burial not only of the permanent inhabitants but also of temporary residents or people who happened to reach the site by chance. It is also possible that the Qumran cemetery served as a central burial place for similar sites in the region, as suggested by Bar-Adon.[226] We may compare the cemetery of Qumran to the huge Nabatean cemetery of Khirbet Qazone, which, according to the excavator, Dino Politis, served three Nabatean settlements on the Lisan Peninsula: al-Mazra'a, al-Haditha, and Khirbet Sekine.[227] The cemetery of Qumran may likewise have served the inhabitants of sites close to Qumran, such as 'Ein Feshkha, Khirbet Mazin, and Rujum el-Baḥr.

To sum up, the Herodian complex revealed at Qumran is a large, well-built structure extending over an area of 4,800 m². The complex does not appear to have been a center for people living in the nearby caves. Systematic survey of the caves has shown that they were used as temporary shelters and for hiding objects rather than for permanent residence. On the other hand, the site does not appear to have been a fortress. The tower surrounded by a revetment made the site defensible, but the living quarters, featuring several entrances and irregular construction, are characteristic of a civilian complex. The industrial installations and the nearby tracts of cultivated land prove that the principal occupation of the inhabitants was agriculture and agricultural processing. The integration of the tower, living quarters, and installations indicates that Qumran, like similar sites in Judea, was a fortified manor house. It may be assumed that the desert oases south of Qumran, 'Ein Feshkha and perhaps also 'Ein el-Ghuweir and 'Ein et-Turabeh, were part of the lands belonging to the estate of Qumran.

The annexation of Judea to the Roman Empire in 6 C.E. did not change the status of landowners such as the family that owned the Qumran estate. In the remains at the site, there are no discernible signs of change or the cessation of its inhabitants' routine activity. Indeed, Josephus mentions various estates and towers owned by the Jewish aristocracy in the first century C.E.[228]

The First Revolt (66–70 C.E.) brought about the absolute end of Qumran. The Romans methodically destroyed the foci of Jewish resistance, including the fortified manor houses. The suppression of the revolt brought about the complete elimination of the settlement pattern that had characterized Herodian Judea, that is, choice tracts of land

---

[226] Bar-Adon 1981, 351.

[227] Politis 1998a, 612; 1999.

[228] A well-known example of this is the "tower" *(pyrgos)* that belonged to Agrippa I (37–44 C.E.) at Malatha in southern Judea. According to Josephus *(Ant.* 18.147–148), Agrippa reached the place with his wife and children, and it thus seems likely that it was in the possession of the family. Elsewhere Josephus mentions an estate in Transjordan that belonged to Crispus, the governor of the city of Tiberias during the reign of Agrippa I *(Life* 33). On the continuity of the land regime of Judea after 6 C.E., see Goodman 1987, 59–60.

that were under the ownership of aristocratic families close to the king, on which tenant farmers and hired laborers were employed.[229] The social structure of the Jewish populace in Judea changed irrevocably after the revolt.

3.5. Qumran after 68 C.E. (Stratum IV)

Qumran Stratum III suffered a violent destruction by fire, which de Vaux attributed to the Roman army at the time of the First Revolt.[230] The damage was evident throughout the site. The area to the south of the tower (Loci 12, 13, and 17) and other rooms in the main building were filled with the collapse of the walls and roofs to a height of 1.2 to 1.5 m. Iron arrowheads found in the debris indicate that there was resistance and that the destruction was caused by armed conflict. The arrowheads, which have three barbed wingtips, are the characteristic Roman type of the first century C.E.

De Vaux used the numismatic evidence and Josephus's description to date the destruction of Qumran to 68 C.E. According to Josephus, the Roman army under Vespasian took Jericho in June 68.[231] The Jewish rebels and the local population were defeated by the Roman military units, who pursued them along the Jordan River and on the Dead Sea in boats. It may be assumed that Qumran, 'Ein Feshkha, and the entire northwestern region of the Dead Sea were occupied by the Roman authorities at that time.

During the excavations, de Vaux found seventy-eight Jewish coins of the First Revolt. The latest among them date from year three of the revolt, that is, 68/69 C.E.[232] This marks the end of Jewish dominion of the site of Qumran. Overall, the literary and archaeological evidence for the Roman destruction supports de Vaux's dating. But de Vaux's suggestion that the subsequent occupation of the site lasted for only six years, until the fall of Masada in 73 C.E., is less secure.

Joan Taylor at University College London has shed new light on the importance of Qumran in the period between the First and Second Revolts, that is, between about 68 and 130 C.E.[233] The numismatic evidence from Qumran and 'Ein Feshkha supports Taylor's theory. The coin assemblage of Qumran includes twenty-nine coins from the period after the revolt. These include three silver coins of Trajan (98–117 C.E.) and four Nabatean coins of the first century C.E.[234] As an aside, Magness suggests that the few potsherds described by de Vaux as "Islamic" are in fact of a type known as Nabatean cream ware and dating to this period.[235] A hoard of ten coins of the Second Revolt, the Bar Kokhba revolt (132–135 C.E.), marks the end of the site.[236]

---

[229] On the changes that took place in Judea after the First Revolt, see Hirschfeld 1995.

[230] de Vaux 1973, 41–44; Magness 2002, 61–62.

[231] Josephus, *J.W.* 4.8, 446–451.

[232] Kenael 1958, 168; Murphy 2002, 305–9.

[233] Taylor 2002b.

[234] The description of the numismatic evidence is based on the list of coins in Laperrousaz 1976, 151–54.

[235] Magness 2002, 63.

[236] de Vaux 1973, 45.

The numismatic evidence from 'Ein Feshkha displays a similar picture. Among the coins found by de Vaux at the site, seventeen are from the reign of the Jewish king Agrippa II (78–95 C.E.), one is a Roman coin of Domitian (81–96), and three are Jewish coins of the Second Revolt.[237] This supports Taylor's claim that the "materials in and around the site [of Qumran] and at 'Ein Feshkha in fact suggest that a small population continued to live at the site into the early decades of the second century and possibly through to 135 without a break in the middle of Period III."[238]

The destruction of Qumran and 'Ein Feshkha was apparently an act of war. Signs of violent destruction have been found in all the sites identified as Jewish manor houses throughout the country. The Romans were determined to crush the Jewish rebels, and since Qumran provided a good lookout position, as de Vaux noted, the Romans occupied and destroyed it. They also sought out Jewish rebels and refugees hiding in caves near the site. Evidence for this is provided by discoveries in the caves, as well as about sixty nails from Roman *caligae* (legionary sandals) along the ancient road leading to Qumran from the north.[239]

The west wing of the Herodian complex was destroyed in 68 C.E. and completely abandoned. On the other hand, analysis of the results of de Vaux's excavation shows that the main building was rebuilt as a Roman fortress. The size of the site in this period was close to that of the Hasmonean period (ca. 1,400 m^2). One may calculate from this that the Roman military unit stationed at the site between the two revolts numbered about twenty soldiers.[240]

According to de Vaux, the Roman soldiers inhabited only part of the main building (fig. 89). This included the tower and several rooms in the north and west wings of the original building. The wall enclosing the northern side of the site to the west of the tower was doubled in width. A solid wall, 1 m thick, was built across the courtyard in a north-south orientation. An opening in the wall, 1.4 m wide, enabled access from one part of the courtyard to the other. The Romans cleared the rooms in the area south of the tower and reoccupied them with minor changes, mainly the division of the rooms into smaller spaces.

According to de Vaux, the soldiers also made use of the dining room (Locus 77) of the Herodian phase. The renovation of the water supply system, which in this phase was based on the large immersion pool (Locus 71) on the southeastern edge of the site, confirms this. The pool was filled by a new channel that connected with the old channel in the area of the now destroyed west wing. The new channel used the original conduit from Wadi Qumran. It was built along the southern wall of the dining hall and over the large reservoir (Locus 91), which was filled with debris to support the channel that crossed it.

Our reconstruction of the plan of the Roman fortress at Qumran derives from de Vaux's description of the remains. The plan of de Vaux's Period III, drawn during the excavations, reveals the remains of fairly well preserved walls enclosing the eastern side of the main building.[241] The central pillar of the staircase of the Herodian period (Locus 35) can be seen as well in the southeastern corner of the courtyard. From these remains, the

---

[237] Laperrousaz 1976, 153–54.

[238] Taylor 2002b, 6.

[239] Broshi and Eshel 1999b, 339–40. The local population wore simple sandals of the *solea* type, i.e., without nails. Some of these were found at Qumran; see Sussmann and Peled 1993, 112–13.

[240] See above, n. 47.

[241] See, e.g., de Vaux 1961, pl. XXII.

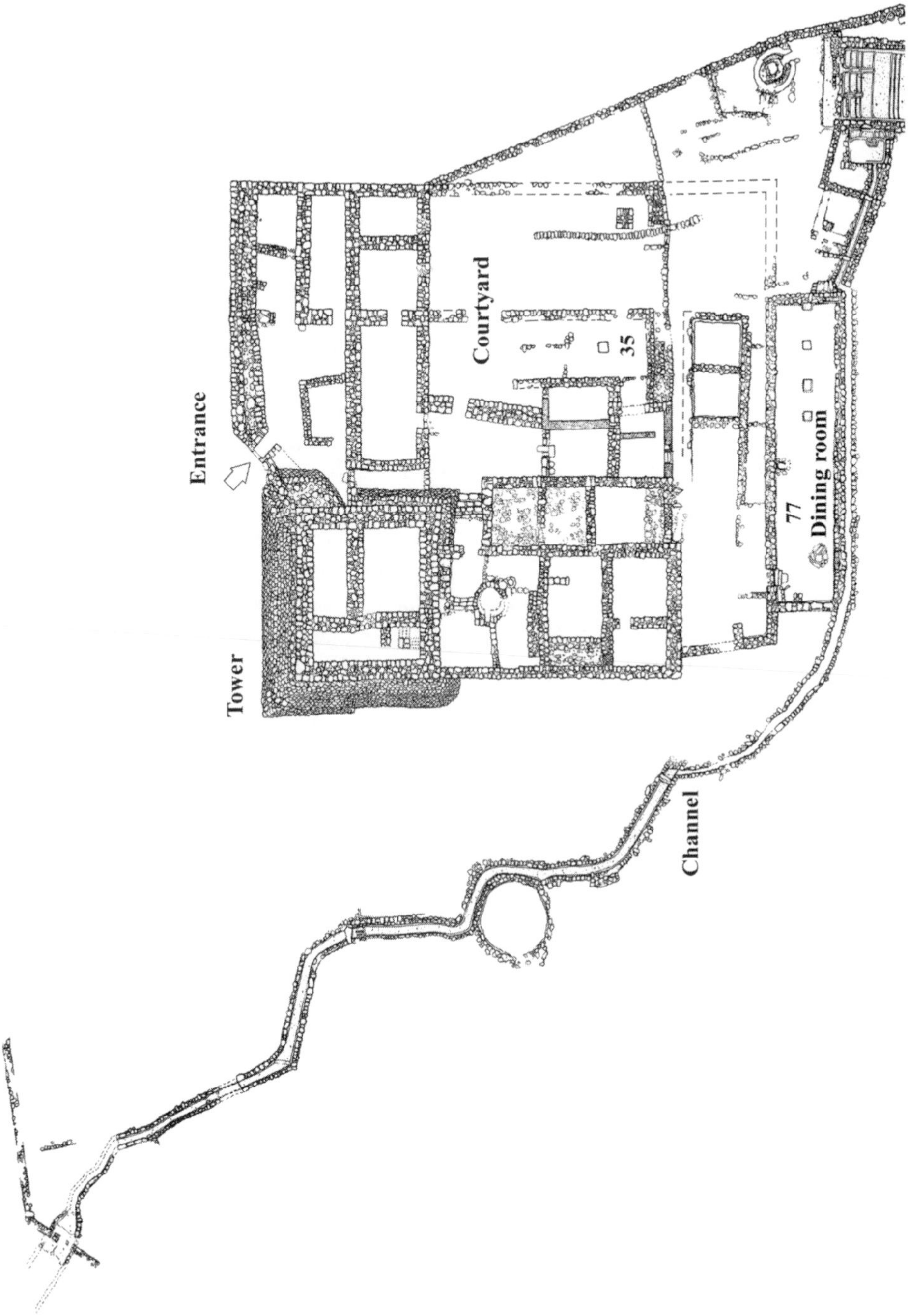

Figure 89. Plan of Qumran after 68 C.E.

Roman fortress at Qumran can be reconstructed as a right-angled building fortified by a tower in one corner and equipped with a large reservoir in another. It is conceivable that the old reservoir and immersion pools under the foundations of the south wing (Loci 56–58) and the east wing (Locus 48/49) of the main building were cleared and still filled up with water as well.

Romans continued to occupy Qumran until 130 C.E. The occupation of Qumran by the Romans between 70 and 130 C.E. accords with the general picture of the settlements in the Dead Sea region. In the winter palace of Jericho, excavators found the remains of a Roman private house that was probably the center of the estate near the palace. According to the excavator, Ehud Netzer at Hebrew University, it was built after the First Revolt and was destroyed by fire during the Second Revolt.[242] The small finds discovered in the house, such as oil lamps, indicate the affluence of its owner.

Similar evidence was uncovered at En-Gedi. In the excavations headed by Benjamin Mazar, a Roman bathhouse was discovered not far from the shoreline.[243] The structure, which is typical of Roman military bathhouses throughout the empire, was in use between the two Jewish revolts. From the archive found by Yigael Yadin in a cave in Nahal Hever, we know that a Roman military unit was stationed in En-Gedi after the First Revolt. In the documents the village of En-Gedi is called "the village of our lord the Emperor."[244]

Pliny the Elder, describing the balsam planted by the Roman *fiscus* ("treasury"), writes in about 75 C.E. that there "has never been such quantity."[245] Pliny is referring to changes in the cultivation and exploitation of balsam that were introduced in his time, perhaps after damage caused to the balsam groves by Jewish rebels during the First Revolt.[246] Pliny's account clearly shows that the Romans had appropriated the rich balsam plantations. If balsam was grown in the northwestern margins of the Dead Sea, it would have provided a strong economic motive for the Romans to take control of the entire region from Jericho to En-Gedi. This would explain the Roman presence at Qumran and 'Ein Feshkha after 68 C.E.

The site may have fallen into the hands of the Jewish rebels of the Second (Bar Kokhba) Revolt in 132–135 C.E. The main evidence for the Second Revolt is a hoard of ten coins found under the floor of a ground floor room (Locus 29) in the tower.[247] This may attest to a small-scale occupation of Qumran during the revolt. A few late Roman and Byzantine coins recovered in the excavations were probably dropped by passersby during the centuries that followed.

In all the stages of Qumran's existence, from the Late Iron Age through the Hasmonean, Herodian, and Roman periods, its location and the economic potential of the nearby oasis of 'Ein Feshkha influenced the archaeology of the site. This is the fascinating and little-explored subject of the next chapter.

---

[242] Netzer 1993, 691.

[243] Mazar 1993, 404–5.

[244] The translation is taken from Cotton 2001, 139.

[245] Pliny, *Nat. hist.* 12.54 (113).

[246] For more details, see Cotton 2001, 142–46.

[247] de Vaux 1973, 45.

Figure 90. A flood in Nahal 'Arugot near En-Gedi in the winter of 2001.

Figure 91. The oasis at 'Ein Feshkha, looking south, bounded by the cliff of Ras Feshkha.

Figure 92. The interior of Cave 4, looking south.

Figure 93. Remains of the long wall running from Qumran to 'Ein Feshkha, looking south.

Figure 94. Remains of an Iron Age tower above 'Ein Feshkha, looking northeast.

Figure 95. The round cistern (Locus 110), looking west.

Figure 96. View from Qumran toward the Dead Sea and beyond, looking east.

Figure 97. A reservoir under the foundation of St. Anthony's monastery in Egypt today. Note the ceiling beams.

Figure 98. Carved stone vessels ("measuring cups") from Qumran. (Courtesy of R. Donceel and P. Donceel-Voûte. "Les Ruines de Qumran Reinterprétés," *Archeologia* 298, 1994: 32.)

Figure 99. Ovoid bag-shaped jars as found in Qumran.
(Courtesy of Israel Antiquities Authority.)

Figure 100. Perfume juglets found at Qumran. (Courtesy of R. Donceel and P. Donceel-Voûte. "Les Ruines de Qumran Reinterprétés," *Archeologia* 298, 1994: 33.)

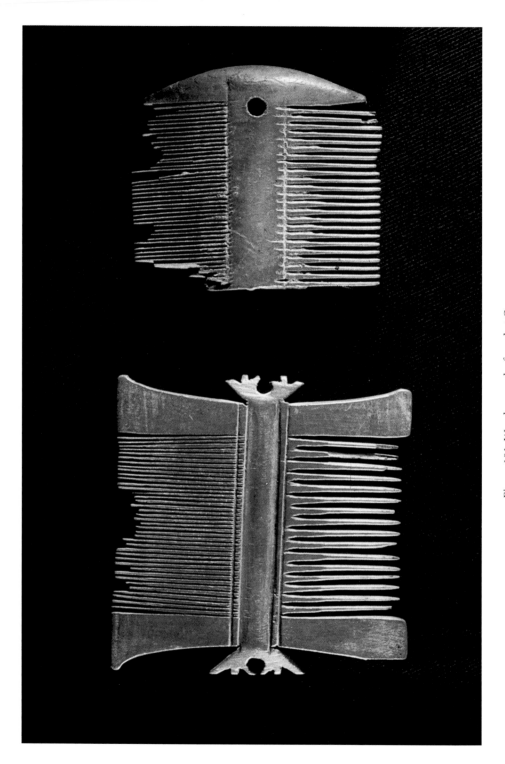

Figure 101. Wooden combs found at Qumran. (Courtesy of Israel Antiquities Authority.)

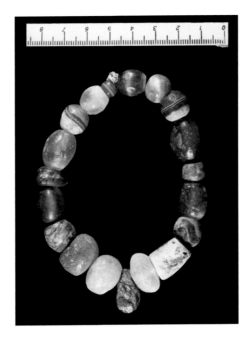

Figure 102. Necklace from a woman's grave at Qumran.
(Courtesy of Israel Antiquities Authority.)

Figure 103. Hoard of eight coins of Mattathias Antigonus, found at 'Ein Feshkha.

Figure 104. Irrigation system at 'Ein Feshkha, looking south.

Figure 105. Gideon Hadas sitting on a lump of bitumen floating in the Dead Sea. (Courtesy of G. Hadas.)

Figure 106. General view of the "Essene site" at En-Gedi, looking south.

CHAPTER 4

The Estate of Qumran
at 'Ein Feshkha

4.1. The Oasis

Herodian Qumran had a little-known companion site 3 km to the south: the oasis of 'Ein Feshkha. Without a consideration of its remains, any reconstruction of Qumran during the Herodian period is simply incomplete. The two sites were contemporary and were linked by the long boundary wall that de Vaux called "the long wall."[1] The purpose of this wall was to enclose an agricultural estate for the cultivation of date palms and balsam.

'Ein Feshkha ('Enot Tsuqim) is the largest and most abundantly watered oasis along the western shore of the Dead Sea Valley.[2] Its Arabic name, meaning "the broken spring," derives from the large quantities of broken blocks of rock that lie at the foot of the cliffs at the boundary of the oasis.[3] The oasis is about 2.5 km long and between 0.3 and 0.6 km wide and lies at 390 m below sea level, 65 m lower than Qumran. Within it are three main springs: 'Ein Ghazal ('Enot Qumran), 'Ein et-Tannur ('Enot Tanur), and 'Ein Feshkha (fig. 107). The three springs are east of the ancient road (the modern Route 90) that runs south to En-Gedi. The main Herodian site of 'Ein Feshkha is located about 100 m north of the spring and only a few meters from the steep slope that borders the oasis on the west. The water supply was not based on the existing spring, which is 3–5 m lower than the site, but apparently came from a spring, at a higher elevation farther north, that has now dried up. Because it originated at a level higher than that of the present spring, the water was probably sweet rather than brackish.[4]

---

[1] de Vaux 1959b, 237; 1973, 59–60. In her discussion of the remains of 'Ein Feshkha, Magness (2002, 210–20) overlooks the existence of the boundary wall physically linking the site with Qumran and consequently arrives at the erroneous conclusion that there was no connection between the two sites.

[2] For the agricultural potential of the oasis, see Farmer 1955; Zeuner 1960, 33–36; Har-El 2000, 15.

[3] Palmer 1881, 349.

[4] Magness 2002, 214. On page 21 of the same publication Magness contradicts herself by describing the springs of 'Ein Feshkha in the past and present as brackish. On the quality of the water in the 'Ein Feshkha oasis, see Mazor and Molcho 1972; Raz 1993, 156; Mazor 1997.

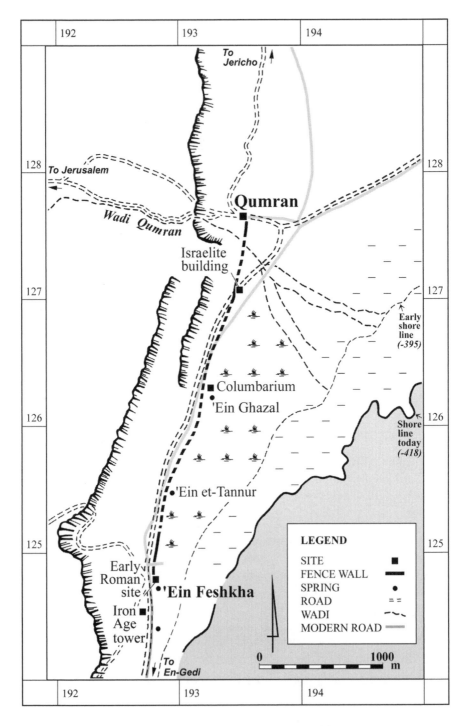

Figure 107. Map of the oasis of 'Ein Feshkha.

The combination of fresh water and abundant sunlight made the oasis of 'Ein Feshkha, like others in the Dead Sea Valley, fertile and suitable for agriculture (fig. 104, color). De Vaux aptly writes that "with a minimum of adaptation a palm-grove could be grown in the terrain irrigated by the springs."[5] He also mentions flocks of sheep, goats, and camels that passed by and slaked their thirst at the springs of the oasis. The site contains industrial installations that may be connected with perfume production. Lumps of bitumen found on the floor of the Herodian building discovered here indicate that its inhabitants exploited the products of the Dead Sea, one of which was bitumen. They may have also harvested edible salt, used in the preservation and flavoring of food.

In the long, narrow area enclosed by the "long wall," that is, between the wall and the Dead Sea, the ancient inhabitants left behind the remains of their agricultural activity. To the north of 'Ein Ghazal, Joseph Porath of the Israel Antiquities Authority has surveyed remains of water channels and enclosure walls of agricultural plots.[6] Trial excavations uncovered potsherds of the first century B.C.E. and the first century C.E.

Closer to the spring of 'Ein Ghazal, de Vaux discovered remains of a structure that he designated "the isolated building" (fig. 108).[7] Today little of this building survives, but according to de Vaux it was a square structure (12 × 12 m) with an entrance on the east (fig. 109). The walls are thick (1.1 m) and are built in straight lines and at right angles to one another. A partition wall divided the internal space into two. In the northeastern and southeastern corners were pillarlike constructions to strengthen the building.

Comparison of the building's plan with similar structures at other sites suggests that it may have been a dovecote (Latin: *columbarium*). Though *columbarium* towers are usually round, square examples also exist. For example, a square *columbarium* tower was uncovered in the palace complex at Jericho (fig. 110).[8] At Masada also, two square *columbarium* towers were found. Most of the known *columbarium* towers belong to sites of the early Roman period in which remains of gardens and agricultural estates have been found,[9] which is logical because the main function of the *columbarium* was to supply pigeon fertilizer for agricultural use. The discovery of a *columbarium* in the area between 'Ein Feshkha and Qumran supports the assumption that in the early Roman period this area served as an estate in which balsam shrubs and date palms, the two main crops of the Dead Sea area in this period, were grown.

4.2. The Herodian *villa rustica*

During his last excavation season at Qumran in 1956, de Vaux cleared one room at 'Ein Feshkha. After finding pottery and coins identical to those of his Period II at Qumran, he conducted large-scale excavations in 1958.[10] In April 2001 I conducted a short season of

---

[5] de Vaux 1973, 84–85.
[6] Porath 1998.
[7] de Vaux 1959b, 237; 1973, 59–60.
[8] Netzer 2001b, 90–91.
[9] Teffer 1986; Zissu 1995, 56–69.
[10] de Vaux 1959b, 246–55.

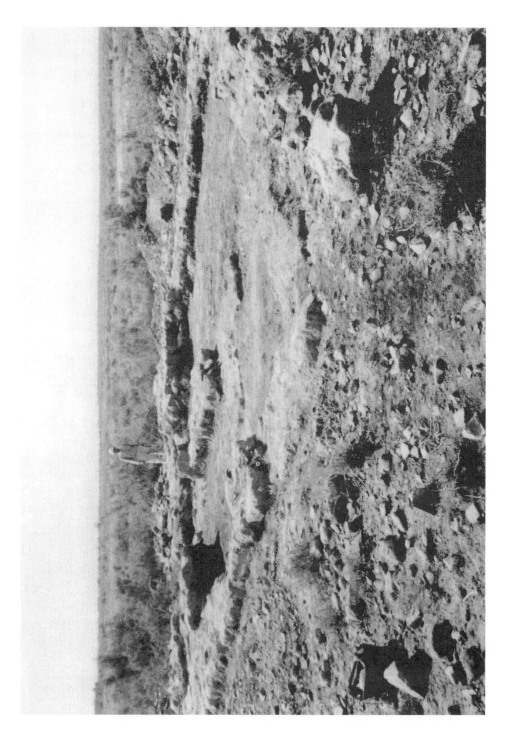

Figure 108. Remains of the isolated building at 'Ein Feshkha as found by de Vaux. (Courtesy of École Biblique.)

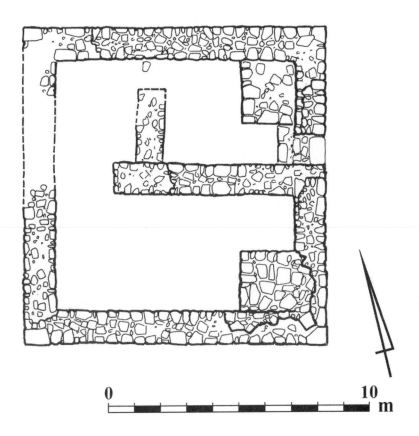

Figure 109. Plan of the columbarium at 'Ein Feshkha.

Figure 110. A squarish columbarium at the winter palace at Jericho. (After E. Netzer.)

surveying and excavations in the oasis of ʿEin Feshkha.[11] The excavations focused on the building of the early Roman period that de Vaux had excavated in 1958. The remains include a main building, an industrial area to the north of the main building, and an enclosure with a pen running the length of its western side (fig. 111). Since the modern road (Route 90) was built over the enclosure, its remains have been almost completely obliterated. The main building and the industrial installations, however, are well preserved and are now accessible to the public.

From the stratigraphic data, it appears that the site was in use for a fairly short period. In probes I conducted under the floors of the main building, no evidence for earlier stages was uncovered. The earliest objects were eight coins (fig. 103, color) of Mattathias Antigonus, the last Hasmonean ruler (40–37 B.C.E.). The coins were found together under a threshold of one of the entrances in the main building. It seems that this was a hoard buried at the beginning of Herod's reign in 37 B.C.E. Consequently, the building and its associated structure were not constructed in stages as de Vaux assumed but, rather, were erected simultaneously as a complex with a coherent plan. De Vaux associated the two phases that he discerned at ʿEin Feshkha with his Period I and Period II at Qumran, implying that at ʿEin Feshkha also there was a settlement gap of thirty years between the two phases. But the minor building changes seen at ʿEin Feshkha, such as a few walls in the courtyard and the blocking of one of the doorways, may be dated to the period of the building's use, that is, the first century C.E.[12] At ʿEn Boqeq a building of almost identical plan and dimensions was constructed during this period.[13] Both sites were centers for local plantations of date palms and balsam.

The main building at ʿEin Feshkha yielded evidence of its destruction in a fierce fire in the second half of the first century, almost certainly in the First Revolt. Judging from the numismatic evidence, it seems that the site was resettled after the First Revolt. Two stamped bricks of the Roman legion were found in addition to about twenty coins of the late first and early second centuries C.E.[14] Similar numismatic evidence from Qumran indicates that it, too, was occupied in this period. Both sites were finally abandoned during the Second Revolt (132–135 C.E.).

De Vaux reported that a lamp and a storage jar of the Byzantine period were found in the excavations of ʿEin Feshkha.[15] On the basis of these finds, he suggested that the Byzantine remains at the site should be associated with the garden of the monastery of

---

[11] Hirschfeld 2004a.

[12] Neither assumption is supported by the evidence. In the final report on ʿEin Feshkha, the two so-called phases of the main building at ʿEin Feshkha are presented; see Humbert and Chambon 1994, 238, pl. LXIV. If one compares the plans of the two phases, practically no differences can be discerned because, in my opinion, the structure was built and used in a single period (the Herodian period). The numismatic finds of de Vaux's excavation confirm this conclusion. According to de Vaux (de Vaux 1959b, 245–48), his excavations at ʿEin Feshkha yielded 143 coins, 59 of which could be identified. Of these, one (a coin of Ptolemy II of the mid-third century B.C.E.) was anomalous; all the rest ranged from the reign of Mattathias Antigonus to the Second Revolt, with the majority dating from the first century C.E.

[13] Fischer, Gichon, and Tal 2000.

[14] Laperrousaz 1976, 153–54. On the small finds from ʿEin Feshkha, see Murphy 2002, 345–46.

[15] de Vaux 1959b, 253–54.

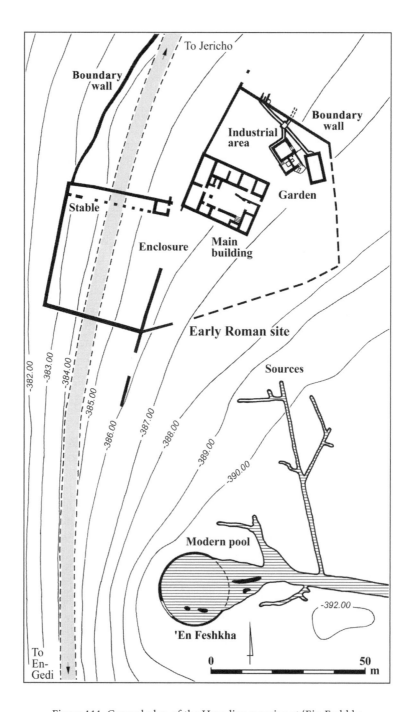

Figure 111. General plan of the Herodian remains at 'Ein Feshkha.

Marda mentioned in the works of an early-seventh-century Judean Desert monk, John Moschus, who wrote a book called *Pratum spirituale (The Spiritual Meadow)*, a collection of several anecdotes about monastic life in the desert. In one of his anecdotes he tells us about Marda, a monastery of anchorites who maintained a garden outside the monastery. De Vaux identified the monastery of Marda with the monastery that was built at Hyrcania (Hirbet el-Mird) during the Byzantine period, and he identified the garden with the Byzantine remains at 'Ein Feshkha. The monastery at Hyrcania at this period, however, was not an anchorite monastery *(laura)* but, rather, a communal type of monastery *(coenobium)*.[16] Besides, we have evidence that the level of the Dead Sea in the Byzantine period was much higher than it was during the Second Temple period, since it was a wetter period, and the Dead Sea covered most of the oasis of 'Ein Feshkha. Therefore agriculture would have been almost impossible. The Byzantine remains that de Vaux identified, if they were such, might be of a small hermitage. The description of the anchorites of Marda fits the monastic remains that Yadin found at Masada very well.[17] Even the garden that is mentioned by John Moschus may be identified near a spring called 'Ein 'Anevah in Nahal Zeelim north of Masada.

I will begin by describing the remains of the main building at 'Ein Feshkha and then will discuss the industrial complex and the few surviving remnants of the square enclosure.

The Main Building

The main building is a well-built courtyard house that has straight walls and a rectangular plan (fig. 112). It was fairly large, with external dimensions of 18 × 24 m, and its total area, including the courtyard, was 432 m[2] (fig. 113). The walls are well preserved and reach a height of 2 m or more. The building techniques are similar to those of Qumran: the doorways are built of ashlars and the walls of fieldstones. The exterior walls are 1 m thick and constructed of medium-sized and large fieldstones, straightened by small stones bound with mortar. The doorways are built of dressed ashlars of sandstone of the Samra formation. On some of them the typical stone dressing of the early Roman period, with prominent bosses and margins 8–10 cm wide, is discernible. The rooms were probably roofed with palm trunks that are abundant in the region. Stone lintels were not found at all, most likely because the lintels of doorways and windows as well were made from palm planks that did not survive. The floor of the courtyard, at an elevation of –386 m, was made of tamped clay. In contrast, the floors of most of the rooms consisted of a thick layer (0.2–0.3 m) of tamped stones covered with a thin layer of earth.

The entrance to the building was through two adjacent doorways on the eastern side. A similar arrangement of two doorways side by side is found at Qumran; it was apparently designed to separate the functions of main entrance and subsidiary entrance for the passage of goods and animals.[18]

The wing along the north side of the courtyard comprises three rooms whose doorways open on the courtyard. An exceptional window was preserved in the southern wall of the largest room (fig. 114), which was apparently a stable. It faces the courtyard and is very

---

[16] On the monastery at Hyrcania, see Patrich 1995, 137–44.

[17] Hirschfeld 1992, 262; 2001–2002.

[18] de Vaux 1973, 61; Magness 2002, 211.

Figure 112. The main building at 'Ein Feshkha, looking east.

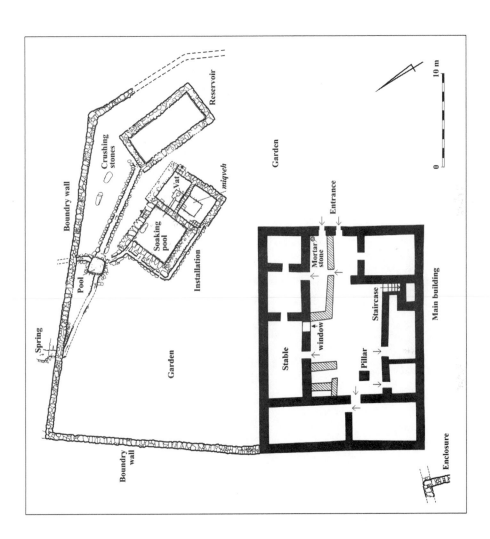

Figure 113. Plan of the main building and industrial installation at 'Ein Feshkha.

Figure 114. The window in the north wing of the main building, looking east.

wide (about 80 cm). The sill is very low, only 0.7 m above a paved ramp in the courtyard below it. A trough was once placed on it, and an animal could reach it from either the inside or the outside. In the window jambs are holes for tethering animals. To the east of the stable are two rooms with a common entrance. Below the threshold of this entrance we found a hoard of eight coins of Mattathias Antigonus (40–37 C.E.).[19] De Vaux suggested that these rooms and those on the south side of the courtyard were storerooms.

The two rooms on the south side of the courtyard were paved with small stones. On the floor of the western room, lumps of bitumen were found, as were a large number of potsherds and some fragments of stone vessels. In the eastern room a cylindrical weight was found with the letters ΛEB (LEB) inscribed on its flat face.[20]

A staircase in the southeastern corner of the building provided access to a roof terrace above the rooms on the north and south sides of the courtyard. Six stone steps belonging to the staircase were preserved (fig. 115). In the proposed reconstruction (fig. 116), a second story is shown above the rooms of the west wing, whose walls are thicker than those of the other wings.

The west wing consists of two fairly large rooms. The facade wall contains a single doorway opening into the southern room. Large amounts of pottery, including an inkwell, were found in this room. A doorway in the north wall provided access to the northern room. A rectangular basalt grinding stone (fig. 117) was found on the floor close to the corner, which may suggest that this room was a kitchen.

The inner courtyard was fairly spacious (92 m²) and occupied one-fifth of the structure's area. A square pier on the courtyard's west side supported a balcony at the second-story level. The second story must have had doorways opening onto this balcony, which served as a passage connecting the roof terraces above rooms of the north and south wings. In the opposite corner of the courtyard, a stone mortar was found in situ. I have found similar mortars in the courtyards of late Roman houses that I have recently excavated at En-Gedi. The mortar was probably used for grinding spices or burghul (cracked wheat), according to ethnoarchaeological research.

Fragments of stone vessels were found in several rooms. These include a large urn (71 cm high) that had apparently fallen from the second story (fig. 118).[21] A similar urn, though less well preserved, was found at Qumran. A number of carefully cut stone tiles were found in various rooms.[22] The square and triangular tiles, made of local gray bituminous limestone (fig. 119), attest to the existence of an *opus sectile* floor, probably in the rooms of the upper story. As noted, floors of this kind have been found in Hasmonean and Herodian palaces and are unmistakable signs of a luxurious lifestyle.[23] The fact that ten similar tiles were found in the excavation of Qumran may support the supposition that the

---

[19] For the chronological significance of this hoard, see Bijovski 2004.

[20] de Vaux (1973, 67–8) suggested that the letter Λ is the Greek symbol for "year," E has the numerical value of 5, and B either has the numerical value of 2 or is an abbreviation for βασιλεύς (*basileus*, "king").

[21] A photograph of this urn appears in Roitman 1997, 41. See also Lemaire 2003, 379.

[22] Humbert and Chambon 1994, 246, photo 458. See also Chambon 2003, 460–63.

[23] Netzer 2001b, 54–55 (Jericho), 73–74 (Cypros), 95–96 (Masada), 112 (Herodium). I am grateful to Ehud Netzer, who examined the tiles from 'Ein Feshkha and confirmed that they are similar to the tiles from these palaces.

Figure 115. The staircase in the south wing, looking south.

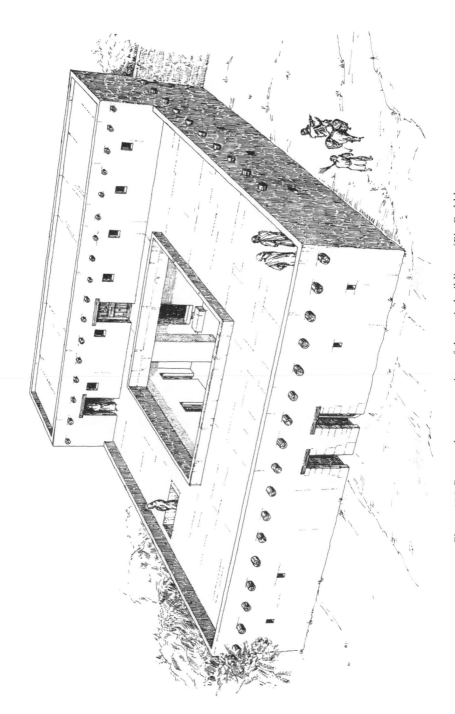

Figure 116. Proposed reconstruction of the main building at 'Ein Feshkha.

Figure 117. Grinding stone found at the Herodian villa at 'Ein Feshkha.

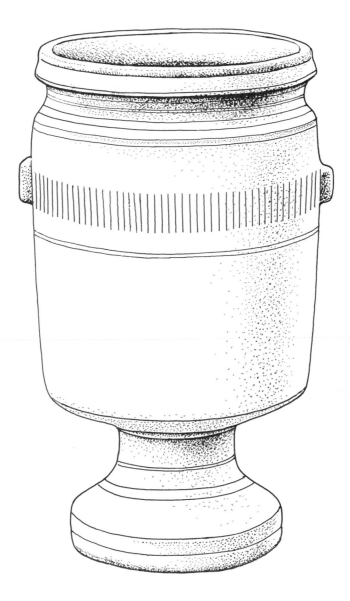

Figure 118. Drawing of a stone urn found at 'Ein Feshkha.
(After R. de Vaux.)

Figure 119. *Opus sectile* tiles found at 'Ein Feshkha.

same person owned Qumran and 'Ein Feshkha. The *opus sectile* tiles discovered in the main building of 'Ein Feshkha indicate that activity in the structure was not limited to domestic concerns but extended to recreation and leisure. On the basis of this find, as well as other finds such as fine stone vessels, weights, and seals, Donceel and Donceel-Voûte have proposed that, like the main building at Qumran, the complex at 'Ein Feshkha should be seen as a kind of *villa rustica,* a combination of a domestic building and industrial installations with elements of luxury.[24]

In contrast, de Vaux wrote, "This building was clearly not a private residence, and was suited to the needs of a religious community."[25] This claim raises a number of questions. Why was the building not a private residence, and in what way was it more suited to the needs of a religious community? The "religious community" is presumably the Essene community that, in de Vaux's opinion, lived in the surroundings of Qumran, but as should now be clear, this is no more than a conjecture. Moreover, de Vaux believed that the main building served not for accommodation but for administration and storage. No support for de Vaux's assumptions, however, was found during our work. On the contrary, the architectural remains and the small finds from the structure attest that this was a residential building in which ordinary people lived, ate, and stored their belongings while also carrying out their daily activities.

The Industrial Complex

The industrial complex is located to the northeast of the main building (fig. 120). Two boundary walls, preserved to a height of about 1 m, enclose the area; since their width is 0.7 m, their original height may be reconstructed as about 2 m, more than the height of a man. The area enclosed by the boundary walls, about 2,000 m², may have been an outer yard or an agricultural plot. In a trial probe that we conducted east of the main building, we encountered a thick layer of homogeneous organic matter (animal waste with its telltale dark color) mixed with a scattering of stones. Beneath this layer of rich organic matter was a stone surface, and below this a layer of soil containing numerous pebbles. Because of the modest dimensions of the probe (2 × 4 m), the nature of the stone surface could not be clarified.

The industrial complex includes a system of channels leading water from a spring (or springs) that in the past existed north of the site. The channels are built of fieldstones and plastered with whitish hydraulic plaster. Two channels that cross the northern boundary wall drain into a small, well-preserved pool. The pool is square, measuring 1.7 × 1.7 m and about 1 m deep. Two channels lead from the pool, the longer one (10 m) to a reservoir and the shorter one (2.5 m) to an installation the identity of which has intrigued scholars for more than fifty years.

The reservoir is 10 m long and 3.2 m wide. It is at least 3 m deep (we did not succeed in excavating its full depth), and consequently its capacity was at least 80 m³. Since no staircase was found, we believe that it was intended for water storage rather than bathing.

---

[24] Donceel and Donceel–Voûte 1994, 27–28.
[25] de Vaux 1993, 1240.

Figure 120. The industrial complex at 'Ein Feshkha, looking northwest.

The installation, which is in an excellent state of preservation, consists of a large pool with two adjacent cells, each containing an additional small pool. The large pool is almost square, measuring 4.4 × 4.5 m and 1.3 m deep. Its walls are about 1 m thick. Patches of whitish hydraulic plaster are preserved on the floor and walls of the pool. Two steps in the northern wall provided access to the pool's floor. A large cylindrical stone, 1.48 m long and 0.6 m in diameter, was found on the floor, close to the step. It probably had a crushing function of some kind in the operation of the installation. Two additional cylindrical stones were found on the stone pavement north of the channel leading to the reservoir. Cylindrical crushing stones were also found in similar industrial installations uncovered in the estate of the winter palace complex at Jericho.[26]

The floor of the large pool sloped down slightly toward a drainage opening in the base of the eastern wall. The round opening, 10 cm in diameter, could be blocked when necessary. The water was drained through a channel that ran into the gathering vat in the cell on the other side of the wall. The northern cell is fairly small (2.3 × 3.5 m) and can be directly accessed from the outside. The vat is square, measuring 0.9 × 1 m and 1.4 m deep and with a capacity of 1.26 m³. At the end of the channel is a protruding stone that served as a spout to direct the liquid to the jar (fig. 121). A column drum 0.3 m in diameter and 0.35 m high was found in situ on the floor; it was perhaps used as a stand for vessels that received the liquid (fig. 122).

The southern cell is larger than the northern cell; its internal dimensions are 2.8 × 3.7 m, and its capacity is 10.3 m². It is accessed by four steps 0.6 m wide leading down from the southwestern corner. In the floor of the cell, adjacent to the wall that divides the two cells, is a small pool; there is no connection between it and the vat on the other side of the wall. The pool measures 1.5 × 1.8 m and is 0.9 m deep, and its capacity is 2.4 m³ (fig. 123). A channel that branches off from the short channel mentioned above feeds the pool. Within the pool is a narrow staircase (0.4 m wide) permitting descent to the floor. In view of the steps, it seems likely that this pool was a mikveh. The inclusion of a ritual bath in an agricultural installation enabled the operators of the installation to purify themselves before or during their work.[27] A similar arrangement was found at Qumran.

From the high-quality construction of the installation and its location within the enclosure, it is clear that it was used for the production of a commodity of high commercial value. Although the installation is similar to a winepress, its connection to a water supply system is unique. Its use as a winepress cannot be ruled out, but other possibilities should be considered. Any proposal must take into account two factors: 1) its connection by channels to a source of running water implies that the process demanded considerable quantities of water; and 2) the presence of three crushing stones, one within the installation and two outside it, attests to some kind of crushing activity as part of the process.

No less than five proposals have been made so far for the function of the installation. The first was made by de Vaux, who believed that the installation was a tannery where skins were processed for the parchment scrolls found in the caves near Qumran.[28] Not only does this proposal lack support from the sources; it is also inherently unlikely, since

---

[26] Netzer 2001a, 14–15; 2002a.

[27] Reich 1990, 122–23.

[28] de Vaux 1959b, 233–37. Poole and Read (1961) rejected de Vaux's interpretation.

Figure 121. The collecting vat at 'Ein Feshkha, looking west.
The protruding stone in the wall (center) directed the liquid to a jar below.

Figure 122. Proposed reconstruction of the installation at 'Ein Feshkha in cross-section.

Figure 123. The pool in the southern cell at ʿEin Feshkha, looking west.

the region of 'Ein Feshkha has never been used on a large scale to pasture the sheep, goats, or cattle from whose skins parchment would have been prepared.[29] The second proposal, put forward by F. E. Zeuner, is that the pools at the site were used to raise fish, but this proposal, too, lacks support from the sources or the archaeological finds.[30] The third proposal, made recently by Mireille Bélis, is that it was used for the production of blue dye from the indigo plant that grew in the vicinity.[31] But although there are historical sources for the cultivation of this plant, they all date from the early Muslim period (tenth to eleventh centuries),[32] and none are from the period under discussion. A fourth suggestion, made recently by Netzer, is that similar installations found in the palaces at Jericho were used for the production of date wine.[33] According to him, these installations consist of a crushing stone, a pool, and a gathering vat. After removal of their stones, the dates were brought to the pool, and a large quantity of water was added. The mixture was crushed with cylindrical crushing stones (which have been found in each of the installations) to produce a liquid. The liquid was then left in the pool to ferment. After fermentation, the stopper at the end of the pipe was removed, and the liquid (i.e., the date wine) flowed into the gathering vat. The fifth suggestion, made recently by Gideon Hadas,[34] differs from that of Netzer in proposing that these installations were used for the production not of date wine but of the date honey mentioned by Josephus (*J.W.* 4.468–469).

I would like to make a sixth proposal, which may complement the suggestions put forward by Netzer and Hadas: that the installations at Jericho and 'Ein Feshkha also played a role in the perfume industry for which the Dead Sea region was renowned in the early Roman period. This proposal takes into consideration the fact that agricultural installations in antiquity were not used for one purpose only. For example, the oil presses in ancient Palestine were also used to crush wheat.[35] The historical sources repeatedly mention the balsam shrubs that were grown in the area of Jericho and the Dead Sea and from which the most costly perfumes were manufactured.[36] The most detailed description is that of Pliny the Elder (23–79 C.E.) (*Nat. hist.* 12.54 [112–118]). According to him, balsam is a small tree from which two qualities of perfume are extracted: *opobalsamon* and the less costly *xylobalsamon*. The former was collected in the form of sap by making cuts in the trunk and was marketed in its natural form. The latter was produced from the pruned branches of the tree and underwent a process of compounding with oils, just as most perfumes are produced to this day. In her article on the perfume industry in the Dead Sea

---

[29] A rock–carved inscription discovered near Hebron by David Amit mentions Zonenos, a tanner from Ascalon who lived in the region (Amit 1989/1090). The location of the tanner's inscription accords with the character of the Hebron area, which supplies ample grazing for sheep, goats, and cattle to the present day. In the rocks near the inscription were quarried installations, perhaps part of a tanning complex.

[30] Zeuner 1960, 34–36.

[31] Bélis 2002, 7.

[32] Amar 1997, 311–12.

[33] Netzer 2002a.

[34] Hadas 2002, 170–71.

[35] On the production of cereal groats in ancient Palestine, see Eitam 1996.

[36] For detailed discussion of the production of balsam perfume in the Dead Sea region, particularly at 'En Boqeq, see Dayagi-Mendels 1993, 107–12; Gichon 2000, 94–95.

region, Donceel-Voûte describes the processes of crushing and soaking by which the perfume essence was produced.[37] According to her, the installations in which the various perfume essences were produced vary, but all contain four elements: 1) a crushing apparatus, 2) shallow containers to soak the material in water for short periods, 3) deeper containers to receive and store the essences, and 4) ovens and hearths for heating the concoction together with oil to produce the finished product.[38]

The first three items in this list are present in the installation at 'Ein Feshkha: the crushing stones, the large pool (which we interpret as a soaking pool), and the gathering vat. Figure 122, above, presents a proposed reconstruction of the installation in operation. The process began with the pruning of the balsam shrubs and the concentration of the branches near the installation. The next step was crushing, first outside the installation with the two stones found on the upper stone surface and then within the soaking pool, in which the third stone was found. It seems likely that this pool was exposed to the sun to accelerate the concentration of the essence. The two cells on the other side of the soaking pool were probably roofed, in the case of the northern cell to protect the precious essence that was collected in the vat and in the case of the southern cell to provide privacy for bathers during ritual immersion.

The fourth element, ovens and furnaces, is lacking in the industrial complex of 'Ein Feshkha. We attempted to locate them in the yard to the east of the main building but without success. One possible explanation for this may lie in the proximity of 'Ein Feshkha to Qumran. De Vaux rightly claimed that the complex at 'Ein Feshkha was connected with that of Qumran, where a remarkable abundance of ovens and furnaces was found.[39] Consequently, one may raise the hypothesis that the perfume essence was produced in the installation at 'Ein Feshkha and that the finished product was manufactured at Qumran and from there was transported to the markets of Judea and beyond.

The Square Enclosure

Very little remains of the square enclosure uncovered by de Vaux.[40] Its walls have been covered by soil eroded from the slopes, and as noted, the modern road to En-Gedi (Route 90) was built over it. The enclosure consists of a square yard (34 × 34 m, 1,156 m²) enclosed by walls 0.7 m thick. The entrance was apparently in the eastern wall facing the main building. On the northern side of the enclosure, de Vaux uncovered a row of about ten pillars with a constant distance of about 2 m between them. The long, narrow space between the pillars and the outer wall of the enclosure (measuring 3.5 × 27 m) probably served as a pen for sheep, goats, cows, and donkeys. This reminds us that in Qumran, bones from all of these animals were found throughout the dig and in the "deposits." At the eastern end of the stable is a small room (internal dimensions 3 × 3.5 m) used for

---

[37] Donceel–Voûte 1998, 96–100.

[38] Ibid., 106.

[39] de Vaux 1973, 84. On the ovens and furnaces at Qumran, see Donceel and Donceel–Voûte 1998, 24–26.

[40] de Vaux 1959b, 228–30; Humbert and Chambon 1994, 260–62, 358–61.

accommodation or storage. The entrance to the room is on the east. This is the room where de Vaux found the Byzantine pottery.

A boundary wall runs from each of two corners of the enclosure. One of them, exposed for a length of 12 m, starts at the southeastern corner and runs to the northeast toward the wall on the east of the industrial complex. It seems likely that these two walls joined to form a single wall and enclosed the yard to the east of the main building. The second boundary wall, de Vaux's "long wall," starts at the northwestern corner of the square enclosure and runs north for about 200 m toward Qumran.

In conclusion, the estate boundary wall that connects Qumran with ʿEin Feshkha attests that the two sites were connected; in other words, the same person owned them. Neither Qumran nor ʿEin Feshkha has yielded evidence for the presence of members of a cult. From the rich finds at both sites, the estate's owner appears to have been a wealthy upper-class Judean, probably a Jerusalemite. The residents of the estate were the estate manager, servants, and slaves, whose task was to work the estate and to extract maximal profits from it. The complex at ʿEin Feshkha is smaller than that at Qumran and was principally intended for agricultural activity. The industrial installation found at ʿEin Feshkha was used, in my opinion, for the production of balsam perfume essence in addition to date wine and date honey. Finds attesting to wealth and luxury were found in the nearby residential building, indicating that it was also used for recreation, on the model of the Western *villa rustica*. The complex at Qumran is larger and is equipped with installations such as ovens and furnaces, which were not found at ʿEin Feshkha. It seems likely that Qumran was the main center of production of the perfume industry and the point from which the goods were sent to markets in Judea and elsewhere.

CHAPTER **5**

Qumran in Context:
The Dead Sea Valley in
the Second Temple Period

5.1. The Settlement Picture

Qumran and its inhabitants should be viewed in the context of the general picture of the region. During the Second Temple period, the Dead Sea Valley was a meeting place for people from different ends of the social spectrum. Kings and influential men had economic interests in the natural resources of the region. The Judean kings, first the Hasmoneans and later the members of the Herodian dynasty, founded palaces and fortresses around the Dead Sea and cultivated large estates as economic concerns. There were also wealthy landowners, many from priestly families and the Jerusalem aristocracy, who wished to enjoy the mild winter climate of the Dead Sea and built pleasure houses, particularly in Jericho. Their estates were worked by the local peasants, who became tenant farmers and took part in the prosperity of the region.

Beside the landowners and the peasants, there were dozens, perhaps hundreds, of ascetics who had abandoned society and retreated to the wilderness to seek spiritual redemption. The sources tell of figures, such as John the Baptist and the Essenes, who lived an isolated and ascetic life near the Jordan River or in the cliffs above the Dead Sea. The sources reveal that these folks, who had voluntarily chosen a life of poverty, were sometimes the object of admiration. Unlike that of the kings and landowners, their physical stamp on the landscape is barely discernible. But their spiritual heritage, as a result of historical events, has lasted until today. A discussion of the members of these four social classes, so different from one another, will help to demonstrate that the site of Qumran was not isolated but part and parcel of the general settlement picture of the region.

During the Second Temple period, the Dead Sea region was divided between two kingdoms: its eastern part belonged to the Nabatean kingdom, and the western part belonged to the Judean kingdom. The regional capital was Jericho, northwest of the Dead Sea, where the Hasmonean rulers built palaces that Herod eventually inherited. Zoar, the principal settlement of the southern Dead Sea, was in Nabatean territory.[1] The other settlements around the Dead Sea varied in size and importance. The three main settlements on the eastern shore were those of the Lisan Peninsula, al-Mazra'a, al-Haditha, and Khirbet Sekine, which sources describe as Nabatean. As noted, the central cemetery of the peninsula settlements, containing thousands of burials, has recently been excavated at Khirbet Qazone.[2] Another important settlement on the eastern shore was Callirrhoe, to the north of the peninsula. Callirrhoe was the harbor for the fortress of Machaerus and was—and is to this day—a medicinal spa thanks to its hot springs (its Greek name means "good waters").[3] Excavations at Callirrhoe have revealed a palace from the period of Herod the Great and a large agricultural estate.[4]

The most important oases on the western shore were En-Gedi, 'Ein Feshkha, and Qumran in the north and 'En Boqeq in the south. En-Gedi contained a fairly large village and royal estates.[5] At Qumran, 'Ein Feshkha, and 'En Boqeq, excavations have revealed the remains of farmhouses and installations attesting to intensive cultivation and processing of agricultural produce.[6] In addition, there were a number of smaller sites, all located close to springs. The northernmost of these is Rujum el-Baḥr, next to the spring of 'Ein ej-Jahir. Traveling south, the next is Khirbet Mazin south of 'Ein Feshkha. About 15 km to the south is a Second Temple period structure near 'Ein el-Ghuweir ('Enot Qaneh), and not far to the south is a larger structure, Qasr et-Turabeh, near the spring of 'Ein et-Turabeh ('Enot Samar). Pesah Bar-Adon studied these four sites in the 1970s.[7]

New plans and sections were made during my survey of Khirbet Mazin in April 2001. It was during this survey that an assemblage of 2,500 bronze coins was found along the shore near the site,[8] and this is only the tip of the iceberg. Every time we return, we find more—the sea does the "excavating" for us, exposing the coins on the shoreline with its waves. In recent decades, thousands of the same type of coins appeared in markets as

---

[1] Netzer (2001a; 2001b, 13–63) excavated the palace complex at Jericho. Zoar at the southern end of the Dead Sea has not yet been excavated; for a survey of its archaeological remains, see Politis 1998b.

[2] For Khirbet Qazone as the central cemetery of the settlements in the region, see Politis 1998a; 1999.

[3] Josephus (J.W. 1.657; Ant. 17.171) relates that King Herod went to the hot baths at Callirrhoe before his death. A depiction of the town appears in the Madaba mosaic map; Avi–Yonah 1954, 40.

[4] The palatial complex at Callirrhoe appears in Clamer 1997. For the remains of the harbor, see Strobel and Clamer 1986; Schult 1966, 142–48.

[5] Mazar (Mazar 1993) excavated the remains of the Second Temple period at Tel Goren in En-Gedi. For historical surveys of En-Gedi in this period, see Mazar, Dothan, and Dunayevsky 1996, 4–7; Cotton 2001.

[6] Fischer, Gichon, and Tal (2000) have recently published the remains of the Second Temple period at 'En Boqeq.

[7] Bar-Adon 1989. Schult (1966, 139–42) suveyed the remains at Rujum el-Baḥr. For further information on Khirbet Mazin, see Netzer 2001b, 77–78. For 'Ein el-Ghuweir, see Bar-Adon 1977. Bar-Adon (1989, 41–43) suggested that the site at Qasr et-Turabeh should be dated to the Late Iron Age. The assemblage from under the foundation of the building, however, also includes pottery of the late Hellenistic and early Roman periods. Since the building belongs to only one period, it seems best to relate its dating to that of the pottery of the Second Temple period that was found under its foundations.

[8] Hirschfeld 2002; Hirschfeld and Ariel, forthcoming.

"widow's mites" (after the New Testament story of the "two small copper coins" of Mark 12:42 and Luke 21:2) to attract potential buyers. There is good reason to believe that they all came from the Dead Sea area. Presumably, these coins, embossed with an anchor, were intended as payment for the mercenaries who, Josephus tells us, were an important component of the army of John Hyrcanus and Alexander Jannaeus (*Ant.* 13.249). Jannaeus probably chose the anchor motif for the coin to emphasize his Dead Sea maritime activity. The huge number of coins is another demonstration of the centrality and extensive military presence in the area at this time. In other words, we need to imagine Qumran as on the margins of an oasis that was a veritable maelstrom of activity rather than an isolated ascetic site—the exact opposite of the life that anchorites sought.

In addition to the coastal settlements, a chain of fortresses was constructed on the high clifftops of the Judean Desert to the east and west of the Dead Sea. The Hasmonean rulers of Judea built these fortresses to defend the approaches to Jerusalem and ensure Jewish control of the region. The fortress of Dok is perched on Mount Qarantal west of Jericho. A little to the south are a pair of fortresses on either side of the ancient road to Jerusalem, Nuseib el-'Uweishira on the north and Cypros (Tel 'Aqaba) on the south.[9] On the road leading from Jerusalem to Qumran, John Hyrcanus I (134–104 B.C.E.) founded the fortress of Hyrcania.[10] At Tel Goren in the oasis of En-Gedi, the remains of a Hasmonean fortress that defended the oasis were uncovered.[11] To the south of En-Gedi, on a towering plateau, the Hasmoneans founded Masada, "a fortress of redoubtable strength," in the words of Josephus.[12]

The Hasmoneans began to fortify Judea as early as the days of Jonathan the high priest, in the mid-second century B.C.E. From 129 B.C.E. onward, the great Hasmonean kings, John Hyrcanus I and his son Alexander Jannaeus, expanded the kingdom with campaigns of conquest of Transjordan and the eastern Dead Sea shore. After the conquest of the northeastern Dead Sea region and the Transjordanian heights, Jannaeus founded the fortress of Machaerus on a mountaintop east of Callirrhoe.[13] This fortress was of great military importance, since from it there was eye contact with the fortresses on the western side of the Dead Sea. Alexander Jannaeus founded another fortress, Alexandrium, which bears his name, in the Jordan Valley north of Jericho.[14] Herod inherited the fortresses from the Hasmoneans and utilized his energies and the considerable financial resources at his disposal to strengthen them and build magnificent palaces in the most important of them, such as Masada and Machaerus. This was in addition to his main palace at the western end

---

[9] Josephus, *Ant.* 13.183 mentions the Hasmonean fortifications of Judea. On the Judean Desert fortresses of the Second Temple period, see Tsafrir 1982. For the different sites in and around Jericho, see Netzer 2001b, 68–76.

[10] For the archaeological remains at Hyrcania, see Patrich 1993; 2002.

[11] Mazar 1993, 403–4. In previous publications Mazar and his colleagues dated the fortress on Tel Goren to the reign of Alexander Jannaeus; Mazar, Dothan, and Dunayevsky 1966, 68–72.

[12] Josephus, *J.W.* 4.398. According to Josephus (*J.W.* 7.285), Jonathan the High Priest (152–142 B.C.E.) built the Hasmonean fortress at Masada.

[13] Josephus, *J.W.* 7.171–172. The Franciscan archaeologist Virgilio Corbo (Corbo 1978) excavated the site.

[14] Josephus mentions Alexandrium several times in his writings as one of the most important of the Hasmonean palaces. For its archaeological remains, see Tsafrir and Magen 1993.

of the Jericho oasis. He also built smaller palaces at the fortresses of Alexandrium in the Jordan Valley and Tell 'Aqaba southwest of Jericho (the latter fortress was named Cypros in memory of Herod's mother) and also Herodium, the fortified palace named after himself southeast of Bethlehem.[15] The fairly extensive excavation of all these sites has led to the discovery of impressive remains of the Second Temple period.

The rich and varied archaeological record of the Dead Sea Valley and the Judean Desert in the Second Temple period owes nothing to chance—the region enjoyed an unprecedented economic boom in the Hasmonean and Herodian periods. Josephus tells of large areas, in the vicinity of Phasaelis and Archaelais north of Jericho, that had previously been wilderness but were cultivated during this period.[16] There were four main sources of income in the region: balsam, dates, and the two most significant products of the Dead Sea, bitumen and cooking salt.[17] Groves of date palms were planted in every possible place, in the Jordan Valley and in the oases of Jericho and the Dead Sea shore, much as they are today. According to the sources, the first balsam plantations were at Jericho and En-Gedi. As early as the fourth century B.C.E., Theophrastus reports on two plantations in the area, one large and one small, the larger one apparently at Jericho and the smaller one at En-Gedi.[18] Pliny also mentions the plantations.[19] Strabo, a geographer of the first century C.E., also describes the balsam plantation near the royal palace in Jericho.[20]

After the battle of Actium in 31 B.C.E., when Augustus granted control of most of the Dead Sea region to Herod, a new phase of economic prosperity and increased settlement in the region was ushered in. It is likely that in this period the cultivation and processing of balsam was extended to the smaller oases of 'Ein Feshkha and 'En Boqeq, as attested by the archaeological finds. At both of these sites, as noted, excavation has revealed the remains of agricultural systems, living quarters, and industrial installations for the processing of agricultural produce, together with small finds, such as perfume juglets and glass bottles, that can be linked with the perfume industry.[21]

Let us not forget that the sites around the Dead Sea were linked by an extensive road system. There was a close economic relationship between the Jews and the Nabateans in the Dead Sea region of this period, as shown, for example, by the Nabatean coins and cream ware pottery found in the settlements of the western shore.[22] In the Nahal Hever documents, dating from the period after the First Revolt, there is also ample evidence of a close relationship between En-Gedi, the neighboring settlements, and the Nabatean town of Zoar.[23]

---

[15] On the palace of Herod at Cypros, see Netzer 2001b, 72–74.

[16] Josephus, *Ant.* 16.145 (Phasaelis); *Ant.* 17.340 (Archelais).

[17] The best summary of the sources of income in the Dead Sea region is Gichon 2000.

[18] Theophrastus, *Hist. plant.* 9.6.1. Many scholars accept the identification of the two plantations with Jericho and En-Gedi; see Patrich 1997, 140. Feliks (1997, 284) lists the sources that relate to balsam; for additional discussion of the terms used for the parts of the plant, see Patrich and Arubas 1989.

[19] Pliny, *Nat. hist.* 12.54 (111).

[20] Strabo, *Geogr.* 16.2.41.

[21] Fischer, Gichon, and Tal 2000, 40–41 (for 'En Boqeq); Donceel-Voûte 1994, 32–33 (for Qumran).

[22] E.g., at 'En Boqeq; Fischer and Tal 2002, 39–40.

[23] Cotton 2001.

Although today it may be difficult to imagine, the most convenient route between the settlements of the western shore and Callirrhoe and Machaerus on the eastern shore was by sea in Second Temple times. Three harbors were built around the Dead Sea at that time, one at Rujum el-Bahr in the north, another at Khirbet Mazin south of 'Ein Feshkha, and the third at Callirrhoe on the eastern shore. At Rujum el-Bahr remains of a tower and an anchorage were discovered (fig. 124).[24] From the large quantities of stone rubble, it appears that the tower was very high (20–25 m); it may even have been a lighthouse (fig. 125). The tower stood on an artificial island. Its foundations were enclosed by walls at a height of 1 m above the sea level of the time; in it mooring stones for boats were integrated.

At Khirbet Mazin, a complex that included a tower, a pier, and a large dock was discovered. The complex was large (1,500 m[2]) and was constructed from massive building stones (fig. 126). Here, on a stretch of the shore opposite the complex, is where the thousands of Alexander Jannaeus period coins were found.[25] Since Jannaeus founded the fortress of Machaerus, it seems likely that the fortified harbor of Khirbet Mazin was also founded during his reign (fig. 127). From here one could sail across the Dead Sea to the harbor of Callirrhoe and ascend the steep road to the fortress, remains of which can still be seen.[26] Remains of a harbor have also been discovered at En-Gedi.[27] Each of the settlements along the Dead Sea shore probably had a harbor of some kind.

These harbors were useful not only for marine transport but also for the collection of bitumen. The lumps of bitumen that occasionally surface in the Dead Sea were much sought after in antiquity for building, for caulking boats, for medicinal purposes, and even for the embalming industry of Egypt.[28] From the testimonies of Diodorus Siculus and Josephus, we learn that the inhabitants of the Dead Sea region harvested the lumps of bitumen by sailing to them and pulling them from the water.[29] The settlements along the coast probably competed to reach the bitumen, with boats at the ready to set sail and lookouts on duty on the shore. The towers that are typical of the Dead Sea sites of the Second Temple period may have been used, inter alia, as lookout posts for spotting lumps of floating bitumen.

The interest in bitumen persisted until modern times. The kibbutzniks of En-Gedi told me that they collected lumps of bitumen to make pharmacological products. Gideon Hadas, an archaeologist from En-Gedi, gave me a slide of himself as a young person sitting on a large lump of bitumen in the 1960s (fig. 105, color).

After the annexation of the Judean kingdom to the Roman Empire in 6 C.E., the Romans took control of the balsam plantations of Jericho and En-Gedi.[30] In the palace complex of Jericho, the remains of a Roman villa were found, attesting to the continued

---

[24] Bar-Adon 1989, 1–14.

[25] Hirschfeld 2000c.

[26] On the ancient road from Callirrhoe to Machaerus, see Strobel 1977; on Callirrhoe's harbor, see Schult 1966, 141–48.

[27] Hadas 1993.

[28] On the bitumen, see Hammond 1959; Gichon 2000, 96–97.

[29] Diodorus Siculus, *Bibl. hist.* 2.48.6–8; Josephus, *J.W.* 4.479–480.

[30] Goodman 1987, 59; Cotton 2001, 142–46.

Figure 124. Remains of a tower and anchorage at Rujum el-Bahr, looking south.

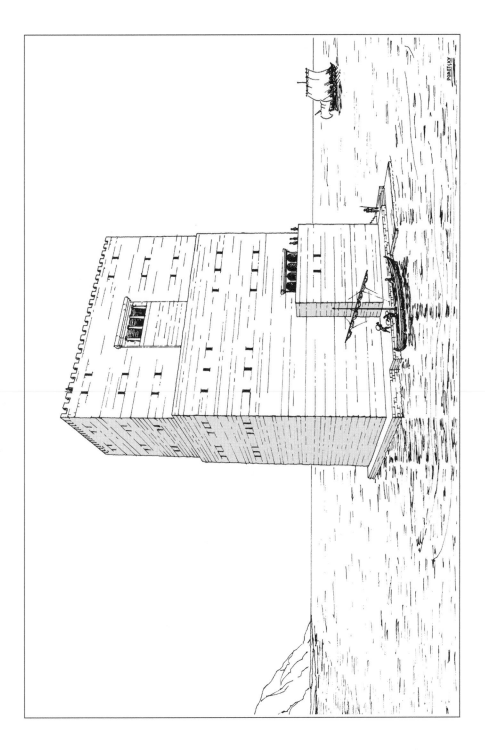

Figure 125. Proposed reconstruction of Rujum el Bahr.

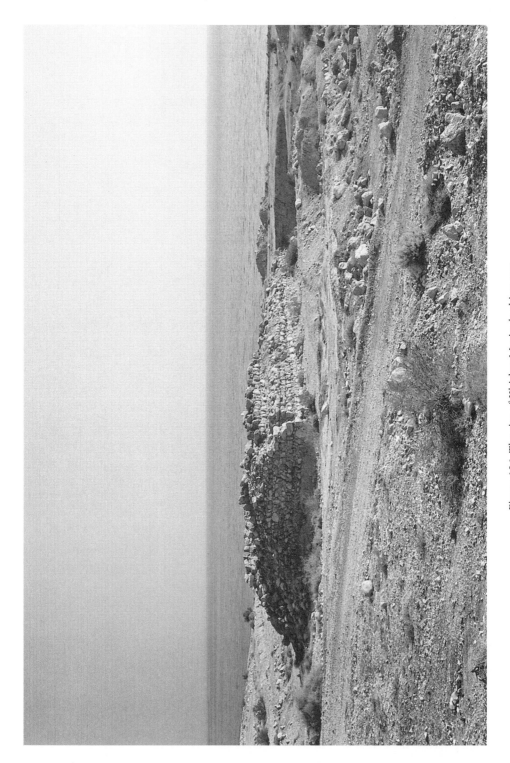

Figure 126. The site of Khirbet Mazin, looking east.

Figure 127. Proposed reconstruction of Khirbet Mazin.

cultivation of the estate's plantations.[31] In the Nahal Hever documents, En-Gedi is called "the village of our lord the Emperor," indicating that the whole village with its plantations of balsam and dates was transferred to the Roman treasury (fiscus).[32] The fiscus made a heavy investment in the development of the balsam plantations. According to Pliny, the plantations that covered the slopes contributed a large annual income to the Roman treasury. During the First Revolt, the Jews attempted to destroy the plantations and made a determined attack on each plant.[33]

Although the Roman authorities annexed the royal estates of Jericho and En-Gedi as crown land (patrimonium), there is no reason to believe that the smaller estates, such as those of Qumran and 'En Boqeq, also passed to the Roman crown. Roman rule was generally restrained and deliberate and did not violate the property rights of the local population. On the contrary, the local leadership of the provinces generally enjoyed the support of the Roman authorities. Its members were able to receive Roman citizenship and serve in the army.[34] The estates of Qumran and 'En Boqeq, which archaeological evidence dictates were founded during the reign of Herod, were probably in private ownership and consequently remained in Jewish hands until their destruction during the First Revolt.

The knowledge needed for the cultivation and processing of balsam accumulated in local Jewish families and was transmitted from generation to generation. After the First Revolt, the Romans permitted the Jews to resettle the main sites around the Dead Sea. From the documents of Nahal Hever and Wadi Murabba'at, it is clear that there was continuity in the cultivation of dates and balsam.[35] A Roman military unit was stationed at En-Gedi, presumably to secure the balsam plantations of the area. At that time, En-Gedi belonged to the region of which Jericho was the capital. It seems likely that the Roman fiscus allowed the Jewish peasants, who knew how to produce the precious balsam, to remain in the desert oases of the Dead Sea. Pliny attests to the existence of the central site of the Essenes in the mountains above En-Gedi in the period after the destruction of the temple.[36] Remains of this site have been identified, though not with certainty, during my excavations at En-Gedi.[37] It is likely that the Essenes, who are known to have subsisted primarily from agriculture, were permitted to settle here on condition of their participation in the local agrarian economy.[38] The archaeological finds at Qumran and 'Ein Feshkha point to a continuous Roman presence between the two revolts, and the balsam and date plantations of En-Gedi and Jericho presumably continued in existence until their destruction in the Second Revolt.

---

[31] Netzer 1993, 691; 2001a, 281–85.

[32] Cotton 2001, 139.

[33] Pliny, Nat. hist. 12.54 (112–113).

[34] Stern 1974, 330–31; Goodman 1987, 34–37, 59–60.

[35] Cotton 2001.

[36] Pliny, Nat. hist. 5.15 (73). The excavator of Qumran, de Vaux (de Vaux 1973, 133–35), believed that the settlement of the Essenes should be located not at En-Gedi but to its north; this issue will be discussed below.

[37] Hirschfeld 2000b.

[38] The description of the Essenes as farmers is based on Philo of Alexandria; see Sandmel 1979, 32; Schürer 1979, 562–63.

In conclusion, Qumran fits well into the division, suggested by the excavators of 'En Boqeq, of the Dead Sea settlements in the Second Temple period into four typological groups:[39]

1. Central settlements. Jericho, En-Gedi, and Zoar served as administrative and economic centers of the region. They were established in large and well-watered desert oases that enabled the development of substantial settlements.

2. Palace complexes. This group included Jericho, Masada, Machaerus, and the smaller sites of Alexandrium, Cypros, Callirrhoe, and perhaps also En-Gedi.[40] The excavations of Jericho and Callirrhoe revealed large agricultural estates enclosed by boundary walls beside the palaces and villas. The winter palace of the Judean kings at Jericho functioned as a branch of the main palace in Jerusalem.

3. Fortified estates. This group includes Qumran, 'Ein Feshkha, 'Ein el-Ghuweir, and 'En Boqeq, located along the western coast road of the Dead Sea. A combination of living quarters and agricultural installations was found in all of them. Some of them, such as Qumran and 'En Boqeq, contain towers. These settlements were situated close to the shore, enabling their inhabitants to exploit the natural resources of the Dead Sea. The structures served both as the administrative center of the estate and also as the domicile of the landowner during his visits and of his staff, including the estate manager, the servants, and the slaves.

4. Military forts. This group consists of three sites close to the shore—Rujum el-Bahr, Khirbet Mazin, and Qasr et-Turabeh—and also Qumran in its Hasmonean phase. Prominent in all of them is the presence of a tower, which both provided security and served as a striking physical expression of the power of the regime. The forts were principally intended to secure both the transport route along the western shore of the Dead Sea and the harbors for marine traffic (such as Rujum el-Bahr and Khirbet Mazin). The Hasmonean forts were part of the chain of fortifications that defended the eastern frontier of Judea against the Nabateans. They joined the large fortresses built on the hilltops: Alexandrium, Dok, Hyrcania, and Masada on the western side of the Dead Sea, and Machaerus on the eastern side.

The graduation of the settlements of the Dead Sea points to an interdependence among the different settlement types. Jericho and En-Gedi were political and administrative centers, and the large estates they contained were the property of the Judean or Roman crown. The palaces served the kings both as dwellings and for the production of commercial produce. Alongside them were sites such as Qumran, Callirrhoe, and 'En Boqeq, which were in private ownership and served similar purposes, both as dwellings and as a source of income. The fortresses on the roads and the hilltops defended the area and guarded the traffic on its roads and the routes to Jerusalem.

---

[39] Fischer, Gichon, and Tal 2002, 143–44.

[40] The archaeological evidence that may point to the existence of a palace at En-Gedi consists of about ten Herodian capitals found in secondary use in the Roman bathhouse of the late first century C.E.; see Mazar 1993, 404–505.

When Herod ascended to the Judean throne, he inherited the Hasmonean fortifications and added some of his own. But from Josephus' descriptions, it seems that the method of controlling the fortresses changed in Herod's day, with the king granting estates to his favorites throughout the kingdom.[41] In this way he maintained the system characteristic of the Hellenistic kings: the building of an army of reservists by granting estates and tracts of land in return for military service when it was required. An example of this is the estate of Ptolemy, one of Herod's senior ministers and a close friend. This estate, the remains of which Shimon Dar at Bar Ilan University located in the heart of the Samarian Hills, included large tracts of land with a fortified manor house at the center.[42]

Qumran of the Herodian period fits well into this model of the manor house.[43] The square plan of the main building is reminiscent of manor houses found at various sites like Horvat 'Aqav and Qasr e-Leja in northwestern Samaria, 'Ofarim in western Samaria, Khirbet el-Muraq (Hilkiya's palace) and Rujum el-Hamiri in the Hebron hills and Tel Aroer in southern Judea (fig. 128). Most of the manor houses have a corner tower. A good example is Horvat 'Aqav at Ramat Hanadiv, which has a tower in one corner and agricultural installations, such as wine and oil presses, both inside and outside the complex (fig. 129). The tower at Rujum el-Hamiri in the Hebron Hills has a sloping stone revetment like that of Qumran (fig. 130). The revetment reinforced the foundations and gave the tower a more massive appearance.

The social structure of Judea during the reign of Herod is very reminiscent of the feudal order of medieval Europe. At the top of the pyramid sat the king, and below him was a broad aristocratic class that included princes, close associates, and army veterans, all of whom helped the king to manage his affairs. In exchange for their loyalty, the king gave them large tracts of land, which included villages and farmsteads populated by tenant farmers. The manor houses boasted walls and towers and stood on elevations in the centers of their estates, similar to the settings of medieval castles. Thus, together with the royal palaces, these manor houses became a dominant feature of the rural landscape of Herodian Judea.

The Second Temple period offers abundant evidence for wealthy estate owners. Josephus describes the early-second-century B.C.E. estate of Hyrcanus son of Tobias at Tyros in Transjordan. In the center of the estate, Hyrcanus built a solid stone "castle" (Greek: *baris*) surrounded by a moat, and around it ornamental courtyards, banquet halls hewn in the rock, and "vastly large gardens."[44] Ptolemy, Herod's court minister, mentioned above, owned a large estate (Greek: *ktēma*) in the heart of Samaria, where, as noted by Josephus, the village of Arus (Haris) was located.[45] Thus, Ptolemy's estate appears to have been spread over a large area that included several villages whose inhabitants were land tenants. In his study of Ptolemy's estate, Dar estimates its area at about 900 hectares

---

[41] On the allocation of land in Herod's day, see Jones 1938, 77–83; Goodman 1987, 38–42; Pastor 1997, 99–102.

[42] On the identification of Ptolemy's estate, see Dar 1993; for more details on Ptolemy, see Roller 1998, 63–64.

[43] See Hirschfeld 1998; 2000a, 709–20; 2000d.

[44] Josephus, *Ant.* 12.230–232. On the estate of Tyros, see Nielsen 1994, 141–43; Netzer 2001b, 137.

[45] Josephus, *J.W.* 2.69.

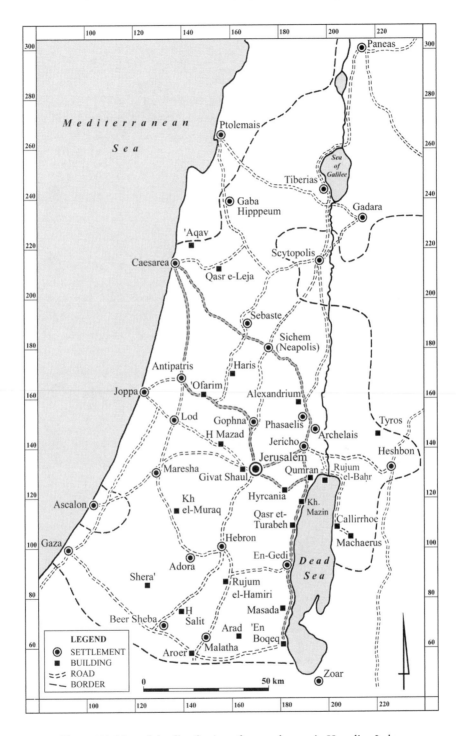

Figure 128. Map of the distribution of manor houses in Herodian Judea.

Figure 129. Proposed reconstruction of Horvat 'Aqav at Ramat Hanadiv.

Figure 130. The stone revetment around the tower of Rujum el-Hamiri, looking north.

(3,600 acres), a significant tract of land that was Ptolemy's main source of power and wealth.[46] Josephus' testimony makes it clear that Ptolemy's permanent place of residence was Jerusalem, so it is likely that he visited his estate only occasionally. The absentee land-owner appears to have been the usual model, although some estate owners probably reversed the pattern, living permanently on the estate and only occasionally visiting the city on business.

Herod often bestowed land estates on army veterans. Josephus mentions two settlements of veterans, one at Gaba Hippeum near the Carmel Range and the other at Heshbon in Transjordan.[47] The two main regions of settlement for Herod's military veterans were Samaria, where lands were granted to the inhabitants of the city of Sebaste, and in Idumea, where lands were granted to about two thousand Edomites who were Herod's loyal subjects.[48] Josephus relates that in his will Herod bequeathed many tracts of land to his family members, friends, and army veterans.[49]

Estate owners in Judea often figure in allegories in the New Testament. For instance, we are told of an absentee landlord who sent his servants to bring in the harvest.[50] Elsewhere we hear of a wealthy man whose steward (Latin: *villicus*) was charged with his properties.[51] The term "Herodians" appears frequently in the New Testament, referring to loyal subjects of the king who enjoyed various economic rewards.[52] One may assume from the sources that the wealthy landowners continued to expand their estates by deception and oppression, increasing the resentment of the people toward them. As a result, the social polarity that characterized Judea at the end of the Second Temple period was exacerbated, and the number of bandits increased.[53] The fortified manor houses of Judea thus reflect a lack of internal security; unlike Roman villas, which were open to the landscape, these were closed buildings equipped with defensive walls and towers.

The Judean manor houses are not palaces; their architecture is simple and utilitarian. Many of them, like Qumran, were the local version of the Roman villa, which was a rural complex consisting of a manor house, servants' quarters, and farm buildings and was a prominent feature of Roman life.[54] Roman agronomists described the distinction between the *pars urbana,* which was the domestic quarters of the owner (Latin: *dominus*), his family, and his guests, and the *pars rustica* or *pars fructuaria,* where the servants' quarters, workshops, barns and other outbuildings and garden were located. For the Romans, the

---

[46] Dar 1993, 46–47.

[47] Josephus, *Ant.* 15.292.

[48] Josephus, *Ant.* 15.296 (for Sebaste); *J.W.* 2.57 (for Idumea). On the status of Herod's military veterans, see Shatzman 1991, 171–83.

[49] Josephus, *J.W.* 2.646.

[50] Matt 21:33–40.

[51] Luke 16:1.

[52] On the significance of the term "Herodians," see Schalit 1964, 237–38; Charlesworth 1988, 146–48.

[53] On the social polarity of Judea, see Theissen 1977, 47–49; Goodman 1987, 38–42. On banditry, see Isaac 1984, 177–80.

[54] Fernández Castro 1982, 310. Smith (1997, XXXI) defines the villa as "the principal house(s) of a country estate or farm." According to Ellis 2000, 11, "a Roman villa is a country estate with a richly decorated house."

villa was a luxurious summer or winter residence (depending on the climate) in association with a country estate. It was viewed as a haven of peace, but this does not contradict the estate's having an important economic function.

The precise layout of the villa depended on a number of factors, such as its particular location, its function, and the preferences of its owner. Nevertheless, unlike the royal palaces and the luxurious *villae maritimae* (open to a beautiful vista, which in Italy often meant the sea, hence the name), which were not numerous, most of the villas of early Roman Judea were of fairly standard type. Many of them, like Qumran, were decorated with columns and *opus sectile* paving.

In Judea a large manor house was apparently called in Greek a *baris* (Hebrew: *birah*). This term, of early Semitic origin, was usually given to fortified palaces that also functioned as regional administrative centers.[55] But *baris* is also the term used by Josephus to describe the palace of Hyrcanus son of Tobias in Transjordan, mentioned above, and elsewhere he also uses it to describe a tall residential building resembling a tower.[56] The term, in the meaning of a fortified manor house, also appears in historical and epigraphic finds throughout the Hellenistic world.[57] It reflects both the physical shape of the house and its socioeconomic role.

Another word that appears in the sources as a general term for this type of building is the Greek *pyrgos* ("tower"). For example, Josephus tells us of the arrival of Agrippa I about 40 C.E. at a *pyrgos* belonging to him and his family in Malatha in southern Judea.[58] Since we are told that Agrippa arrived with his wife and children, we may surmise that this was not a military stronghold but, rather, a privately owned building intended to provide shelter to its owners. The term *pyrgos,* which was later transmuted in rabbinic literature to *burganin* or *burgasin,* usually appears in a context of agricultural activity and protection of the harvest.[59] Another term given to manor houses in these sources is the Hebrew *'ir* ("city") or, more precisely, *'ir shel yakhid* ("city of an individual"). In rabbinic literature *'ir* refers to privately owned property, including the compound of a farmhouse or manor house that was not necessarily fortified.[60] The multiplicity of the terms used to denote them reflects the great diversity of manor houses in Second Temple period Judea.

The combination of a tower and an inner courtyard surrounded by rooms (fig. 131) characterizes the fortified manor houses of Judea. Agricultural installations, such as wine and oil presses, were found in several of these buildings, indicating that they were working farms. In the manor house at Tel Aroer in southern Judea, excavations uncovered an ostracon that contained a record of the wages of agricultural laborers.[61] Another ostracon dealing with agricultural matters (the so-called Yahad Ostracon) was found at Qumran.[62]

---

[55] On the origin of the term *baris,* see Will 1987; on its Hebrew equivalent, *birah,* see Mendel 1992.

[56] Josephus, *Life* 48.

[57] On the widespread use of the term *baris,* see Lawrence 1979, 292–93; Hopwood 1986, 348.

[58] Josephus, *Ant.* 18.147.

[59] Sperber 1976. On the significance of the term *burgii,* e.g., in *m. ʿErub.* 5.6, see Isaac 1993.

[60] On the term *'ir* in rabbinic literature, see Applebaum 1976, 641–43.

[61] See Naveh 1985, 121.

[62] See Cross and Eshel 1997.

Figure 131. Comparison of plans for manor houses in Herodian Judea
with a manor house at Chersonesos.

Fortified manor houses are usually located on elevations that command their surroundings and are near the main roads passing through the region. Consequently, the scholarly literature often interprets these structures as fortresses.[63] Close examination of manor houses and fortresses of the Hellenistic and Roman periods, however, reveals essential differences between them. Military fortresses usually have a large inner courtyard to accommodate troops and also to provide temporary shelter for refugees in times of need.[64] In contrast, fortified manor houses have a relatively small courtyard surrounded by rooms and halls that served the daily needs of their inhabitants. Although many of them had defensive features such as walls, towers, and guardhouses, these should be viewed as playing civilian rather than military roles. The location of the manor houses near major traffic arteries enabled their inhabitants both to market their agricultural products and to maintain control of the area.

The tower was a primary feature of the fortified manor house in Judea and elsewhere. The tower played a variety of roles, serving simultaneously as a dwelling, a watchtower, a safe repository for valuables, and, in times of need, a refuge for the estate's inhabitants.[65] The tower's height and strength was a matter of prestige, as an architectural expression of the status and affluence of the landowner.

Comparable manor houses with towers are found mostly in mainland Greece and areas colonized by the Greeks along the shores of the Mediterranean and the Black Sea. Such structures are known in Greece from the fifth century B.C.E. onward.[66] The closest parallels to the Judean manor houses, however, are those of the Hellenistic period in Chersonesos; this Greek colony on the Crimean Peninsula, on the Black Sea shore, as noted, contains one of the best examples of a corner tower, and a courtyard surrounded by rooms.[67] The similarity between this complex and those of Judea, such as Qasr e-Leja, 'Ofarim, Rujum el-Hamiri, and Qumran, cannot be coincidental. It is probable that estate owners in Judea adopted a model, known throughout the Hellenistic world, that met their social and economic needs.

On the basis of this evidence, one can reasonably assume that the complex at Qumran, which was constructed as a road-station and fort during the Hasmonean period, was handed over to one of the king's favorites (one who had survived Herod's tendency to prune the aristocracy and leave behind those loyal to him) during his reign. I believe that from that time onward and until its destruction during the First Revolt, Qumran functioned as a fortified rural estate complex, occupied by the landowner during his visits to the estate and by his farm manager, servants, and slaves. The living quarters for the owner, his family, and his guests were in the central building, and the staff of servants and slaves lived in the service wings around it.[68]

---

[63] See, e.g., Barouch 1996. Shatzman (1991, 266) notes that "many of these [fortified sites] were civilian settlements equipped with appropriate defensive installations and troops."

[64] On the characteristics of fortresses, see Lawrence 1979, 172.

[65] See Nowicka 1975, 119–21.

[66] On farm and manor houses in Greece, see Young 1956.

[67] On the fortified manor houses with towers in the Crimean Peninsula, see Nowicka 1975, 113–18. On the fortified villa in the late Republican period, see McKay 1975, 102–3.

[68] On the separation of the residential area intended for the owner of the house and his guests *(pars urbana)* from the service area of farm buildings *(pars rustica)*, see Percival 1996, 68–69; Hirschfeld 1998, 181–82.

Qumran can therefore be defined as the center of an agricultural estate rather than the communal center of the writers of the scrolls. Since not a single scroll was discovered at the site itself, but only in the nearby caves, it can be assumed that the scrolls originated in Jerusalem.[69]

5.2. The Essenes and the Dead Sea Ascetics

The widely held view is that Qumran was a cult center for members of the Essene sect. The description of the Essenes as freely choosing poverty and a frugal life, however, clearly contradicts the nature of the remains and finds at the site. Josephus comments that the Essenes despised wealth, and Philo of Alexandria explicitly states that "they do not store up treasures of silver and of gold, nor do they acquire vast sections of the earth out of a desire for ample revenues."[70] The group of Essenes that, according to Pliny the Elder, lived above En-Gedi was especially stringent in its ascetic way of life: "The solitary tribe of the Essenes . . . has no women and has renounced all sexual desire, has no money and has only palm trees for company."[71]

Advocates of the Qumran-Essene theory, to explain elements indicating the wealth at Qumran, resort to the monastic model in the Byzantine period, according to which the monks themselves lived a life of abstinence and penury, having surrendered their worldly possessions to the abbot, although their monasteries were large and rather splendid.[72] We do have impressive remains of such monasteries, such as the Martyrius Monastery at Ma'aleh Adummim in the Judean Desert east of Jerusalem. We also have evidence for this way of life from the story of Sabas, a fifth-century Judean Desert monk who, when he joined the monastery as a novice, gave three gold coins to the abbot.[73] This anecdote reminds us of what Josephus tells us about the Essenes and what the *Rule of the Community* relates about the Dead Sea sect—that they gave their private property to the community and had a common treasury.

There are many similarities between the Essenes as they are described by Josephus and Philo, and in particular as they are described by Pliny, and the first Christians as the New Testament portrays them. For instance, both practiced the sharing of possessions and a communal life. The Essenes' way of life was certainly a source of inspiration for the earliest followers of Jesus.

---

[69] Golb 1994; 1995; 1999; Cansdale 1997, 189–90.

[70] Philo, *Every Good Man Is Free*, 689. For Josephus's description of the Essenes, see *J.W.* 2.122 (Thackeray, 369). On the Essenes' poverty and rejection of wealth, see Theissen 1977, 82; Boccaccini 1998, 32–34; Broshi 2000, 633–34.

[71] Pliny, *Nat. hist.* 5.15 (73) (Rackham).

[72] Safrai (2000, 42), e.g., writing about the contradiction inherent in a rich sect with poor members, mentions communities of Christian monks. He reaches the absurd conclusion that the Essenes who lived at Qumran enjoyed a high standard of living that included, inter alia, "long banquets" and the "eating of several meat courses" (p. 47).

[73] On the monastery of Martyrius and other monasteries in the Judean Desert, see Hirschfeld 1992, 42–45.

In addition to withdrawal from society, poverty, and celibacy as a matter of choice, Pliny focuses specifically on "the company of palm trees"—closeness to nature—when describing the ascetic way of life. As early as the third and fourth centuries, we have historical and archaeological evidence for Christian hermits, who are considered the founders of the Christian monastic movement, living in the desert in the same lifestyle as the Essenes, such as Saint Anthony in Egypt, Hilarion in the desert region of Gaza, and Chariton in the Judean Desert. In this sense, the heritage of the Essenes in the Dead Sea region has been branded into the consciousness of Christianity from that day to this.

The supposed similarities between Byzantine monastic life, Qumran, and the Essenes sound convincing. But they are completely misleading. The real wealth of the later monasteries did not come from "the coins of Sabas." It came from the heart of the ecclesiastical establishment in Jerusalem and Constantinople. Many of the monks were appointed to high offices in the church, and several of them even became patriarchs. In contrast, the Essenes are described as a small sect living on the periphery of Jewish society, without access to the Jewish administrative establishment in Jerusalem. Another important difference between the Byzantine model and the Essenes is the fact that some of the wealth of the Byzantine monks came from rich pilgrims whereas visitors to the Essenes were, as far as we know, in the main, poor people. Jesus, John the Baptist, and their followers, who retreated to the Dead Sea region and the desert, as related in the New Testament and by Josephus, are good examples of the kind of people likely to have visited the Essenes.[74] On the other hand, we have the example of Josephus himself, who came from a priestly family and joined Bannus in the desert for three years. But even Josephus, at the age of sixteen, would not have possessed property of his own to give.

From the surviving ancient sources, we learn that during the late Second Temple period, particularly in the first century C.E., there was a widespread movement of retreat to the desert.[75] Social and economic distress, together with messianic fervor, apparently motivated many people to leave their homes and settle in the Judean Desert and the Dead Sea Valley. They voluntarily chose an ascetic life whose principles were renunciation of property, celibacy, rigid observance of the laws of purity by means of immersion, and extreme frugality.

Josephus tells of several occasions when people from all over Judea followed their leaders to the deserts of Judea and the Jordan Valley in the first century C.E., before the revolt.[76] As already mentioned, Josephus himself spent three years in the wilderness with Bannus, one of these asectics. Bannus reportedly ate only wild plants, wore clothes made of tree bark, and immersed himself frequently in cold water.[77] Though this description of Bannus is remarkably similar to Pliny's account of the Essenes, he was not a member of this group, since Josephus joined Bannus only after he had studied the ways of the Essenes.

Among those who retreated to the desert were numerous Essenes, as we learn from Pliny the Elder, who wrote about 75 C.E. (a few years before his death in the eruption of Vesuvius),

---

[74] Matt 3:1–13; Josephus, *Ant.* 18.116.

[75] On ascetic hermits and the messianic movements that emerged in the Judean Desert in the first century C.E., see Goodman 1987, 79–80; Schwartz 1992, 29–31; Theissen 1977, 48–50.

[76] Josephus, *Ant.* 20.97, 167; *J.W.* 2.116.

[77] Josephus, *Life* 11–12.

On the west side of the Dead Sea, but out of range of the noxious exhalations of the coast, is the solitary tribe *[gens]* of the Essenes *[Esseni],* which is remarkable beyond all other tribes in the whole world, as it has no women and has renounced all sexual desire, has no money, and only palm-trees for company. Day by day, the throng of refugees is recruited to an equal number by numerous accessions of persons tired of life and driven thither by the waves of fortune to adopt their manners. Thus through thousand of ages (incredible to relate) a race in which no one is born lives on forever, so prolific for their advantage is other men's weariness of life![78]

Pliny tells us exactly where to look for the Essenes:

Lying below *[infra]* the Essenes [*hos;* literally, "these"] was formerly the town of Engedi, second only to Jerusalem in the fertility of its land and in its groves of palm-trees, but now like Jerusalem a heap of ashes.[79]

De Vaux, like many other scholars after him, believed that the Essene settlement should be located at Qumran, north of En-Gedi, because, in his view, the Latin term *infra hos* should be understood as meaning either "to the south of these" or "downstream of these."[80] By this interpretation, En-Gedi is to the south of the Essene settlement, in the direction of the Jordan's flow, and consequently the settlement should be sought in the northwestern Dead Sea region, that is, at Qumran.

Pliny's testimony is the only one that locates the Essenes in the Dead Sea region and consequently is of great importance. Close examination of the passage describing the area shows that both of the proposed translations of *infra hos* are implausible. At the beginning of the passage dedicated to Judea, Pliny describes the source of the Jordan and its flow through the Sea of Galilee to the Dead Sea (the "Asphalites").[81] He goes on to mention various settlements around the Sea of Galilee (Bethsaida [Julia], Hippos [Susita], Tarichea, and Tiberias) before returning to the Dead Sea. After describing the Dead Sea itself, Pliny mentions several places on the eastern side. He reports on the fortress of Machaerus, whose strength is exceeded only by Jerusalem, in the mountains of Moab and describes Callirrhoe and its springs. Only then does he cross to the western side of the Dead Sea and describe the Essenes and two other sites of interest, En-Gedi and Masada. From this it is clear that Pliny is not describing a straightforward itinerary from north to south but is giving an account of various places and settlements around the Dead Sea from the literary sources at his disposal.[82]

Nowhere in his account is there any sense of a systematic description in the direction of the Jordan's flow. Moreover, his description of the river ends well before he deals with the settlements around the Dead Sea. Nor is it plausible to translate *infra hos* as "to the

---

[78] Pliny, *Nat. hist.* 5.15 (73) (Rackham).

[79] Ibid. The reference to Jerusalem is probably a copyist's error for Jericho, whose fertile soil was renowned.

[80] de Vaux 1973, 134–35.

[81] Pliny, *Nat. hist.* 5.15 (71–72).

[82] Before the discovery of the scrolls, there were no doubts among scholars that the Essene settlement should be located in the En-Gedi area; see, e.g., Abel 1938, 316–17. For an analysis of Pliny's description, see Hutchesson 2000, 26–28. A new reading of the Essenes passage is suggested by Kraft 2001, 257.

south of." When Pliny wants to indicate the explicit directional term "to the south of," as in describing the location of Tarichea on the Sea of Galilee in relation to Hippos and Bethsaida and of Arabia south of Machaerus, he uses the words *a meridie*. It is likely that if it had been his intention to indicate a direction, Pliny would have used this same term once again to describe the location of En-Gedi relative to the Essene settlement.

The straightforward translation of Pliny's term *infra hos* is "below these" in the topographical sense. If this interpretation, which appears in most of the modern translations, is correct, then the location of the Essene settlement should be sought on one of the mountain slopes above En-Gedi and not at Qumran. Such a location is supported by the fact that the remains at Qumran contrast with the description of the Essenes as celibate ascetics.

If Qumran was not the center of the Essenes that Pliny describes, where was their settlement? During 1998–1999 I excavated a site above En-Gedi that may provide an answer to this question.[83] It is located on a natural rock terrace on the margin of the oasis of En-Gedi, about 200 m above the ancient site and about 220 m above the current level of the Dead Sea (fig. 106, color). The remains at the site, unlike those of Qumran, accord with the ascetic character of the Essenes as it is described in the sources.

The "Essene site," as I have called it, extends over a long, narrow terrace about 300 m long and 20–25 m wide. This relatively large area (about 7,500 m²) was sparsely occupied (fig. 132). The principal remains consist of twenty-eight small cells without courtyards. There is no connection between the cells, and each has a separate entrance. They are irregular in form and scattered in a random pattern over the area. The inner space of the cells is only 2–3 m² in area, indicating that each had a single occupant. The cell walls are generally preserved to a height of 1 m; in some cases the preserved height reaches 2 m. A good example is the northernmost cell, which is in a good state of preservation (fig. 133). The walls, about 0.8 m thick, are constructed, without bonding materials, from the natural boulders that occur in the vicinity. The floors consist of tamped marl. Since no signs of roofing were discovered in the excavation, it seems likely that the cells were roofed by palm branches (fig. 134). The cells are arranged on either side of an ancient path that leads down to the village of En-Gedi.

Three structures in the center of the site are exceptional in their larger size and the higher quality of their construction. One of them consists of two rooms. Unlike the other cells, which are built entirely from unworked fieldstones, these structures have corners and openings built from roughly dressed stones. They are also regular in plan, with right-angled corners. These structures, which probably served communal purposes of some kind, are located on the eastern side of the path that bisects the site from north to south.

Opposite them, on the western side of the path, are two pools, one above the other. To this day, a small spring wells up in the floor of the upper pool. The pool has an irregular shape that conforms to the topography of the surrounding rock formations. The pool is plastered with several layers of the gray hydraulic plaster typical of the Herodian period. The hewers of the pool deliberately left a kind of ramp to enable descent to the floor of the pool (fig. 135). According to Jewish law, the descent to the mikveh had to be dignified, by

---

[83] Hirschfeld 2000b.

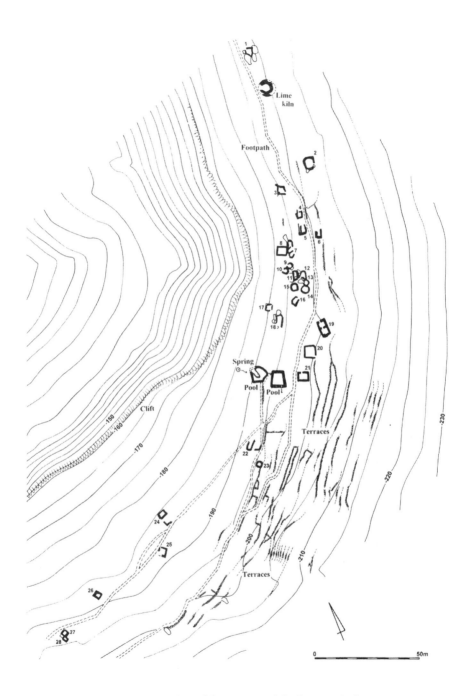

Figure 132. Plan of the remains of the "Essene site."

Figure 133. The northernmost cell of the "Essene area," looking south.

Figure 134. Proposed reconstruction of life in an Essene cell.

Figure 135. The upper pool in the "Essene area," looking west.
Note the rock-hewn ramp descending to the floor of the pool.

means of either steps, a ramp, or a moderate incline if it was a natural source such as a lake, a pool, or a stream. Because of the ramp, I have suggested that the upper pool was a mikveh. The lower pool is square and plastered with the light-colored hydraulic plaster that is characteristic of En-Gedi in the Byzantine period. It thus seems that this pool was added in the later period of the site's occupation in the Byzantine period and is dated, on the numismatic evidence, to the fourth–sixth centuries C.E.

Excavation in the cells uncovered pottery and glass that are characteristic of the second half of the first century and the first half of the second century C.E. The pottery assemblage consisted mainly of storage jars (including some that are of Nabatean origin), jugs, juglets, plates, and bowls. The numismatic evidence confirms this dating, showing that the site was occupied during the first century and up to the Second Revolt (132–135 C.E.). The dating is in accord with the testimony of Pliny, who wrote his composition after the fall of Jerusalem in 70 C.E. His account is written in the present tense, demonstrating that the Essene settlement was in existence after the destruction of Jerusalem. This rules out the possibility that Qumran, which was destroyed in 68 C.E., was the site of the Essene settlement. The continued existence, after the revolt, of the site that I excavated above En-Gedi conforms with Pliny's description.

The architectural remains of the site correspond with Pliny's description of the Essene settlement. The cells may well have been those of ascetics, since their small dimensions would permit occupation by only one person. The location of the site on the margin of the oasis of En-Gedi would have been suitable for ascetics who had withdrawn from society. The suggestion that the site was occupied by simple laborers working in the oasis is unacceptable;[84] ordinary hired laborers would have chosen to live in the center of the oasis, close to its agricultural plots. The secluded location of the site, 200 m above the village of En-Gedi, is an indication that the site was occupied by ascetics.

The finds of the excavation were few and utilitarian: local pottery vessels, small quantities of glass, and four coins. Another striking feature of the finds is the total lack of animal bones; despite careful excavation and sieving of all the earth removed, no bones at all were found. This fact is significant, since meat was an important dietary item in antiquity, as shown by the large quantities of bones found at ancient sites, particularly in desert areas. For instance, in my excavations in the village of En-Gedi, we uncovered more than three thousand animal bones. We can conclude from this that the inhabitants of the site above En-Gedi in the first and second centuries were vegetarians. This conclusion, as noted, accords with evidence from the sources that the Essenes were vegetarians.

There are numerous similar ascetic sites below the cliffs along the western shore of the Dead Sea (fig. 136). Bar-Adon identified sixteen such sites, all dating from the Roman period[85] and consisting of a cluster of cells, in his 1968 survey of the area of Qumran and En-Gedi. These sites are situated at the foot of the cliff or on the natural rock terrace that runs along it. The cells are similar in form to those of the "Essene site" above En-Gedi. The number of cells varies from site to site. In some there are as few as two cells, while in others there are ten to twelve; the average is six. The site above En-Gedi is outstanding in having

---

84 Amit and Magness 2000.

85 Hirschfeld 2000b, 139–43.

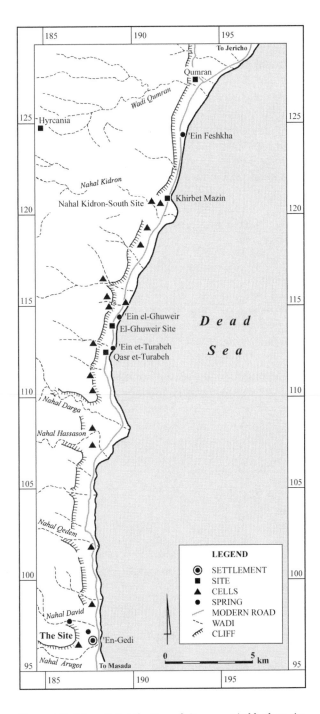

Figure 136. Map of distribution of sites occupied by hermits
between En-Gedi and Qumran.

twenty-eight cells. Analysis of Pliny's testimony supports the assumption that the site above En-Gedi and similar sites were part of a general phenomenon of ascetic colonies along the western shore of the Dead Sea in the Second Temple period.

In the unique settlement pattern characteristic of the Dead Sea region in the Second Temple period, one element consisted of wealthy estate owners, such as those at Qumran, Jericho, and En-Gedi. Another element comprised ascetics who lived on the fringes of the estates, leading a solitary life of contemplation while also working for their subsistence on the nearby estates. For the estate owners, they were a source of cheap and available labor for the various agricultural tasks. The cultivation of the date and balsam plantations required a large workforce all year round to undertake the backbreaking labor. It was in the interest of the estate owners to tolerate the existence of hermit communities on the fringes of the estates. Their employment in these estates enabled the ascetics of the Dead Sea to subsist, since even frugal ascetics needed an income to satisfy their basic needs and to live a life of purity in the desert.

Conclusions

The archaeological picture that emerges from the excavations at Qumran and 'Ein Feshkha does not accord with the historical descriptions of the Essenes and other Jewish ascetics living in the region. The Herodian complex is a large, well-built structure. At its center stood a massive tower surrounded by a stone revetment, in clear contradiction to the literary description of the Essenes as a sect of pacifists. From the rich finds of the excavation, it seems that the owner of Qumran not only was affluent but also had social and economic ties with centers of administration within and beyond Judea.

It thus seems that a complete distinction should be made between the Essenes and the permanent inhabitants of the site of Qumran. The Essenes who, according to Pliny, lived on the western shore of the Dead Sea should be regarded as part of a popular movement whose members took up residence in the Judean Desert for religious reasons. Josephus mentions large groups of people who descended to the desert in their search for messianic redemption, and he relates that he himself lived in the company of ascetics for three years in the desert. The New Testament narratives about the ascetic John the Baptist, who lived near the Jordan River north of the Dead Sea, should be understood as part of this phenomenon. There is no reason to assume that such poor ascetics were able to acquire or maintain a site as large and rich as Qumran, but they could have worked there.

Although the Herodian complex of Qumran is well built and fortified, its numerous doorways argue against its identification as a fort. From the various industrial installations found at the site, such as ovens and soaking pools, and the *columbarium* and processing installations revealed at nearby 'Ein Feshkha, we learn that the main occupation of the inhabitants of Qumran was agriculture and the processing of agricultural produce. The combination of all these elements—the fortified tower, residential wings, and industrial installations—indicates that in the Herodian stage of its existence Qumran functioned as the center of an estate, although in the Hasmonean period it may have served as a fort, a way-station, and a center of the economic activity fostered by the royal dynasty of this period.

Once the significance of Qumran's valuable location at the junction of roads from Jerusalem and Jericho to En-Gedi is recognized, one may then reasonably conjecture that the kings of the Hasmonean dynasty initially established the site as a fort. In this context, as we have seen, Qumran and other fortified sites along the Dead Sea played a key role. The

Hasmonean fortifications were multipurpose structures that served simultaneously as forts to protect the boundaries and ensure safe travel on the roads and as administrative centers and strongholds for the safeguarding of royal revenues. It seems likely that Hasmonean Qumran was built as a *baris,* a fort, and that its inhabitants had the king's confidence.

In the time of Herod, Qumran was rebuilt as a fortified manor house; it continued to function as such until the First Jewish Revolt. The landowner *(dominus)* was probably a member of the Herodian elite who enjoyed close ties with the king. Among the Herodian aristocracy were priestly families from Alexandria and Babylon and old-established Jerusalemite priestly families, such as that of Josephus.[1] Such families were granted lands in various parts of the kingdom, as attested by Josephus regarding his own.[2] Against this background, it may be conjectured that one of the affluent priestly families in Jerusalem owned Qumran and its estate. This assumption may explain the strict observance of the laws of ritual purity by the inhabitants of Qumran (as expressed by the ritual baths and stone vessels found at the site).

The sources indicate that the annexation of Judea to the Roman Empire in 6 C.E. did not change the status of landowners such as the family that owned the Qumran estate. Josephus mentions various estates and towers owned by the Jewish aristocracy in the first century C.E.[3] And no discernible signs of change in the routine activity of the inhabitants of Qumran are evident from the remains. These Jews, strictly observant according to the finds, continued to live at Qumran up to the First Revolt, a crucial fact for any proposal of a scenario explaining the origins of the Dead Sea Scrolls.

We have sought to establish an identity for the residents of Qumran. Now the question must be asked: who were the people who hid the scrolls? In recent years, more scholars have seen the connection between the sectarian scrolls of the Qumran Caves and Sadducean halakah.[4] In some of the scrolls, for example, opposition to the temple might reflect an old Sadducean-Hasmonean feud rather than Essene beliefs, as is usually thought. The Sadducees, a dynasty founded in biblical days (e.g., 2 Sam 8:17, 1 Chr 29:22), produced most of Jerusalem's rich priestly families. Herod replaced these old families with nouveau riche Sadducean "newcomers" who were loyal to him. Nevertheless, some of the older families retained their wealth, among them Josephus, who we know was related to the priestly Hasmoneans. The Sadducees mentioned in the New Testament (e.g., Matt 22:34, Acts 5:17) are a mixture of both these groups.

The word "priests" can sometimes be misleading. These were the most sophisticated, affluent, and fashionable of Jerusalem's citizens and the most romanized. The excavations of Nahman Avigad in Jerusalem reflect their opulent upper-class lifestyle.[5] The priestly

---

[1] On the priestly families in Herod's day, see Stern 1976, 600–612; Schürer 1979, 227–36; Goodman 1987, 60.

[2] According to Josephus's independent testimony, his family had estates in the vicinity of Jerusalem (*Life* 422). After the suppression of the revolt, Titus granted Josephus an estate on the coastal plain in place of the ones that he had lost in the Jerusalem area (*Life* 426).

[3] On the continuity of the land regime of Judea after 6 C.E., see Goodman 1987, 59–60.

[4] See, e.g., Baumgarten 1997; Schiffman 1975; 1990; 2001; and Sussman 1992.

[5] Avigad 1983.

cemetery of Second Temple Jericho, excavated by Rachel Hachlili and Anne Killebrew, contains much evidence of this wealth.[6] The results of both these excavations show that although these people were wealthy and romanized, they were also meticulous in following the halakah and in questions of ritual immersion and ritual purity. The archaeological findings at Qumran, indicating wealth and Roman culture, on the one hand, and mikvehs of the Jerusalem type and stone implements, on the other, suit these families exactly.

We can imagine that after the beginning of the revolt in 66 and before the capture of Jericho in 68 and the beginning of the siege of Jerusalem, priests in Jerusalem of Saddu-cean origin decided to do what they could to save their holy books—the Bible and the Apocrypha—that were in Jerusalem's libraries. They delivered them from the doomed city to someone close to them, apparently of the same social status, the owner of the estate at Qumran. He may have also supplied the jars in which some of the scrolls were found.

Because of the enormous number of scrolls, we can imagine that a whole convoy of pack animals was needed to deliver them to Qumran. The owner of Qumran, probably familiar with the area, helped locate the most suitable caves in which to conceal the scrolls. The mission was accomplished—the scrolls remained hidden for almost nineteen centuries and, thanks to the ironies of history, eventually came back into Jewish hands in Jerusalem.

Some of these same books were taken at this time to the Jewish community in Egypt, where they were saved and copied. Over the course of time, they were forgotten in the attic of the Cairo Synagogue, where Solomon Shechter found them at the end of the nineteenth century. This is the famous Cairo Genizah.

What about the Essenes? Although they did not live in the Qumran estate, or on the other estates along the Dead Sea, or even in the village of En Gedi, we may assume that they lived on the fringes of these oases not far from the date and balsam plantations. The Essenes were certainly part of the settlement picture in the Dead Sea Valley at the end of the Second Temple period, as were other Jewish ascetics who chose to live on the fringes of the region. Here they could be close to God and in harmony with nature but also earn their keep by working in plantations such as those of Qumran, 'Ein Feshka, En-Gedi, and Jericho. Although they worked to maintain themselves, their presence in the desert was a spiritual statement of simple folk at the bottom of the social ladder.

The upper class who lived in sites such as Qumran left amazing remains of architecture and rich assemblages of objects. But these finds have been largely ignored at Qumran and elsewhere. Why? These people, who were Sadducees and belonged to the wealthy class, did not survive the social turmoil of the Second Temple period. It was the heritage of the Pharisees, the Essenes, Jesus, and John the Baptist that won out; ironically, they have left few remains of their existence. In order to understand the period fully, we must put back into context the role played by the wealthy class all over Judea. Excavations at Qumran and elsewhere assist us in this task.

---

[6] Hachlili and Killebrew 1999.

Bibliography

Abel, F. M. 1938. *Géographie de la Palestine.* Vol. 2. Paris: Gabalda.

Adkins, L., and R. Adkins. 1994. *Handbook to Life in Ancient Rome.* New York: Facts on File.

Albani, M., U. Glessmer, and G. Grasshoff. 1997. An Instrument for Determining the Hours of the Day and the Seasons (Sundial). Pages 20–24 in *A Day at Qumran: The Dead Sea Sect and Its Scrolls.* Edited by A. Roitman. Jerusalem: Israel Museum.

Allegro, J. M. 1956. *The Dead Sea Scrolls.* Harmondsworth, Engl.: Penguin.

———. 1960. *The Treasure of the Copper Scroll.* New York: Routledge & Kegan Paul.

———. 1968. *Qumran Cave 4.I.* Discoveries in the Judaean Desert of Jordan 5. Oxford: Clarendon.

Amar, Z. 1997. Agricultural Products in the Jordan Valley during the Middle Ages. (In Hebrew.) Pages 297–326 in *The Village in Ancient Israel.* Edited by E. Dar and Z. Safrai. Tel Aviv: Eretz.

———. 1998a. The Production of Salt and Sulphur from the Dead Sea Region in the Tenth Century according to At-Tamimi. *Palestine Exploration Quarterly* 130:3–7.

———. 1998b. The Ash and the Red Material from Qumran. *Dead Sea Discoveries* 5:1–15.

Amiram, D. H. K. 1997. The Madaba Mosaic Map as a Climate Indicator for the Sixth Century. *Israel Exploration Journal* 47:97–99.

Amit, D. 1989/1990. Khirbet Dah-Dah. *Excavations and Surveys in Israel* 9:162–63.

———. 1993. Ritual Baths (Mikva'ot) from the Second Temple Period in the Hebron Mountains. (In Hebrew.) *Judea and Samaria Research Studies* 3:157–89.

Amit, D., and J. Magness. 2000. Not a Settlement of Hermits or Essenes: A Response to Y. Hirschfeld, "A Settlement of Hermits above 'En Gedi." *Tel Aviv* 27:273–85.

Amit, D., J. Patrich, and Y. Hirschfeld, eds. 2002. *The Aqueducts of Israel.* Journal of Roman Archaeology: Supplementary Series 46. Portsmouth, R.I.: Journal of Roman Archaeology.

Amit, D., J. Zeligman, and I. Zilberbrod. 2001. A Quarry and Workshop for the Production of Stone Vessels on the Eastern Slope of Mount Scopus. (In Hebrew.) *Qadmoniot* 34:102–10.

'Amr, K., et al. 1996. Archaeological Survey of the East Coast of the Dead Sea. *Annual of the Department of Antiquities in Jordan* 40:429–48.

Applebaum, S. 1976. Economic Life in Palestine. Pages 631–700 in *The Jewish People in the First Century.* Edited by S. Safrai and M. Stern. Assen, Neth.: Van Gorcum.

Arensburg, B., and P. Smith. 1983. The Jewish Population of Jericho, 100 B.C.–70 A.D. *Palestine Exploration Quarterly* 115:133–39.

Ariel, D. T. 1993. Hoard of Coins. Pages 86–89 in *Scrolls from the Dead Sea.* Edited by A. Sussmann and R. Peled. Washington, D.C.: Library of Congress.

Avigad, N. 1983. *Discovering Jerusalem.* Jerusalem: Shikmona.

Avi-Yonah, M. 1954. *The Madaba Mosaic Map.* Jerusalem: Israel Exploration Society.

———. 1966. *The Holy Land: A Historical Geography.* Grand Rapids: Baker.

Ayalon, E. 1987. *The Palm Tree: Tree of Life.* (In Hebrew.) Tel Aviv: Eretz Israel Museum.

Bar-Adon, P. 1977. Another Settlement of the Judean Desert Sect at ʿEin el-Ghuweir on the Shores of the Dead Sea. *Bulletin of the American Schools of Oriental Research* 227:1–26.

———. 1981. The Hasmonean Fortresses and the Status of Khirbet Qumran. (In Hebrew.) *Eretz-Israel* 15:349–52.

———. 1989. *Excavations in the Judean Desert.* (In Hebrew with English summary.) ʿ*Atiqot* 9. Jerusalem: Israel Antiquities Authority.

Bar-Nathan, R. 1981. Pottery and Stone Vessels of the Herodian Period. Pages 54–70 in *Greater Herodium.* Qedem 13. Edited by E. Netzer. Jerusalem: Hebrew University of Jerusalem Press.

———. 2002. *The Pottery.* Vol. 3 of *Hasmonean and Herodian Palaces at Jericho.* Jerusalem: Israel Exploration Society.

Barouch, Y. 1996. Road Stations in Judea during the Second Temple Period. (In Hebrew.) *Judea and Samaria Research Studies* 6:125–36.

Baumgarten, A. I. 1997. The Zadokite Priests at Qumran: A Reconsideration. *Dead Sea Discoveries* 4:137–56.

———. 1998. Graeco-Roman Voluntary Associations and Ancient Jewish Sects. Pages 93–111 in *Jews in a Graeco-Roman World.* Edited by M. Goodman. Oxford: Clarendon.

Beit-Arieh, I. 1996. The Dead Sea Region: An Archaeological Perspective. Pages 249–51 in *The Dead Sea.* Edited by T. M. Niemi, Z. Ben-Avraham, and J. R. Gat. New York: Oxford University Press.

Bélis, M. 2002. The Workshops at ʿEin Feshkha: A New Hypothesis. Page 7 in *Qumran: The Site of the Dead Sea Scrolls.* Edited by K. Galor and J. Zangenberg. Providence: Brown University Press.

———. 2003. Des textiles catalogues et commentaires. Pages 207–76 in vol. 2 of *Khirbet Qumrân et ʿAïn Feshkha.* Edited by J.-B. Humbert and J. Gunneweg. Göttingen: Academic Press Fribourg.

Benoit, P., J. T. Milik, and R. de Vaux. 1961. *Les grottes de Murabbaʿat.* Discoveries in the Judaean Desert 2. Oxford: Clarendon.

Berlin, A. 1997. Between Large Forces: Palestine in the Hellenistic Period. *Biblical Archaeologist* 60:3–51.

Bijovsky, G. 2004. A Hoard of Coins of Mattathias Antigonus from ʿEin Feshkha. *Israel Exploration Journal* 53 (in press).

Blake, M. I. 1966. Rivage occidentale de la mer Morte. *Revue biblique* 73:564–66.

Boccaccini, G. 1998. *Beyond the Essenes Hypothesis: The Parting of the Ways between Qumran and Enochic Judaism.* Grand Rapids: Eerdmans.

Braun, O. 1901. Ein Brief des Katholikos Timotheus I über biblische Studien des 9 Jahrhunderts. *Oriens Christianus* 1:299–313.

Broshi, M. 1980. The Population of Western Palestine in the Roman-Byzantine Period. *Bulletin of the American Schools of Oriental Research* 236:1–10.

———. 1992. The Archaeology of Qumran: A Reconsideration. Pages 103–15 in *The Dead Sea Scrolls: Forty Years of Research.* Edited by D. Dimant and U. Rappaport. Leiden: Brill.

———. 1998. Was Qumran, Indeed, a Monastery? Pages 19–37 in *Caves of Enlightenment.* Edited by J. H. Charlesworth. North Richland Hills, Tex.: D. & F. Scott.

———. 1999. Was Qumran a Crossroads? *Revue de Qumran* 19:273–76.

———. 2000. Matrimony and Poverty: Jesus and the Essenes. *Revue de Qumran* 19:629–34.

———. 2001. Qumran and Its Scrolls: Stocktaking. (In Hebrew.) *Cathedra* 100:165–82.

Broshi, M., and H. Eshel. 1999a. How and Where Did the Qumranites Live? *Studies on the Texts of the Desert of Judah* 30:267–72.

———. 1999b. Residential Caves at Qumran. *Dead Sea Discoveries* 6:328–48.

———. 2003. Whose Bones? *Biblical Archaeology Review* 29:26–33, 71.

Burdajewicz, M. 2001. Typology of the Pottery from Khirbet Qumran (French Excavations, 1953–1956). *American Schools of Oriental Research Newsletter* 51:14.

Burgmann, H. 1989. The Saduccean *Torah.* Pages 257–63 in *Temple Scroll Studies.* Edited by G. J. Brooke. Sheffield, Engl.: Sheffield Academic Press.

Campbell, J. 1999. The Qumran Sectarian Writings. Pages 798–821 in *The Early Roman Period.* Vol. 3 of *The Cambridge History of Judaism.* Edited by W. D. Davies and L. Finkelstein. Cambridge: Cambridge University Press.

Cansdale, L. 1997. *Qumran and the Essenes: A Re-evaluation of the Evidence.* Tübingen: J. C. B. Mohr (Paul Siebeck).

———. 2000. The Metamorphosis of the Name Qumran. Pages 631–36 in *The Dead Sea Scrolls: Fifty Years after Their Discovery.* Edited by L. H. Schiffman, E. Tov, and J. C. VanderKam. Jerusalem: Israel Exploration Society.

Carswell, J. 1965. Fastenings on the Qumrân Manuscripts. *Discoveries in the Judean Desert* 4:23–28.

Casson, L. 2001. *Libraries in the Ancient World.* New Haven: Yale University Press.

Chambon, A. 2003. Catalogue des blocs d'architecture localisés ou erratiques. Pages 445–65 in vol. 2 of *Khirbet Qumrân et 'Aïn Feshkha.* Edited by J.-B. Humbert and J. Gunneweg. Göttingen: Academic Press Fribourg.

Charlesworth, J. H. 1988. *Jesus within Judaism.* New York: Doubleday.

Clamer, C. 1997. *Fouilles archéologiques de 'Ain ez-Zâra/Callirrhoë.* Beirut: Institut Français d'Archéologie du Proche Orient.

———. 2003. Jewellery Finds from the Cemetery. Pages 171–83 in vol. 2 of *Khirbet Qumrân et 'Aïn Feshkha.* Edited by J.-B. Humbert and J. Gunneweg. Göttingen: Academic Press Fribourg.

Clermont-Ganneau, C. 1899. *Archaeological Research in Palestine during the Years 1873–1874.* Vol. 2. London: Palestine Exploration Society.

Conder, C. R., and H. H. Kitchener. 1883. *Judaea.* Vol. 3 of *The Survey of Western Palestine.* London: Palestine Exploration Society.

Corbo, V. 1978. La fortezza di Macheronte. *Liber annuus* 28:217–31.

Cotton, H. M. 2001. Ein Gedi between the Two Revolts. *Scripta classica israelica* 20:139–54.

Cotton, H. M., and J. Geiger. 1989. *Masada II, The Yigal Yadin Excavations, 1963–1965, Final Reports: The Latin and Greek Documents.* Jerusalem: Israel Exploration Society.

Cotton, H. M., and A. Yardeni. 1997. *Aramaic, Hebrew, and Greek Documentary Texts from Nahal Hever and Other Sites.* Discoveries in the Judaean Desert 27. Oxford: Clarendon.

Cross, F. M. 1958. *The Ancient Library of Qumran and Modern Biblical Studies.* New York: Doubleday.

Cross, F. M., and E. Eshel. 1997. Ostraca from Khirbet Qumran. *Israel Exploration Journal* 47:17–28.

Cross, F. M., and J. T. Milik. 1956. Explorations in the Judaean Beqeʻah. *Bulletin of the American Schools of Oriental Research* 142:2–17.

Crowfoot, G. M. 1955. The Linen Textiles. Pages 18–38 in *Qumran Cave 1.* By D. Barthélemy and J. T. Milik. Discoveries in the Judaean Desert 1. Oxford: Clarendon.

Dahari, U., and U. Ad. 1998. Shoham Bypass Road. (In Hebrew.) *Hadashot Arkheologiyot* 109:79–83.

Dalman, G. 1914. *Palästinajahrbuch des deutschen evangelischen Instituts für Altertumswissenschaft des heiligen Landes zu Jerusalem.* Vol. 10. Berlin: E. S. Mittler und Sohn.

Dar, S. 1993. The Estate of Ptolemy, Senior Minister of Herod. (In Hebrew.) Pages 36–50 in *Jews and Judaism in the Second Temple, Mishna, and Talmud Period.* (In Hebrew.) Edited by I. Gafni, A. Oppenheimer, and M. Stern. Jerusalem: Yad Izhak Ben Zvi.

Davies, P. R. 1983. *The Damascus Covenant.* Sheffield, Engl.: Sheffield Academic Press.

———. 1988. How Not to Do Archaeology: The Story of Qumran. *Biblical Archaeologist* 51:203–7.

———. 1990. The Birthplace of the Essenes: Where Is Damascus? *Revue de Qumran* 14:503–19.

Dayagi-Mendels, M. 1993. *Perfumes and Cosmetics in the Ancient World.* Jerusalem: Israel Museum.

Dimant, D. 2000. The Library of Qumran: Its Content and Character. Pages 170–76 in *The Dead Sea Scrolls: Fifty Years after Their Discovery.* Edited by L. H. Schiffman, E. Tov, and J. C. VanderKam. Jerusalem: Israel Exploration Society.

Donceel, R. 1997. Qumran. Pages 392–96 in vol. 4 of *The Oxford Encyclopedia of Archaeology in the Near East.* Edited by E. M. Meyers. New York: Oxford University Press.

———. 1998. Poursuites des travaux de publication du matériel archéologique de Khirbet Qumrân: Les lampes en terre-cuite. Pages 87–104 in *Mogilany 1995: Papers on the Dead Sea Scrolls.* Edited by Z. J. Kapera. Kraków: Enigma Press.

———. 1999/2000. Antique Glass from Khirbet Qumrân. *Bulletin de l'Institut royale du patrimoine artistique* 28:9–40.

———. 2002. *Synthèse des observations faites en fouillant les tombes des nécropoles de Khirbet Qumrân et des environs.* Qumran Chronicle 10. Kraków: Enigma Press.

Donceel, R., and P. Donceel-Voûte. 1994. The Archaeology of Khirbet Qumran. Pages 1–38 in *Methods of Investigation of the Dead Sea Scrolls and the Khirbet Qumran Site.* Edited by M. O. Wise et al. New York: New York Academy of Sciences.

Donceel-Voûte, P. 1992. "Coenaculum": La salle à l'étage du locus 30 à Khirbet Qumrân sur la mer Morte. *Res orientales* 4:61–84.

———. 1994. Les ruines de Qumran réinterprétées. *Archeologia* 298:24–35.

———. 1998. Traces of Fragrance along the Dead Sea. *Res orientales* 11:93–117.

Dorsey, D. A. 1991. *The Roads and Highways of Ancient Israel.* Baltimore: Johns Hopkins University Press.

Driver, G. R. 1951. *The Hebrew Scrolls from the Neighbourhood of Jericho and the Dead Sea.* London: Oxford University Press.

Dupont-Sommer, A. 1954. *The Jewish Sect of Qumran and the Essenes.* London: Macmillan.

Eisenberg, E. 2001. Nahal Yarmut. (In Hebrew.) *Hadashot Arkheologiyot* 112:91–93.

Eitam, D. 1996. Mass Production of Cereal Groats in Ancient Israel during the Roman and Byzantine Periods. (In Hebrew.) *Judea and Samaria Research Studies* 6:192–202.

Elder, L. B. 1994. The Woman Question and Female Ascetics among Essenes. *Biblical Archaeologist* 57:220–34.

Elderen, B. van. 1998. Early Christian Libraries. Pages 45–59 in *The Bible as Book.* Edited by J. L. Sharpe and K. van Kampen. London: British Library.

Ellis, S. P. 2000. *Roman Housing.* London: Duckworth.

Eshel, E., H. Eshel, and A. Yardeni. 1992. A Qumran Composition Containing Part of Ps. 154 and a Prayer for the Welfare of King Jonathan and His Kingdom. *Israel Exploration Journal* 42:199–229.

Eshel, H. 1995. A Note on Joshua 15:61–62 and the Identification of the City of Salt. *Israel Exploration Journal* 45:37–40.

———. 2000. The Date of the Founding of Aelia Capitolina. Pages 637–43 in *The Dead Sea Scrolls: Fifty Years after Their Discovery.* Edited by L. H. Schiffman, E. Tov, and J. C. VanderKam. Jerusalem: Israel Exploration Society.

Eshel, H., and B. Zissu. 2000. Ketef Jericho. Pages 3–20 in *Miscellaneous Texts from the Judaean Desert.* By J. Charlesworth et al. Discoveries in the Judaean Desert 38. Oxford: Clarendon.

Farmer, W. R. 1955. The Economic Basis of the Qumran Community. *Theologische Zeitschrift* 11:295–308.

Fassbeck, G. 2000. Die Archäologie Qumrans und ihre Interpretationen: Bemerkungen zur aktuellen Diskussion. Pages 111–28 in *Jericho und Qumran.* Edited by B. Mayer. Regensburg: Friedrich Pustet.

Feliks, Y. 1997. The History of Balsamon Cultivation in the Land of Israel. Pages 275–96 in *The Village in Ancient Israel.* Edited by S. Dar and Z. Safrai. Ramat Gan: Eretz-Geographic Research and Publications.

Fernández Castro, M. C. 1982. *Villas romanas en España.* Madrid: Ministerio de Cultura.

Finkelstein, I. 1990. A Few Notes on Demographic Data from Recent Generations and Ethnoarchaeology. *Palestine Exploration Quarterly* 22:47–52.

Fischer, M., M. Gichon, and O. Tal. 2000. *The Officina.* Vol. 2 of *'En Boqeq, Excavations in an Oasis on the Dead Sea.* Mainz am Rhein: P. von Zabern.

Fischer, M., and O. Tal. 2000. Pottery. Pages 29–68 in *The Officina.* Vol. 2 of *'En Boqeq: Excavations in an Oasis on the Dead Sea.* By M. Fischer, M. Gichon, and O. Tal. Mainz am Rhein: P. von Zabern.

Foerster, G. 1981. The Conquest of John Hyrcanus I in Moab and the Identification of Samaga-Samoge. (In Hebrew.) *Eretz-Israel* 19:353–55.

———. 1995. *Masada V, the Yigal Yadin Excavations, 1963–1965, Final Reports: Art and Architecture.* Jerusalem: Israel Exploration Society.

Frankel, R. 2003. The Olynthus Mill, Its Origin and Diffusion: Typology and Distribution. *American Journal of Archaeology* 107:1–21.

Frumkin, A. 1997. The Holocene History of Dead Sea Levels. Pages 237–48 in *The Dead Sea: The Lake and Its Setting.* Edited by T. M. Niemi, Z. Ben-Avraham, and J. R. Gat. New York: Oxford University Press.

Frumkin, A., and Y. Elitzur. 2001. The Rise and Fall of the Dead Sea. *Biblical Archaeology Review* 27:43–50.

Galor, K. 2002. Qumran's Plastered Installations: Cisterns or Immersion Pools? Pages 33–46 in *Cura aquarum in Israel.* Edited by C. Ohlig. Y. Peleg, and T. Tsuk. Schriften der Deutschen Wasserhistorischen Gesellschaft 1. Siegburg, Germany: Deutsch Wasserhistoricsche Gesellschaft.

———. 2003. Plastered Pools: A New Perspective. Pages 291–320 in vol. 2 of *Khirbet Qumrân et 'Aïn Feshkha.* Edited by J.-B. Humbert and J. Gunneweg. Göttingen: Academic Press Fribourg.

Galor, K., Humbert, J.-B., Zangenberg, J., eds. Forthcoming. *The Site of the Dead Sea Scrolls: Archaeological Interpretations and Debates. Proceedings of the Conference Held at Brown University, November 17–19, 2002.* Leiden: E. J. Brill.

Garbrecht G., and Y. Peleg. 1994. The Water Supply of the Desert Fortresses in the Jordan Valley. *Biblical Archaeologist* 57:161–70.

Gat, Z., and O. Karni. 1998. The Evaporation Regime over the Samaria and Judea. (In Hebrew.) *Judea and Samaria Research Studies* 8:257–74.

Gibson, S. 1983. The Stone Vessels Industry at Hizma. *Israel Exploration Journal* 31:176–88.

———. 1994. The Tel el-Judeideh (Tel Goded) Excavations: A Reappraisal Based on Archival Records in the Palestinian Exploration Fund. *Tel Aviv* 21:194–234.

Gichon, M. 2000. The Industry. Pages 93–126 in *The Officina.* Vol. 2 of *'En Boqeq: Excavations in an Oasis on the Dead Sea.* By M. Fischer, M. Gichon, and O. Tal. Mainz am Rhein: P. von Zabern.

Gleason, K. 1993. A Garden Excavation in the Oasis Palace of Herod the Great at Jericho. *Landscape Journal* 12:156–67.

Glessmer, U. 1998. Calendars in the Qumran Scrolls. Pages 213–78 in vol. 1 of *The Dead Sea Scrolls after Fifty Years: A Comprehensive Assessment.* Edited by P. W. Flint and J. C. VanderKam. Boston: E. J. Brill.

Glessmer, U., and M. Abani. 1999. An Astronomical Measuring Instrument from Qumran. *Studies on the Texts of the Desert of Judah* 30:407–42.

Golb, N. 1994. Khirbet Qumran and the Manuscript Finds of the Judean Wilderness. Pages 51–72 in *Methods of Investigation of the Dead Sea Scrolls and the Khirbet Qumran Site.* Edited by M. O. Wise et al. New York: New York Academy of Sciences.

———. 1995. *Who Wrote the Dead Sea Scrolls?* New York: Scribner.

———. 1999. The Dead Sea Scrolls and Pre-Tannaitic Judaism. Pages 822–51 in *The Early Roman Period.* Vol. 3 of *The Cambridge History of Judaism.* Edited by W. D. Davies and L. Finkelstein. Cambridge: Cambridge University Press.

Goodman, M. 1987. *The Ruling Class of Judaea.* Cambridge: Cambridge University Press.

———. 1995. A Note on the Qumran Sectarians, the Essenes, and Josephus. *Journal of Jewish Studies* 46:161–66.

Goranson, S. 1992. An Inkwell from Qumran. *Michmanim* 6:37–40.

———. 1994. Qumran: A Hive of Scribal Activity? *Biblical Archaeology Review* 20:37–39.

Gunneweg, G. and M. Balla. 2003. Neutron Activation Analysis of Scroll Jars and Common Ware. Pages 3–53 in vol. 2 of *Khirbet Qumrân et 'Aïn Feshkha*. Edited by J.-B. Humbert and J. Gunneweg. Göttingen: Academic Press Fribourg.

Hachlili, R. 1993. Burial Practices at Qumran. *Revue de Qumran* 16:247–64.

———. 2000. The Qumran Cemetery: A Reconsideration. Pages 661–72 in *The Dead Sea Scrolls: Fifty Years after Their Discovery*. Edited by L. H. Schiffman, E. Tov, and J. C. VanderKam. Jerusalem: Israel Exploration Society.

Hachlili, R., and A. Killebrew. 1999. *Jericho: The Jewish Cemetery of the Second Temple Period*. IAA Reports 7. Jerusalem: Israel Antiquities Authority.

Hadas, G. 1993. Where Was the Harbour of 'En-Gedi Situated? *Israel Exploration Journal* 43:45–49.

———. 1994. *Nine Tombs of the Second Temple Period at 'En Gedi*. ʿAtiqot 24. Jerusalem: Israel Antiquities Authority.

———. 2002. Irrigation Agriculture in the Oasis of Ein Gedi and Its Parallels in the Oases around the Dead Sea during the Roman-Byzantine Period. (In Hebrew.) Ph.D. diss., Hebrew University of Jerusalem.

Hammond, P. C. 1959. The Nabatean Bitumen Industry at the Dead Sea. *Biblical Archaeologist* 27:40–48.

Harding, G. L. 1949. The Dead Sea Scrolls. *Palestine Exploration Quarterly* 81:112–16.

———. 1952. Khirbet Qumran and Wadhy Muraba'at. *Palestine Exploration Quarterly* 84:104–9.

———. 1955. The Archaeological Finds. Pages 3–7 in *Qumran Cave 1*. By D. Barthélemy and J. T. Milik. Discoveries in the Judaean Desert 1. Oxford: Clarendon.

———. 1958. Recent Discoveries in Jordan. *Palestine Exploration Quarterly* 90:7–18.

Har-El, M. 2000. Agriculture. Pages 13–16 in vol. 1 of *Encyclopedia of the Dead Sea Scrolls*. Edited by L. H. Schiffman and J. C. VanderKam. Oxford: Oxford University Press.

Hidiroglou, P. 2000. Aqueducts, Basins, and Cisterns: The Water Systems of Qumran. *Near Eastern Archaeology* 63:138–39.

Hirschfeld, Y. 1991. Gerasimus and His Laura in the Jordan Valley. *Revue biblique* 98:419–30.

———. 1992. *The Judean Desert Monasteries in the Byzantine Period*. New Haven: Yale University Press.

———. 1995. *The Palestinian Dwelling in the Roman-Byzantine Period*. Jerusalem: Franciscan Printing Press.

———. 1998. Early Roman Manor Houses in Judea and the Site of Khirbet Qumran. *Journal of Near Eastern Studies* 57:161–89.

———. 2000a. *Ramat Hanadiv Excavations*. Jerusalem: Israel Exploration Society.

———. 2000b. A Settlement of Hermits above 'En Gedi. *Tel Aviv* 27:103–55.

———. 2000c. The Architectural Context of Qumran. Pages 673–83 in *The Dead Sea Scrolls Fifty Years after Their Discovery*. Edited by L. H. Schiffman, E. Tov, and J. C. VanderKam. Jerusalem: Israel Exploration Society.

———. 2001–02. The Monastery of Marda: Masada in the Byzantine Period. *Bulletin of the Anglo-Israel Archaeological Society* 19–20:119–56.

———. 2002. A Royal Marina on the Dead Sea? *Eretz: The Geographic Magazine from Is-rael* 83:38–43.

———. 2004a. Excavations at 'Ein Feshkha, 2001: Final Report. *Israel Exploration Journal* 54:37–74.

———. 2004b. The Library of King Herod in the Northern Palace of Masada. *Scripta classica israelica* (in press).

———. 2004c. A Climactic Change in the Early Byzantine Period? Some Archaeological Evidence. *Palestine Exploration Quarterly* (in press).

Hirschfeld, Y., and D. T. Ariel. Forthcoming. A Coin Assemblage from the Reign of Alexander Jannaeus (103–76 B.C.E.) Found on the Shore of the Dead Sea. *Israel Exploration Journal.*

Hollenback, G. M. 2000. The Qumran Roundel: An Equatorial Sundial? *Discoveries in the Judean Desert* 7:123–29.

Hopwood, K. 1986. Towers, Territory, and Terror: How the East was Held. Pages 343–56 in vol. 2 of *The Defence of the Roman and Byzantine East.* Edited by P. Freedman and D. Kennedy. BAR International 297. Oxford: British Archaeological Reports.

Humbert, J.-B. 1994. L'espace sacré à Qumrân: Propositions pour l'archéologie. *Revue biblique* 101/102:161–214.

———. 1999. Qumrân, ésseniens, et architecture. Pages 183–96 in *Antikes Judentum und frühes Christentum.* Edited by B. Kollmann, W. Reinbold, and A. Steudel. New York: W. de Gruyter.

———. 2000. Interpreting the Qumran Site. *Near Eastern Archaeology* 63:140–43.

———. 2003. Reconsideration of the Archaeological Interpretation. Pages 419–44 of vol. 2 of *Khirbet Qumrân et 'Aïn Feshkha.* Edited by J.-B. Humbert and J. Gunneweg. Göttingen: Academic Press Fribourg.

Humbert, J.-B., and A. Chambon. 1994. *Fouilles de Khirbet Qumrân et de 'Ain Feshkha.* Vol. 1. Göttingen: Academic Press Fribourg.

Humbert, J.-B., and J. Gunneweg, eds. 2003. *Khirbet Qumrân et 'Aïn Feshkha.* 2 vols. Göttingen: Academic Press Fribourg.

Hutchesson, I. 2000. The Essene Hypothesis after Fifty Years: An Assessment. *Qumran Chronicle* 9:17–34.

Ilan, Z., and D. Amit. 2002. The Aqueduct of Qumran. Pages 380–86 in *The Aqueducts of Israel.* Edited by D. Amit, J. Patrich, and Y. Hirschfeld. Journal of Roman Archaeology: Supplementary Series 46. Portsmouth, R.I.: Journal of Roman Archaeology.

Isaac, B. 1984. Bandits in Judaea and Arabia. *Harvard Studies in Classical Philology* 88:171–203.

———. 1993. The Function of *Burgi* and *Burgarii* (in Hebrew). Pages 235–42 in *Jews and Judaism in the Second Temple, Mishna and Talmud Period.* Edited by I. Gafni, A. Oppenheimer, and M. Stern. Jerusalem: Yad Izhak Ben Zvi.

Israel, I. 1993. Ashqelon. *Excavations and Surveys in Israel* 13:100–105.

Jashemski, W. F. 1979. *The Gardens of Pompeii.* New York: Caratzas Brothers.

———. 1987. Recently Excavated Gardens of the Villas at Boscoreale and Oplontis. Pages 31–76 in *Ancient Roman Villa Gardens.* Edited by E. B. Macdougall. Washington, D.C.: Dumbarton Oaks.

Jones, A. H. M. 1938. *The Herods of Judaea.* Oxford: Oxford University Press.

Josephus. 1926–1965. Translated by H. St. J. Thackeray et al. 10 vols. Loeb Classical Library. Cambridge, Mass.: Harvard University Press.

Kapera, Z. J. 1994. Some Remarks on the Qumran Cemetery. Pages 97–114 in *Methods of Investigation of the Dead Sea Scrolls and the Khirbet Qumran Site*. Edited by M. O. Wise et al. New York: New York Academy of Sciences.

———. 1995. Recent Research on the Qumran Cemetery. *Qumran Chronicle* 5:123–32.

———. 1996. Khirbet Qumran: A Monastic Settlement or a Villa Rustica? *Qumran Chronicle* 6:93–114.

———. 2000. Some Notes on the Statistical Elements in the Interpretation of the Qumran Cemetery. *Qumran Chronicle* 9:139–52.

Kasher, A. 1993. The Wars of Alexander Jannaeus against the Nabateans. (In Hebrew.) Pages 379–92 in *The Hasmonean State*. Edited by U. Rappaport and I. Ronen. Jerusalem: Yad Izhak Ben Zvi.

Kenael, B. 1958. Some Observations on the Chronology of Khirbet Qumran. (In Hebrew.) *Eretz-Israel* 5:165–69.

Khairy, N. I. 1980. Ink-wells of the Roman Period from Jordan. *Levant* 12:155–63.

Kloner, A. 1996. Central-Pillar Spiral Staircases in the Hellenistic Period. (In Hebrew.) *Eretz-Israel* 25:484–89.

Kol-Yaakov, S. 2000. Various Objects from the Hellenistic, Roman, and Byzantine Periods. Pages 473–503 in *Ramat Hanadiv Excavations*. By Y. Hirschfeld. Jerusalem: Israel Exploration Society.

Kraft, R. A. 2001. Pliny on Essenes, Pliny on Jews. *Dead Sea Discoveries* 8:255–61.

Laperrousaz, E. M. 1976. *Qumrân: L'établissement essénien des bords de la mer Morte*. Paris: Picard.

Lapp, P. W. 1961. *Palestine Ceramic Chronology, 200 B.C.–A.D. 70*. New Haven: American Schools of Oriental Research.

Lawrence, A. W. 1979. *Greek Aims in Fortifications*. Oxford: Oxford University Press.

Lemaire, A. 2000. Reflexions sur la fonction du site du Qumrân. Pages 37–42 in *Józef Tadeusz Milik et cinquantaire de la découverte des manuscrits de la mer Morte de Qumrân*. Edited by D. Dlugosz and H. Ralajczak. Warsaw: Centre Scientifique de l'Académie Polonaise des Sciences à Paris.

———. 2003. Inscriptions due Khirbet, des grottes et de ʿAin Feshkha. Pages 341–88 in vol. 2 of *Khirbet Qumrân et ʿAïn Feshkha*. Edited by J.-B. Humbert and J. Gunneweg. Göttingen: Academic Press Fribourg.

Levy, A. 1998. Bad Timing: Time to Get a New Theory. *Biblical Archaeology Review* 24.4:18–23.

Lönnqvist, M., and K. Lönnqvist. 2002. *Archaeology of the Hidden Qumran: The New Paradigm*. Helsinki: Helsinki University Press.

Magen, I., and Y. Peleg. 2002. Important New Findings at Qumran. Page 5 in *Qumran: The Site of the Dead Sea Scrolls*. Edited by K. Galor and J. Zangenberg. Providence: Brown University Press.

Magen, Y. 2002. *The Stone Vessel Industry in the Second Temple Period*. Jerusalem: Israel Exploration Society.

Magness, J. 1995. The Chronology of the Settlement at Qumran in the Herodian Period. *Dead Sea Discoveries* 2:58–65.

———. 1998. Qumran Archaeology: Past Perspectives and Future Prospects. Pages 47–77 in vol. 1 of *The Dead Sea Scrolls after Fifty Years: A Comprehensive Assessment.* Edited by P. W. Flint and J. C. VanderKam. Boston: E. J. Brill.

———. 2000. A Reassessment of the Excavations of Qumran. Pages 708–19 in *The Dead Sea Scrolls: Fifty Years after Their Discovery.* Edited by L. H. Schiffman, E. Tov, and J. C. VanderKam. Jerusalem: Israel Exploration Society.

———. 2002. *The Archaeology of Qumran and the Dead Sea Scrolls.* Grand Rapids: Eerdmans.

Markus, M. 1970. Rosh Tzuqim. (In Hebrew.) Pages 176–78 in *Israel Guide: The Judean Desert and the Jordan Valley.* Edited by S. Ben Yoseph. Jerusalem: Keter.

———. 1986. *The Northern Judean Desert.* (In Hebrew.) Jerusalem: Israel Nature and Parks Authority.

Martínez, F. G., and D. W. Parry. 1996. *A Bibliography of the Finds in the Desert of Judah, 1970–1995.* Studies on the Texts of the Desert of Judah 19. New York: Brill.

Masterman, E. W. G. 1902. Observation of the Dead Sea Levels, ʿAin el-Feshkha, el-Hajar, el-Asbeh, and Khurbat Kumrân. *Palestine Exploration Fund Quarterly Statement* 27:155–67.

———. 1903. Notes on Some Ruins and a Rock-Cut Aqueduct in the Wady Kumrân. *Palestine Exploration Fund Quarterly Statement* 28:264–67.

Mazar, B. 1993. En-Gedi. Pages 399–405 in vol. 2 of *The New Encyclopedia of Archaeological Excavations in the Holy Land.* Edited by E. Stern. Jerusalem: Israel Exploration Society & Carta.

Mazar, B., T. Dothan, and I. Dunayevsky. 1966. *ʿEn-Gedi: The First and Second Seasons of Excavation, 1961–1962. ʿAtiqot* 5. Jerusalem: Department of Antiquities and Museums.

Mazor, E. 1997. Groundwaters along the Western Dead Sea Shore. Pages 265–75 in *The Dead Sea: The Lake and Its Setting.* Edited by T. M. Niemi, Z. Ben-Avraham, and J. R. Gat. New York: Oxford University Press.

Mazor, E., and M. Molcho. 1972. Geochemical Studies on the Feshcha Springs, Dead Sea Basin. *Journal of Hydrology* 15:37–47.

McKay, A. G. 1975. *Houses, Villas, and Palaces in the Roman World.* London: Thames & Hudson.

McNicholl, A. W. 1997. *Hellenistic Fortifications from the Aegean to the Euphrates.* Oxford: Clarendon.

Mébarki, F. 2000. Józef Tadeusz Milik: Memories of Fieldwork. *Near Eastern Archaeology* 63:131–35.

Mendel, P. 1992. Birah as an Architectural Term in Rabbinic Literature. (In Hebrew.) *Tarbiz* 61:195–217.

Metzger, B. M. 1959. The Furniture in the Scriptorium at Qumran. *Revue de Qumran* 4:509–15.

Milik, J. T. 1959. *Ten Years of Discovery in the Wilderness of Judea.* Studies in Biblical Theology. Naperville, Ill.: Allenson.

———. 1962. Le rouleau de cuivre provenant de la grotte 3Q (3Q 15). Pages 201–302 in *Les "petites grottes" de Qumrân.* By M. Baillet, J. T. Milik, and R. de Vaux. Discoveries in the Judaean Desert of Jordan 3. Oxford: Clarendon.

———. 1977. Qumrân grotte 4: Tefillin, mezuzot, et targums. Pages 33–90 in *Qumrân grotte 4.II.* By R. de Vaux and J. T. Milik. Discoveries in the Judaean Desert 6. Oxford: Clarendon.

Murphy, C. M. 2002. *Wealth in the Dead Sea Scrolls and in the Qumran Community.* Studies on the Texts of the Desert of Judah 40. Boston: E. J. Brill.

Naveh, J. 1985. Published and Unpublished Aramaic Ostraca. *'Atiqot* 17:114–21.

Netzer, E. 1978. Miqvaot (Ritual Baths) of the Second Temple Period at Jericho. (In Hebrew.) *Qadmoniot* 11:54–59.

———. 1991. *Masada III, the Yigal Yadin Excavations, 1963–1965, Final Reports: The Buildings, Stratigraphy and Architecture.* Jerusalem: Israel Exploration Society.

———. 1993. Jericho, Hellenistic to Early Roman Period. Pages 681–91 in vol. 2 of *The New Encyclopedia of Archaeological Excavations in the Holy Land.* Edited by E. Stern. Jerusalem: Israel Exploration Society & Carta.

———. 2001a. *Hasmonean and Herodian Palaces at Jericho: Final Reports of the 1973–1987 Excavations.* Vol. 1. Jerusalem: Israel Exploration Society.

———. 2001b. *The Palaces of the Hasmoneans and Herod the Great.* Jerusalem: Yad Izhak Ben Zvi.

———. 2002a. Date "Winepress" in the Royal Estate at Jericho. (In Hebrew.) *Judea and Samaria Research Studies* 11:69–80.

———. 2002b. A Proposal Concerning the Utilization of the Ritual Bath at Qumran. (In Hebrew.) *Qadmoniot* 35:116–17.

Nielsen, I. 1994. *Hellenistic Palaces: Tradition and Renewal.* Aarhus, Denmark: Aarhus University Press.

Norton, J. 2003. Reassessment of Controversial Studies on the Cemetery. Pages 107–27 in vol. 2 of *Khirbet Qumrân et 'Aïn Feshkha.* Edited by J.-B. Humbert and J. Gunneweg. Göttingen: Academic Press Fribourg.

Nowicka, M. 1975. *Les maisons à tour dans le monde grec.* Wroclaw: Academia Scientiarum Polona.

Ofer, A. 1998. Qumran is Secaca. (In Hebrew.) *Qadmoniot* 31:65.

Oppenheimer, A. 1980. Benevolent Societies in Jerusalem. (In Hebrew.) Pages 178–90 in *Jerusalem in the Second Temple Period.* Edited by A. Oppenheimer, U. Rappaport, and M. Stern. Jerusalem: Yad Izhak Ben Zvi.

Palmer, E. H. 1881. *The Survey of Palestine: Arabic and English Name List.* London: Palestine Exploration Fund.

Parker, S. T. 2000. The Roman 'Aqaba Project: The 1997 and 1998 Campaigns. *Annual of the Department of Antiquities of Jordan* 44:373–94.

Pastor, J. 1997. *Land and Economy in Ancient Palestine.* New York: Routledge.

Patrich, J. 1993. Hyrcania. Pages 639–41 in vol. 2 of *The New Encyclopedia of Archaeological Excavations in the Holy Land.* Edited by E. Stern. Jerusalem: Israel Exploration Society & Carta.

———. 1994a. Khirbet Qumran in Light of New Archaeological Explorations in the Qumran Caves. Pages 73–96 in *Methods of Investigation of the Dead Sea Scrolls and the Khirbet Qumran Site.* Edited by M. O. Wise et al. New York: New York Academy of Sciences.

———. 1994b. Graves and Burial Practices in Talmudic Sources. (In Hebrew.) Pages 190–211 in *Graves and Burial Practices in Israel in the Ancient Period.* Edited by I. Singer. Jerusalem: Yad Izhak Ben Zvi.

———. 1995. *Sabas, Leader of Palestinian Monasticism: A Comparative Study in Eastern Monasticism, Fourth to Seventh Centuries.* Washington, D.C.: Dumbarton Oaks Research Library and Collection.

———. 2000. Did Extra-mural Dwelling Quarters Exist at Qumran? Pages 720–27 in *The Dead Sea Scrolls: Fifty Years after Their Discovery.* Edited by L. H. Schiffman, E. Tov, and J. C. VanderKam. Jerusalem: Israel Exploration Society.

———. 2002. The Aqueducts of Hyrcania-Kastellion. Pages 336–52 in *The Aqueducts of Israel.* Edited by D. Amit, J. Patrich, and Y. Hirschfeld. Journal of Roman Archaeology: Supplementary Series 46. Portsmouth, R.I.: Journal of Roman Archaeology.

Patrich, J., and B. Arubas. 1989. A Juglet Containing Balsam Oil (?) from a Cave near Qumran. *Israel Exploration Journal* 39:43–59.

Percival, J. 1996. Houses in the Country. Pages 65–90 in *Roman Domestic Buildings.* Edited by I. M. Barton. Exeter, Engl.: Exeter University Press.

Pfann, S. 1994. The Wine Press (and Miqveh) at Kh. Qumran (Loc. 75 and 69). *Revue biblique* 101/102:212–14.

———. 2003. *Excavations of Khirbet Qumran and 'Ain Feshkha.* Göttingen: Academic Press Fribourg.

Philo. 1993. Translated by C. D. Yonge. Peabody, Mass.: Hendrickson.

Pliny. *Natural History.* 1942. Translated by H. Rackham. 10 vols. Loeb Classical Library. Cambridge, Mass.: Harvard University Press.

Politis, K. D. 1998a. Rescue Excavations in the Nabatean Cemetery at Khirbet Qazone. *Annual of the Department of Antiquities of Jordan* 42:611–14.

———. 1998b. Survey and Rescue Collections in the Ghawr es-Safi. *Annual of the Department of Antiquities of Jordan* 42:627–33.

———. 1999. The Nabatean Cemetery at Khirbet Qazone. *Near Eastern Archaeology* 62:128.

Poole, J. B., and R. Reed. 1961. The "Tannery" of 'Ain Feshkha. *Palestine Exploration Quarterly* 93:114–23.

Porath, J. 1986. Aspects of the Development of Ancient Irrigation Agriculture in Jericho and Ein Gedi. (In Hebrew.) Pages 127–41 in *Man and Land in Eretz-Israel in Antiquity.* Edited by A. Kasher, A. Oppenheimer, and U. Rappaport. Jerusalem: Yad Izhak Ben Zvi.

———. 1998. Horbat Qumran. *Excavations and Surveys in Israel* 13:84.

Potcher, O. 2000. Environmental and Climatological Aspects of the *Officina.* Pages 21–27 in *The Officina.* Vol. 2 of *'En Boqeq: Excavations in an Oasis on the Dead Sea.* By M. Fischer, M. Gichon, and O. Tal. Mainz am Rhein: P. von Zabern.

Puech, E. 1998. The Necropolis of Khirbet Qumran and 'Ain el-Ghuweir and the Essene Belief in Afterlife. *Bulletin of the American Schools of Oriental Research* 312:21–36.

Rapuano, Y. 2001. The Hasmonean Period "Synagogue" at Jericho and the Council Chamber Building at Qumran. *Israel Exploration Journal* 91:48–56.

Raz, E. 1993. *Sefer Yam Hamelah.* (In Hebrew.) Jerusalem: Nature and Parks Authority.

Reed, W. M. 1954. The Qumran Caves Expedition of March, 1952. *Bulletin of the American Schools of Oriental Research* 135:8–13.

Regev, E. 1996. Ritual Baths of Jewish Groups and Sects in the Second Temple Period. *Cathedra* 79:3–20.

———. 2001. The Individualistic Meaning of Jewish Ossuaries: A Socio-anthropological Perspective on Burial Practice. *Palestine Exploration Quarterly* 133:39–49.

Reich, R. 1988. A Note on Samaritan Ritual Baths. (In Hebrew.) Pages 242–44 in *Jews, Samaritans, and Christians in Byzantine Palestine*. Edited by D. Jacoby and Y. Tsafrir. Jerusalem: Yad Izhak Ben Zvi.

———. 1990. Miqwa'ot (Jewish Ritual Immersion Baths) in Eretz Israel in the Second Temple and the Mishnah and Talmud Periods. (In Hebrew.) Ph.D. diss., Hebrew University of Jerusalem.

———. 1995. A Note on the Function of Room 3 (the "Scriptorium") at Khirbet Qumran. *Journal of Jewish Studies* 46:157–60.

———. 2000. Miqwa'ot at Khirbet Qumran and the Jerusalem Connection. Pages 728–31 in *The Dead Sea Scrolls: Fifty Years after Their Discovery*. Edited by L. H. Schiffman, E. Tov, and J. C. VanderKam. Jerusalem: Israel Exploration Society.

Rengstorf, K. H. 1960. *Hirbet Qumran und die Bibliothek vom Toten Meer*. Stuttgart: Kohlhammer.

Rohrhirsch, F., and O. Röhrer-Ertl. 2001. Die Individuen des Gräberfelder von Hirbet Qumran aus der *Collectio* Kurth: Eine Zusammenfassung. *Zeitschrift des deutschen Palästina-Vereins* 117:164–70.

Roitman, A. 1997. *A Day at Qumran: The Dead Sea Sect and Its Scrolls*. Jerusalem: Israel Museum.

Roller, D. W. 1998. *The Building Program of Herod the Great*. Berkeley: University of California Press.

Rosenthal, R., and R. Sivan. 1978. *Ancient Lamps in the Schloessinger Collection*. Qedem 8. Jerusalem: Hebrew University of Jerusalem.

Roth, C. 1959. Why the Qumran Sect Cannot Have Been Essenes. *Revue de Qumran* 3:417–22.

Safrai, Z. 2000. Qumran or Ein Gedi: Where Did the Dead Sea Sect Live? (In Hebrew.) *Cathedra* 96:41–56.

Sandmel, S. 1979. *Philo of Alexandria: An Introduction*. New York: Oxford University Press.

Sapiro, S. 1997. Concerning the Identification of Qumran. *Qumran Chronicle* 7:91–116, 215–23.

Schalit, A. 1964. *King Herod: Portrait of a Ruler*. (In Hebrew.) Jerusalem: Bialik Press.

Schechter, S. 1910. *Fragments of a Zadokite Work*. Vol. 1. Cambridge: Cambridge University Press.

Schick, T. 1993. Textiles. Pages 118–27 in *Scrolls from the Dead Sea*. Edited by A. Sussmann and R. Peled. Washington, D.C.: Library of Congress.

Schiffman, L. H. 1975. *The Halakhah at Qumran*. Leiden: Brill.

———. 1989. The Temple Scroll and the System of Jewish Law of the Second Temple Period. Pages 239–55 in *Temple Scroll Studies*. Edited by G. J. Brooke. Sheffield, Engl.: Sheffield Academic Press.

————. 1990. A New Halakhic Letter (4Q MMT) and the Origin of the Dead Sea Sect. *Biblical Archaeologist* 53:64–73.

————. 1993. *Law, Custom, and Messianism in the Dead Sea Scrolls.* (In Hebrew.) Jerusalem: Bialik Press.

————. 2001. Pharisaic and Sadducean Halakha in Light of the Dead Sea Scrolls. *Dead Sea Discoveries* 8:285–99.

Schult, H. 1966. Zwei Häfen aus römischer Zeit am Toten Meer: Rujum el-bahr und el-beled (ez-Zara). *Zeitschrift des deutschen Palästina-Vereins* 82:139–48.

Schürer, E. 1979. *The History of the Jewish People in the Age of Jesus Christ (175 B.C.–A.D. 135).* Vol. 2. Edinburgh: Clark.

Schwartz, D. R. 1992. *Studies in the Jewish Background of Christianity.* Tübingen: Mohr.

Seligman, J. 1995. Jerusalem, Kh. Ka'kul. *Excavations and Surveys in Israel* 13:69–70.

Shanks, H. 1998. *The Mystery and Meaning of the Dead Sea Scrolls.* New York: Random House.

————. 2002. Chief Scroll Editor Opens Up. *Biblical Archaeology Review* 28.3:32–35, 62.

Sharabani, M. 1989. Monnaies de Qumrân au Musée Rockefeller de Jérusalem. *Revue biblique* 87:274–84.

Shatzman, I. 1991. *The Armies of the Hasmonaeans and Herod.* Tübingen: Mohr.

Shavit, Y. 1994. The "Qumran Library" in the Light of the Attitude towards Books and Libraries in the Second Temple Period. Pages 299–318 in *Methods of Investigation of the Dead Sea Scrolls and the Khirbet Qumran Site.* Edited by M. O. Wise et al. New York: New York Academy of Sciences.

Silberman, N. A. 1993. *A Prophet from amongst You: The Life of Yigael Yadin, Soldier, Scholar, and Mythmaker of Modern Israel.* Reading, Mass.: Addison-Wesley.

————. 2000. The Scrolls as Scriptures: Qumran and the Popular Religious Imagination in the Late Twentieth Century. Pages 919–26 in *The Dead Sea Scrolls: Fifty Years after Their Discovery.* Edited by L. H. Schiffman, E. Tov, and J. C. VanderKam. Jerusalem: Israel Exploration Society.

Smith, J. T. 1997. *Roman Villas: A Study in Social Structure.* New York: Routledge.

Smith, R. H. 1964. The Household Lamps of Palestine in Intertestamental Times. *Biblical Archaeologist* 27:101–24.

————. 1966. The Household Lamps of Palestine in New Testament Times. *Biblical Archaeologist* 29:2–27.

Sperber, D. 1976. On the πύργος as a Farm Building. *Association for Jewish Studies Review* 1:359–61.

Stager, L. E. 1976. Farming in the Judean Desert during the Iron Age. *Bulletin of the American Schools of Oriental Research* 221:145–58.

Steckoll, S. H. 1968. Preliminary Excavation Report in the Qumran Cemetery. *Revue de Qumran* 6:323–34.

Stegemann, H. 1998. *The Library of Qumran: On the Essenes, Qumran, John the Baptist, and Jesus.* Grand Rapids: Eerdmans.

Stern, E. 1994. The Eastern Border of the Kingdom of Judah in Its Last Days. Pages 399–409 in *Scripture and Other Artifacts: Essays on the Bible and Archaeology.* Edited by M. D. Coogan, J. C. Exum, and L. E. Stager. Louisville: Westminster John Knox.

Stern, M. 1974. The Province of Judaea. Pages 308–76 in vol. 1 of *The Jewish People in the First Century*. Edited by S. Safrai and M. Stern. Assen, Neth.: Van Gorcum.

———. 1976. The Province of Judaea, Aspects of Jewish Society: The Priesthood and Other Classes. Pages 561–630 in *The Jewish People in the First Century*. Edited by S. Safrai and M. Stern. Assen, Neth.: Van Gorcum.

Strobel, A. 1977. Auf den Suche nach Machärus und Kallirrhoe. *Zeitschrift des deutschen Palästina-Vereins* 93:247–67.

Strobel, A., and C. Clamer. 1986. Excavations at ez-Zara. *Annual of the Department of Antiquities of Jordan* 30:381–84.

Sukenik, E. L. 1948. *Megillot Genuzot*. (In Hebrew.) Jerusalem: Magness.

Sumner, W. M. 1979. Estimating Population by Analogy: An Example. Pages 164–74 in *Ethnoarchaeology: Implications of Ethnography for Archaeology*. Edited by C. Kramer. New York: Academia.

Sussmann, A., and R. Peled. 1993. *Scrolls from the Dead Sea*. Washington, D.C.: Library of Congress.

Sussmann, Y. 1992. The History of *Halakha* and the Dead Sea Scrolls. (In Hebrew.) Pages 99–127 in *The Scrolls of the Judean Desert: Forty Years of Research*. Edited by M. Broshi et al. Jerusalem: Bilaik Press.

Sutcliffe, E. F. 1960. *The Monks of Qumran*. Westminster, Md.: Newman.

Tahoon, R. 1990. Around the Dead Sea. (In Hebrew.) Pages 245–57 in *The Dead Sea and Judean Desert*. Edited by M. Naor. Jerusalem: Yad Izhak Ben Zvi.

Taylor, J. E. 1999. The Cemeteries of Khirbet Qumran and Women's Presence at the Site. *Dead Sea Discoveries* 6:265–323.

———. 2002a. Khirbet Qumran in the Nineteenth Century and the Name of the Site. *Palestine Exploration Quarterly* 134:144–64.

———. 2002b. Qumran in Period III. Page 6 in *Qumran: The Site of the Dead Sea Scrolls*. Edited by K. Galor and J. Zangenberg. Providence: Brown University Press.

Taylor, J. E., and T. Higham. 1998. Problems of Qumran's Chronology and the Radiocarbon Dating of Palm Log Samples in Locus 86. *Qumran Chronicle* 8:83–94.

Teffer, Y. 1986. The Rise and Fall of Dove-Raising. (In Hebrew.) Pages 170–96 in *Man and Land in Eretz-Israel in Antiquity*. Edited by A. Kasher, A. Oppenheimer, and V. Rappaport. Jerusalem: Yad Izhak Ben Zvi.

Theissen, G. 1977. *Sociology and Early Palestinian Christianity*. Philadelphia: Fortress.

Thiering, B. 1989. The Date of Composition of the Temple Scroll. Pages 99–120 in *Temple Scroll Studies*. Edited by G. J. Brooke. Sheffield, Engl.: Sheffield Academic Press.

Tov, E. 1998. Scribal Practices and Physical Aspects of the Dead Sea Scrolls. Pages 45–60 in *The Bible as a Book*. Edited by J. L. Sharpe and K. Van Kampen. London: Oak Knoll.

Tsafrir, Y. 1982. The Desert Fortresses of Judaea in the Second Temple Period. Pages 120–45 in vol. 2 of *The Jerusalem Cathedra*. Edited by L. I. Levine. Detroit: Wayne State University Press.

Tsafrir, Y., and Y. Magen. 1993. Sartaba-Alexandrium. Pages 1318–20 in vol. 4 of *The New Encyclopedia of Archaeological Excavations in the Holy Land*. Edited by E. Stern. Jerusalem: Israel Exploration Society & Carta.

Ullmann-Margalit, E. 1998. Writings, Ruins, and Their Reading: The Dead Sea Discoveries as a Case Study in Theory Formation and Scientific Interpretation. *Social Research* 65:839–70.

Underhill, H. W. 1967. Dead Sea Levels and the P.E.F. Mark. *Palestine Exploration Quarterly* 99:43–53.

VanderKam, J. C. 1994. *The Dead Sea Scrolls Today*. Grand Rapids: Eerdmans.

———. 1998. *Calendars in the Dead Sea Scrolls*. New York: Routledge.

Vaux, R. de. 1953a. Fouilles au Khirbet Qumrân: Rapport préliminaire. *Revue biblique* 60:83–106.

———. 1953b. Exploration de la région de Qumrân: Rapport préliminaire. *Revue biblique* 60:540–61.

———. 1954. Fouilles au Khirbet Qumrân: Rapport préliminaire sur la deuxième campagne. *Revue biblique* 61:206–36.

———. 1956. Fouilles au Khirbet Qumrân: Rapport préliminaire sur les 3è, 4è, et 5è campagnes. *Revue biblique* 63:533–77.

———. 1959a. Les manuscrits de Qumrân et l'archéologie. *Revue biblique* 66:87–110.

———. 1959b. Fouilles de Feshkha. *Revue biblique* 66:225–55.

———. 1961. *L'archéologie et les manuscrits de la mer Morte*. London: Oxford University Press.

———. 1962. Archéologie. Pages 3–36 in *Les "petites grottes" de Qumrân*. By M. Baillet, J. T. Milik, and R. de Vaux. Discoveries in the Judaean Desert of Jordan 3. Oxford: Clarendon.

———. 1973. *Archaeology and the Dead Sea Scrolls*. Oxford: Oxford University Press.

———. 1977. Archéologie. Pages 3–22 in *Qumrân grotte 4.II*. By R. de Vaux and J. T. Milik. Discoveries in the Judaean Desert 6. Oxford: Clarendon.

———. 1993. Qumran, Khirbet, and 'Ein Feshkha. Pages 1235–41 in vol. 4 of *The New Encyclopedia of Archaeological Excavations in the Holy Land*. Edited by E. Stern. Jerusalem: Israel Exploration Society & Carta.

Vermes, G. 1956. *Discovery in the Judean Desert*. London: Desclee.

Walker, D. 1993. Notes on Qumran Archaeology: The Geographical Context of the Caves and Tracks. *Qumran Chronicle* 3:93–100.

Weiss, Z. 1989. The Jewish Cemetery in the Galilee in the Mishna and Talmud Period. (In Hebrew.) M.A. diss., Hebrew University of Jerusalem.

Will, E. 1987. Qu'est-ce qu'une *baris? Syria* 64:253–59.

Wolters, A. 1994. History and the Copper Scroll. Pages 285–98 in *Methods of Investigation of the Dead Sea Scrolls and the Khirbet Qumran Site*. Edited by M. O. Wise et al. New York: New York Academy of Sciences.

———. 1998. The Copper Scroll. Pages 302–24 in vol. 1 of *The Dead Sea Scrolls after Fifty Years: A Comprehensive Assessment*. Edited by P. W. Flint and J. C. VanderKam. Boston: E. J. Brill.

Wood, B. G. 1984. To Dip or Sprinkle? The Qumran Cisterns in Perspective. *Bulletin of the American Schools of Oriental Research* 256:45–60.

Woude, A. S. van der. 1998. Fifty Years of Qumran Research. Pages 1–45 in vol. 1 of *The Dead Sea Scrolls after Fifty Years: A Comprehensive Assessment*. Edited by P. W. Flint and J. C. VanderKam. Boston: E. J. Brill.

Yadin, Y. 1957a. *Hamegiloth Hagenuzoth Mimidbar Yehuda*. (In Hebrew.) Tel Aviv: Schocken.

———. 1957b. *The Message of the Scrolls*. London: Weidenfeld & Nicolson.

————. 1969. Tefillin (Phylacteries) from Qumran (7Q ^{Phyl 1–4}). (In Hebrew.) *Eretz-Israel* 9:60–85.

————. 1983. *The Temple Scroll.* Vols. 1–2. Jerusalem: Israel Exploration Society.

Yardeni, A. 1997. A Draft of Deed on an Ostracon from Khirbet Qumran. *Israel Exploration Journal* 47:233–35.

Yeivin, S. 1973. Temples That Were Not. (In Hebrew.) *Eretz-Israel* 11:163–75.

Yellin, J., M. Broshi, and H. Eshel. 2001. Pottery from Qumran and Ein Ghuweir: The First Chemical Exploration of Provenience. *Bulletin of the American Schools of Oriental Research* 321:65–78.

Young, J. H. 1956. Studies in South Attica: Country Estates at Sunion. *Hesperia* 25:122–46.

Zangenberg, J. 2000a. Wildnis unter Palmen? Khirbet Qumran im regionalen Kontext des Toten Meeres. Pages 129–64 in *Jericho und Qumran.* Edited by B. Mayer. Regensburg: Friedrich Pustet.

————. 2000b. Bones of Contention: "New" Bones from Qumran Help Settle Old Questions (and Raise New Ones): Remarks on Two Recent Conferences. *Qumran Chronicle* 9:51–76.

————. Forthcoming. *Opening Up Our View: Khirbet Qumran in a Regional Perspective.*

Zangenberg, J., and K. Galor. 2003. Qumran Archaeology in Transition. *The Qumran Chronicle* 11:1–6.

Zeuner, F. E. 1960. Notes on Qumran. *Palestine Exploration Quarterly* 92:27–36.

Zias, J. E. 2000. The Cemeteries of Qumran and Celibacy: Confusion Laid to Rest? *Dead Sea Discoveries* 7:220–53.

Zissu, B. 1995. Two Herodian Dovecotes: Horvat Abu Haf and Horvat 'Aleq. Pages 56–69 in *The Roman and Byzantine Near East: Some Recent Archaeological Research.* Edited by J. H. Humphrey. Ann Arbor: University of Michigan Press.

————. 1998. "Qumran Type" Graves in Jerusalem: Archaeological Evidence of an Essene Community? *Dead Sea Discoveries* 5:158–71.

————. 2001. The Identification of the Copper Scroll's Kahelet at 'Ein Samiya in the Samaria Desert. *Palestine Exploration Quarterly* 133:145–58.

Zorn, J. R. 1994. Estimating the Population Size of Ancient Settlements: Methods, Problems, Solutions, and a Case Study. *Bulletin of the American Schools of Oriental Research* 295:31–48.

Modern Author Index

General Index